FOODIFESTO

Dan Hunt

To the team

Wookie, Raven, Valko, Sam, Eryl, Heti, Greta, Felipé, Winnie, Tinks, Colin, and the girls.

Plus of course, Weebs and Robert.

"The food system – agriculture, food production, distribution and retail combined – releases more greenhouse gases than any other sector apart from energy. It is responsible for 25–30% of global emissions: a tally that dwarfs, say, the 3.5% contributed by air travel. In the UK, the food system accounts for a fifth of domestic emissions – but that figure rises to around 30% if we factor in the emissions produced by all the food we import"

Henry Dimbleby. National Food Strategy

"We created a society obsessed with food chains and ethics, while disconnecting most people for the practical agricultural and ecological knowledge to make those choices. Now people worry about what *they should eat but have largely lost sight of* how *their local landscapes should be farmed and what foodstuffs they can produce sustainably. Most people are now largely illiterate when it comes to agriculture and ecology. This is a cultural disaster, because the global challenge of how we live sustainably on this planet is really a local challenge."*

James Rebanks, English Pastoral.

"Yes, we can."

Barack Obama, 8th January 2008, New Hampshire.

Contents

Part 4: Tomorrow

Foreword

The light of a new morning peers hesitantly over the top of the high hills behind our smallholding before bursting into the full glory of new dawn. Felipé the chicken hasn't waited for the full chorus. She's awake and going through her repertoire of squawks, calls and clucks at the first sign of the night slinking away. It takes the ducks a while longer to get going, their body clocks run a little behind. They aren't really that chatty until breakfast approaches. For Valko and Sam, the two Shetland ponies that munch their way around our acreage, the new day brings a chance to be vocal about their desire for more grass. Sam's worked out where the humans sleep and if he's grazing on the right side of the house, he'll be in place to call for his first meal before we're out of the door.

For most of the year I'll inevitably need to water something in the kitchen garden, even if it's just the polytunnel. This is my job. Simple, repetitive. All I have to do is get up every day. My wife does the bulk of the animal care because she's good at it. And it takes knowledge. I just turn the hose on or take some nitrogen rich duck water from the pond and make sure nothing green dies. I can do this. What's more, I get to look at the view whilst I'm doing it. As I mindlessly let water tumble onto our potatoes, I can see the land falling away gently once it reaches the end of our smallholding, continuing down towards the distant coast which lies about five miles away. But in between that distant blue line and us lies a multitude of fields, scattered houses, small villages, and hillsides that morph from yellow, to green, to purple, to exposed rugged grey as the year progresses. It's a feast for the eyes that grounds our existence in seasonality. Plus, I can see the rain coming from miles away, so I know when to get the washing off the line.

Once the animals are fed and the plants watered it's time to start work. I may need to harvest some salad leaves, cabbage, or kale to take with me depending on the time of year. Precious green bounty in hand I head off to our sustainable food shop where we sell a range of loose, unpackaged foods and local or otherwise sustainable products in bid to reduce the planetary footprint associated with what we eat. The harvest from home is just part of a wider project to provide an alternative to large supermarkets and heavily packaged and processed foods. It's not easy. The inertia of the existing model is going to take a lot to overcome. Most days it feels good to be trying, even if I'm not always very successful.

Selling food is what I do. I've done it for supermarkets, convenience retailers and myself, as a self-employed business owner. I have seen most of the ways you can sell tins of beans to the masses. It took me a long time to realise the large scale mainstream way of doing it was flawed and damaging. The shop, the land, and this book grew out of that realisation. Collectively we need to sell different beans in different ways for different reasons. That might not sound like an excessively big ambition but once you peel back what that means, it's revolutionary. It is what this book is all about.

It's taken a motley assortment of influences, professional and personal to end up at this spot. This hillside, these accumulated experiences. Together they are the foundation of what follows, the anchor that informs what fills these pages. I couldn't have written this book without these fields, these animals, those tins of beans. As time passes, I find am increasingly of this place, moulded and shaped by an ever deeper knowledge of the land and its inhabitants. From that comes a vision of a different food future for us all. One grounded in our surroundings and yet aware of our place on the largest scales of all. Our challenges our planetary, the solutions are local. The world needs changing but chickens still need feeding.

Introduction

Food. A fundamental part of existence that binds us all to each other. To live is to eat, and to live well is impossible without good food. Often, it is taken for granted, especially in the more affluent parts of the globe. Yet, the events of 2022 have made the topic far more relevant to a greater number of people. How food ends up on our shelves may have seemed an abstract question in previous years and decades. Now it has become a more obviously acute question. War in Europe has shaken the comfortable beliefs of many who presumed such a thing was unthinkable. Widescale sanctions, co-ordinated on a scale previously presumed unlikely, have placed a dead hand on sections of the global economy. Such actions have slowed the endless cycle of finance that acts as the lubricant for global trade. All this impacts on our food.

On a basic level, farmers in Ukraine are unable to harvest already planted crops or prepare for the next round of sowing. Russian growers are finding it harder to bring their goods to the global market. Between them they account for huge swathes of what the planet eats. Before war broke out the Economist noted that 'Russia and Ukraine were the world's first and fifth biggest exporters of wheat, shipping 39m tonnes and 17m tonnes respectively – 28% of the world market'[1]. Countries around the globe including places as disparate as Egypt and Indonesia are suddenly scrabbling to find replacement calories for their populations. The immutable idea that the global market will provide has been heavily dented.

And it's not just food itself that is in short supply. Commodity markets are facing upheaval with Russia the largest producer of agricultural fertilizer in the world. On top of that, global shipping markets still haven't recovered from the impact of the Covid pandemic and La Nina weather patterns are disrupting crops in other areas as well, particularly India. In response, many nations are suddenly imposing export bans on various products, further gumming up the wheels of trade. And there is no guarantee of a return to the old normal, even if war ends tomorrow. Climate change is driving long term changes to weather patterns which threaten to make redundant much of the infrastructure we currently rely on to supply us with our existing smorgasbord of choice here in the western world.

In short, Food is no longer something we can take for granted. Predictions of a perilous tomorrow have become the reality of an uncomfortable today.

Our food never should have been a mere convenience. We have been lulled into a false sense of security by an abundance of easy calories that looked like they would keep coming for as long as we wanted, at ever lower cost. The first half of 2022 rammed home the fallacy of such an arrangement to far more people, yet often we don't see arguments for long term structural change emerging as the answer to the problems now exposed. Instead, we're content to call for short term support to minimise the impact of price rises.

Part of that is because of how we buy our food. In the UK we continue to flock to supermarkets, convinced that any gaps on the shelves are minor inconveniences which will soon be overcome, even as most of us have only the faintest idea how all that food ends up in those shops in the first place. We are divorced from the reality of how our dinner is grown, transported, and sold to us. Despite all that is going on, that status quo is yet to be seriously disrupted.

When that disruption comes (and it will), what will we replace the existing system with? Who will control it? What sort of food will we want to eat? How will we want that to interact with the places we live? All these questions are more pressing than ever and yet, collectively, we have few answers to them. Such is the success of the supermarket era, an alternative to the norm seems unthinkable to many. But the truth is, we need to start thinking now. We have little time to imagine new ways of doing things and bring them to life before the challenges of a changing climate for change upon us, for better or worse.

As the summer of 2022 progressed an overdue government white paper designed to lay out its food strategy finally arrived with minimal fanfare. Its belated appearance summed up the lack of urgency in tackling an issue fundamental to our future security and wellbeing.

The paper was promised at the start of the year as a formal response to the report commissioned by the government on the state of the food sector. The report, written by restaurateur Henry Dimbleby and published in the summer of 2021 as a national food strategy labelled 'The Plan'[2]. It is detailed, well researched and contains a range of strong recommendations that, if implemented fully, would go a long way towards tackling the problems outlined in this book and others. That is not to say it is faultless, but its publication represented a real moment of honest accounting for an industry that had been left to its own devices for too long.

Sadly, the government's response was not just late, it was incredibly weak. Running to just 27 pages[3] and ignoring the bulk of the recommendations from the Dimbleby report, it fails to meet the moment entirely. Just as frustratingly, this failure has passed almost unnoticed as other news stories hog the headlines (sometimes understandably). The questions surrounding our food future remain unanswered, despite a clear opportunity to provide a strong central strategy. This book takes up the challenging of finding what the answers might be. Based on more than twenty years of experience within the food retail industry, including as a sustainable shop owner, and as a smallholder and food producer, I've come to see that wholesale reform of our food landscape is the only way we can build a sustainable tomorrow. One that is resilient enough to withstand future events and keep us supplied with healthy, affordable calories. Such change would amount to a revolution in our relationship with what we eat.

Over the coming pages I'll seek to highlight our existing food reality and how it impacts us and our wider environment before going on to explore more positive ways of producing food, better types of products we could fill our diets with, and how a reshaped retail landscape could look. At the start of each of the four sections of the book, I'll lay out in concise form the changes required to bring a new food reality to life.

Change is needed at all levels. Individuals, companies, local governments, national governments, and international organisations such as the UN or EU. All need to play their part and implement the change appropriate or their level of influence and control. We often hear the weary refrain of how saving a single plastic bottle at a time doesn't really make a difference and that we're all doomed if China doesn't slash its emissions. Bluntly, that's a lazy argument designed to avoid personal responsibility or the direct consequences of our own actions. All choices matter because they all contribute to making the eventual worst case scenario of climate change a little less bad than it would have been if we'd collectively done nothing. We all must act with whatever agency and influence we can muster. The challenge is to resist the urge to be frustrated into inaction when those with power at other levels of society fail to act in a timely manner. Our personal actions should start with the task of educating ourselves as to the size of the challenge. This can be an unpopular call in a world of soundbites and simplification. This is unashamedly a book that wants you to read more books.

The 'Foodifesto' seeks to treat our food problems in a wide holistic sense. We need to improve how and what we farm, how much food we import, how we improve health outcomes associated with what we eat, how we tackle the outrage that is food poverty in a rich nation, where we shop for our food and how we take the democratic action needed to make all that and so much more a reality. It's a daunting list but as we've realised time and time again whilst nurturing our own small patch of food production, we all have to try.

This manifesto for a better food future can be part of rebuilding our connection with the world around us whilst providing better outcomes for all. Action is needed for all those currently shut off from good, healthy choices by the structural barriers that exist within our society. We can build a different tomorrow, but only if we embrace the challenge of making different choices to meet an altered set of priorities. The food we eat is vitally important and the challenge is correspondingly huge. But as daunting as the task seems, if we ask ourselves can we really do all that? Can we write a new story of food for a better future? Is there a positive narrative of change to be grasped? The answer is undoubtedly, yes, we can.

So, we should.

Foundations

Part 1
A Brief History of Food
The World As It Is
What is Sustainability?
Food Beyond the Plate
A Better Support Structure

The Foodifesto

Foundations – Climate & Planet

- ➢ Banning of all non-recyclable packaging.
- ➢ Updated Planning regulations to enforce provision of high quality habitats that support local biodiversity in all large developments.
- ➢ Funding for hedgerow replacement to be increased and linked to reductions in average field/paddock size to encourage regenerative grazing practices and pasture management.
- ➢ Creation of UK wide Nitrate Zone to enforce tough restrictions on nitrate run offs.
- ➢ All government departments and local governments to be required to make the circular economy a first principle of all purchasing decisions.
- ➢ Report into UK wide recycling facilities with a remit to suggest gaps in provision and spending

required to ensure best possible recycling rates are achieved across all of the country.

- ➢ Ban on exporting waste overseas.
- ➢ Bottle exchange scheme launched in rest of the UK (already exists in Scotland) by 2024.
- ➢ Individuals to take personal responsibility for creating a culture of refilling and reusing at home to supersede current mindset that recycling alone is often enough.
- ➢ Individuals to take personal responsibility for reducing meat and other animal products in their diets by making use of the increasing range of alternatives.
- ➢ Funding for increased roll out of Food Hubs aiming for 100 new hubs within 2 years.
- ➢ Funding linked to Food Hub roll out (above) to provide access to electric vans which can be used for circular trips supporting multiple local retailers per journey.
- ➢ Increased roll out of Palm Oil Free towns and cities.
- ➢ Subsidies for home composting kits to change culture of food waste.
- ➢ Establishment (and expansion) of national and global carbon tax regimes.

1

A brief history of food

In the beginning

A story can start in many places. Maybe a history of humankinds' relationship with food should begin with Adam, Eve, and an apple. A foundational tale based on a moment of munching. Maybe we start when nutrients went from being absorbed to consumed. A history of food from the very first bite. Most of us, when we think of the food and the first humans default to the trope of early man (and contrary to recent evidence, it is nearly always depicted as a man) as a hunter gather. The image of the woman sat around a campfire in the doorway of a cave as her bearded, muscular, moderately clothed man drags a freshly killed carcass back to his waiting family is imbued into popular culture and it's as good a place as any to bring our tale to life. We can leave the garden of Eden to theologists while we focus on abundance here on earth.

Before we reached the stage of prehistoric barbecues, our ancestors were nomadic foragers, deeply aware of what was available on a seasonal basis. The idea of permanent settlements where often an anathema as humans followed the migratory flows of the animals that made up the staples of their diets. Tribes roamed over large areas; movements dictated by knowledge handed down verbally through generations. The arrival of fire made food more palatable and saw man through the last Ice Age. But while it didn't reshape those established flows of early humanoids immediately, it did start to confer on us one of our great advantages as a species. Scientists often attribute the advent of cooked food to the evolutionary increase in the size of our brains.

As the ice retreated humanity embarked on the path that made use of those bulging craniums to bend the planet to its will, ushering in what is known as the First Agricultural Revolution (or sometimes, the Neolithic Revolution)[4]. About 11,000 years ago farming began to emerge on the land left behind as the coldness retreated to the poles. As the weather warmed, a 'fertile crescent' emerged which spanned across the southern coast of the Mediterranean and down into modern day Iraq. Faced with such hospitable conditions humans slowly stopped moving and started tending fixed plots that could sustain them, give or take, through an entire year. This moment was a major change in our relationship with food and how it shapes the way we live. The knowledge you need changes, the focus tends towards protecting a home. Raising a family becomes easier. Collaboration and long-term relationships become more sustainable. What we had available to eat, and our ability to harness it, shaped a shift to a world we'd recognise the outlines of today. And from there, in evolutionary terms, it was a short, dizzying hop from settlement, to village, to town, to city.

Once you have cities, you have cemented a whole new way of thinking and whole new way of eating. This is the deep-rooted source of our modern ignorance and another key moment in are entwined relationship with what we eat. In a city, you're no longer finding or growing all your own food, you've arrived in a world of specialisms. Single jobs done with skills honed over a lifetime. This shift is considered to have been present from 3500BC in the city of Uruk, in what is now modern day Iraq, although it would have grown over time to that point across multiple locations. [5]

By the time Uruk was flourishing humans had already been farming grain for 8000 years and rice paddies had existed since around 5000BC. That may sound like a long time, but again, think of the big picture. Homo Sapiens are probably around 250,000 years old. For only 7,000 of those years have we been able to grow rice. Modern, easily consumable calories are a recent development for our species and their arrival drove change. Reliable harvests of grain and rice meant that humans had developed staple sources of food that supplemented their traditional meat heavy diets to further fuel their development. Combine that with the social and economic advantages conferred by being able to put down roots and we can see the development of cities with their potential for growth and the free exchange of ideas as the moment that took the thoughtful apes onto the next level.

Those first cities, and their town sized cousins, gave birth to early markets which have been recorded for as long as humanity has been able to write. They are the logical end product of the consolidation of farming techniques and knowledge which produced a regular surplus beyond the growers needs. Over time, those markets became more formal, structures became more permanent, regular days of the week became the norm and trade flourished. In the UK, permanent markets date back to at least the 12th century, but at their heart was still the idea of single producers selling what they had grown or made to those who had other skills and specialisms. In that sense, while tastes and fashion may have changed alongside the fluctuating fortunes of nations and empires, are relationship with food stayed broadly stable through this period in our history. But that would change when humanity found the key to its next great leap forward.

1750 to 1950 – Industrialisation and the Emergence of the Modern World

Historians generally agree that a second agricultural revolution occurred in the United Kingdom between the 17th and 19th Centuries. An increase in food produced played a large part in the rapid growth of population in England and Wales, from 5.5 million in 1700 to over 9 million by 1801. For much of this period agricultural output grew faster than the population.[6] All this manic growing was powered by innovations such as crop rotation, new ploughs, selective breeding, and the formalisation of the enclosure of land.

Overlapping (and contributing to) this picture of agricultural change was one of the most seismic events in human history. The Industrial Revolution unleashed a wave of growth powered by a newfound ability to harness fossil fuels. This great onset of industrialisation changed our relationship with our food, just as much as new growing techniques and better breeds of cow. How could it not? Emergent industries powered massive economic growth, driving people from the land of their ancestors and into cities such as London and Manchester. The textiles boom generated massive wealth and a need for a new way of accessing food. New modes of transport, such canals and then railways, facilitated the movement of goods further and further from the place they had been grown. Crops chasing after the waves of human migration.

General stores selling a range of dry goods started to appear. These independent forerunners of the corner shops we still have today knew their regulars, responded to local demand, and thrived with the invention of tinned and preserved goods. They even started to stock exotic items from overseas as fossil fuel powered trade started to shrink the globe. Spices, fruits, vegetables, all began to make their way slowly into our national food conversation, even if it was only for the very richest and well connected to begin with. Despite this growth, these general stores still didn't encroach on the territory of the butchers, bakers and fishmongers who maintained their own premises. Specialism survived even with the arrival, during the mid 1800's, of the first Co-op. The Co-operative is the oldest of our recognisable modern brands and the movement traces its heritage back to 1843 and the first store in Rochdale. It was an innovation born of the need to provide decent food to workers in mills who were being fed poorly by their employers. These first retailers that we would recognise today met the need for a different type of food relationship. One based on little direct knowledge of how dinner was grown. Instead, there was a focusing on concepts such as price, trustworthiness, and quality. Values, either real or perceived, began to matter as much as provenance.

If you're focusing on abstract ideas then you create room for marketing. Seen in that light, it's unsurprising that the move towards large, chain food retailers really began in the shrine to consumerism and advertising that is America. The late 19th century saw the rise of the Great Atlantic and Pacific Tea company which had been founded in 1859. This was the first real multiple retailer, with supply chains and generic standards across its stores. A mere half a century later the United States gave us the first supermarket in 1930, flanked by the instantly industry defining slogan; 'Pile it High, Sell it Low.' Opened by a man called Michael Cullen who had seen the future and wanted his existing employer to seize the moment. They demurred so he did it himself. He set up his first store in the Queens area of New York and called it King Kullen.[7]

The concept quickly took off. but it wasn't until 1948 that the UK joined the headlong rush to towards the promised land when the London Co-Operative Society opened its first self-service food shop in Manor Park. By the end of the same year Tesco had jumped on the trend as well and the course of our Americanised future was set even if it did take until 1964 for the first large out of town supermarket to open in Nottingham. Called 'Gem' and built at West Bridgford, it was an offshoot of an existing U.S. brand.[8] Once the UK finally joined the party though there was no stopping us. In the space of the following 30 years the UK added well over a thousand such stores. Before long they had triumphed in a way the founders of the old A&P could only have dreamed of.

But whilst the way we shopped for food was evolving over this period, what we consumed and how it was grown changed as well.

The march of the British Empire across the globe changed how people in Britain ate and how the state saw its role in making sure the population was getting a half decent meal or two a day. Starting with fruits and spices, it would be nice to view this trend as a paternalistic outpouring of social goodwill by Victorian and Edwardian Britons towards their fellow citizens, but it was far more often shaped by war. The first act of parliament requiring school meals for children was passed in 1906 because of the poor health of the average British soldier during the earlier Boer war. The first Minister for Food Control was appointed in 1916 as a direct response to food shortage imposed by the

German U boat blockade during WWI. In 1914, as much as 60% of the UK's food was imported, which was fine in peace time but became a liability as the German navy began targeting shipping bringing supplies to the 'mother country'. The most visible policy of the new Food Minister was the creation of 'National Kitchens' designed to offer a hearty meal of meat and veg for sixpence with none of the stigma of the pre-existing soup kitchens, which were seen as exclusively for the poor.[9] Not only was the government trying to maintain the supply of food it was also trying to demonstrate what a good meal looked like to the masses.

The Food ministry was disbanded in 1921 and that left the stage clear for two of 20th century Britain's mightiest social reformers to move the food debate forward. The first of these figures is the better known. William Beveridge is widely considered the founder of the modern British welfare state. His landmark report in 1942 laid the intellectual foundations for the Atlee government after the second world war. However, that wasn't where his policy interventions began. Berveridge had form as a clarion voice for social equality. He began by writing a history of the Food Control Ministry in 1928, a key act that sought to learn the lessons of a hastily thrown together novelty in case such an entity was needed again. He was the perfect figure for the work, having been an economist in the department when it was set up in 1916. Following on from that, in 1936 he was asked to head a government review primarily looking a food rationing in the event of another war. He went further, pushing for immediate action, convinced of the case for government action to ensure the nation ate properly.[10]

Beveridge shared his wide ranging views on social equality with Seebohm Rowntree, the second figure from this period who had a lasting impact on the way we eat. Rowntree and Lord Astor published a report on the state of British farming in 1935, linking the decline in home grown produce to the wider issues of diet and food security. It was titled The Agricultural Dilemma and laid out the sorry state of a nation producing only a third of its own food.[11] But Rowntree, part of the chocolate making family based in York, went further than this. He set out to chronicle how poor working class diets had been since 1899. In doing so he clearly laid out the staggering impact poverty has on people and laid the platform for the work the Rowntree Foundation does to this day.

By the time the Second World War arrived, the actions of individuals such as Beveridge and Rowntree, along with others whom history has paid scant attention to, laid out the argument for strong intervention to create a food industry that was both resilient in a time of crisis and capable of providing the nutrition required for good health to all parts of society. A food ministry was set up at the start of the conflict and it heavily influenced the first post war government and their work to create a meaningful social safety net. Even with the passing of time, that vision remains relevant today, offering a tantalising glimpse of what might have been an alternative set of forces not been unleashed when hostilities ceased.

1950 – 2020 Productivity and the rule of the invisible hand.

The scars of the second world war were deep and lasting for all sections of society. For food policy, as in much else, there was left a lingering sense of insecurity. The answer to such worries seemed to lie in the miracles of modern science. Boosting productivity and yields on staple crops would allow Britain to be self-sufficient in a time of crisis and demonstrate a viable path to feeding an ever expanding global population. Science, not governments, would ensure the masses were fed.

The introduction of nitrogen based crop feeds transformed how much food could be extracted from a given area. On top of that, modern farming practices, dedicated to the most efficient methods to spread such yield changing substances, transformed how our landscape looked as well. Hedgerows and ditches vanished as large, open fields with minimal obstacles for tractors and other machinery became the standard operating practice for modern farming in western nations. The UK embraced this future whole heartedly, destroying miles of hedges and habitats in the process. We grew more crops but lost much in the process. A forestry commission report estimated that we had 1 million miles of hedges in 1950. By 2007 we had lost 52% of that total.[12] This loss was driven by the Agriculture Act of 1947 which formalised an understandable desire for food independence and neatly illustrated how hard it is to balance the competing needs of mankind and the natural world. The bare figures fail to capture the full impact of this momentous upheaval. Field patterns that had survived generations were ripped apart in a headlong rush for modernisation by many farmers. Those who didn't embrace the siren call of simplification and scale were seen as out of touch and anachronistic. Villages, valleys, and communities were changed, very often not for the better, as our desire for cheaper food and the elimination of hunger drove social change among farming communities that was often out of the sight of those directing such policies from central government. A crucial balance was lost.

Into this heady mix of productivity rises and a future full of useful technology stepped the nascent supermarket industry and they had more than just cheap, widely available staples on their side as the changes to the farming system really kicked in. They also rode the wave of modern, western lifestyles which were starting to obsess over previously unthought of concepts such as convenience. Modern marketing painted a world of time shortages and labour saving devices. The refrigerator made possible processed food in wider shapes and sizes than ever before. Supermarkets sat perfectly at that nexus. A modern invention that capitalised on improved food availability and invention, married to lifestyle changes that demanded time saving miracles for the women who still made up the majority of those doing the food shopping. What wasn't to love? Who needed hedgerows?

As the 1970's gave way to the 80's, for reasons too many and varied to dive into during a brief history of food, the wider social context of what we eat changed again. The interventionist governments of the post war period gave way to the laisse faire gospel of the free market and with them came the hands off approach to food policy that we see today. It is a doctrine that sees responsibility for what we eat scattered between government departments and left to those ever mutable market forces that come with such a disarming lack of accountability. As the fear of hunger and wartime memories receded, the reasons for reigning in the invisible hand of capitalism became lost in a dash for profitability above all else.

That's not to say that all modern developments are bad. We've seen the explosion of ranges for different dietary needs and lifestyle choices. These are positive moves. More questionable are the creation of entire new categories of food. If you look at the cereal aisle in a large retailer today, you'll see all sorts of On-the-Go drinks and pots, designed to fit a fast moving lifestyle. Those products didn't exist ten years ago, it is a category entirely created by modern food producers and sellers in response to a socially driven opportunity (or, if you're more cynical, by the leveraging of their stupendous power to create products we didn't know we wanted until they were stuffed full of sugar and aggressively marketed to us). But the truth remains, no matter what the shade of government, without the technological developments that filled our kitchens with appliances our food buying wouldn't have changed half as much. It wasn't until the 1950's that refrigerators became common in the UK and without them there would be no aisles of yogurts, juices, spreads and continental meats. The same is true for the rise of frozen foods, a category that was very much the child of the supermarket age and a forerunner of the range creation we see today.

A modern supermarket is a miracle of abundance sat at the heart of food system that tries to be invisible to our daily lives otherwise. To our forebears it would be an unimaginable cornucopia, a gaudy display of modern food security for most. But that has a downside too. Food is no longer something we are programmed to see as scarce or even precious. Our behaviours have evolved far, far from our ancestors bartering whatever surplus they could hunt or grow themselves. Providing we have the money (a big if in a country that has normalised the use of food banks), no one must ever think they will go without. It is a sad reflection of how we've lost touch with the food we eat, fully consumed by the sanitized successes of the supermarkets. Modern life is wasteful, superficially convenient, lacking in knowledge previous generations took for granted and trends towards planet damaging decisions. Our modern food retail industry is just a mirror held up to the society we live in, our meals changing as society evolves.

Food Retail Today

Having arrived in the modern world via the fields, farms, and towns of our ancestors, what do we actually spend our money on in this 21st century food industry that surrounds us?

The average UK household spends £300 per month on food, excluding eating out[13]. That's an awful lot of money. In total we spent around £103 billion on food in 2020[14]. No wonder our food retail sector is one of the most competitive in the world.

The UK grocery market is theoretically highly cut-throat. Competition between the largest retailers is fierce and choice is seemingly abundant. The traditional big four, Tesco, Sainsbury, Asda and Morrisons are the recipients of most of our cash but increasingly find themselves locked in a battle for market share as the so called 'discounters' Lidl and Aldi lure shoppers away in ever bigger numbers. A rejuvenated Co-op, back from its near death experience of being dragged under by its own bank, offers nearly 3000 outlets in every conceivable location the length and breadth of the nation. Marks & Spencer continue to sell very nice ready meals and pink pig sweets to a certain demographic. Iceland sells surprisingly good quality and responsible packaged frozen food to another type of customer. And then there are all the other convenience retailers, Costcutter, McColls and so on. And on top of that there's the non-traditional food retailers muscling in, the likes of B&M and Home Bargains who, almost unnoticed, have filled aisles of their stores with edibles. The array of locations where we can buy food is quite astonishing.

The problem with all of this is that it is predominantly homogenous. We've ended up with a myriad of different ways to buy the same foods in pretty much the same way. Our plastic packed, highly sanitised supermarkets have led us to forget what it is to be tactile with the food we buy. Our big food stores don't smell of the fresh food they're selling. They have far more in common with Henry Ford's efficient production lines, moving us swiftly from entrance to till point to exit in a choreographed dance of the trollies, than they do to any sort of food market our forefathers might have recognised. This isn't by accident, it's the plan. Efficiency generates larger profits. The quantity of food sold by genuinely independent retailers dealing in products you can touch, taste and smell is vanishingly small on our crowded little Isles.

So, as we visit these modern retailers, what do we actually eat? Well let's start with the healthy stuff; we eat a lot of apples and bananas, grapes and strawberries. We spend over £500 million on each of those items. That's £2 billion a year just on four types of fruit[15]. And then there's potatoes. Boy do we still love a good spud. In 2019 we bought over £750 million of them. You might also be surprised to know that we spend more on avocados than we do carrots, proving that the rise of the hipster is complete and absolute now. The problem with that statistic goes way beyond the amount of beard oil the UK now consumes. You have to air freight an avocado halfway around the world instead digging it out the ground in the UK. It's a naughty, planet damaging habit we've learned as a result of the supermarket illusion of year round availability. It's one of the key factors we should be using when deciding what non UK fruit and veg we eat; how did it get here? The trouble is, that as consumers we just aren't given that information. In reality, bananas sent on a slow boat, have a relatively low carbon footprint, you can eat those pretty much guilt free. Anything that comes by plane, with the associated high atmosphere emissions, needs to be more of a rare treat.

If we move onto meat, surprisingly, we still just about eat more beef than we do chicken as a nation. This is based on monetary spend so we almost certainly consume more poultry by volume. Even so, when we know meat from ruminants is a major source of greenhouse gases, that figure represents a huge challenge going forward.

The meat section of our supermarkets is also where we see another recent trend at is most pernicious. The creation of homely sounding fake brands that seek to invoke a faintly longed for past, where we knew our butcher and where our meat came from, has proliferated in recent times. It's just marketing, a way to make us feel warm inside whilst essentially making the same choices. It also visible on fruit and veg packaging. The problem is, judged by those numbers we've just seen, it does seem to be working.

Beyond those fresh staples it's all about the biggest, most familiar (real) brands. We shop by habit and by familiarity and the supermarkets stock the shelves on the same basis. If you know you like Heinz beans why take a risk on another brand? And from the opposite end of the equation, if you know your shoppers are happy buying Heinz beans and you have ten years of computerized sales history that shows exactly how many tins of beans you need to drop into each of your 500+ stores each day, why change? It's easier for the retailer and the consumer that way. The trouble is, it makes it extremely hard for a mythical up and coming maker of ethical baked beans to find a way into the places most people buy their food.

We spend more than 50% of our weekly shopping bill on grocery products. Far more of that goes on confectionary, crisps, nuts, and snacks than it does on boring essentials like rice pasta or tins of peas. Cadbury, Nestle and Coca Cola all top more than £1 billion of sales per year in the UK according to 2019 figures from the industry magazine 'The Grocer', with Walkers very close to joining that club as well. That's £5 billion of our £78 billion total spend going to four brands alone[16]. Nowhere is the power of familiarity more clearly signalled. Cadburys don't make the nicest chocolate in the world, but they make acceptable chocolate at an OK price, shaped into products we know and trust. It's the perfect metaphor for how we buy our food, alright quality and low price, wrapped up in familiarity. But it hasn't always been like that, and it doesn't have to be that way going forward.

The biggest shift in food retail over the past 15 years has been the widespread loss of jobs. All the major retailers have restructured their working practices and internal hierarchies to cut staff costs. Both in store and in head offices, large numbers of roles that were commonplace ten years ago now just don't exist. Some of these are down to technology. In store cash office staff are an almost extinct species now that machines can accurately count the cash instead. Every time you see a cashier feed your note into a little slot to the side of the till rather than place it in the cash drawer, you're seeing this in action. That's an automatic cash counting system they are using. No need for someone in an artificially lit, double locked room to be doing that by hand anymore.

Other changes are cost driven. Supermarkets used to be genuine bastions of opportunity and democracy. You really could start off as a part time stock boy at the weekend when in college and end up as a store manager a decade or so later. That was possible because these stores had robust ladders to climb. You might go from standard team member to supervisor to assistant department or section manager. From there you could reach section manager, deputy store manager on to the peak of running your own store. Supermarkets, almost unnoticed, were an engine of social mobility. Now, an awful lot of those rungs on the ladder are gone and entry to the senior roles is increasingly limited to graduates. That's not to say these systems were perfect. The higher you went the more there was a clear divide between the sexes. Senior level supermarket management was (and still is) very male dominated. But they provided a real outlet for those who wanted to work hard and had a decent amount of common sense. It's not clear that the care sector, where a lot of these jobs have migrated to, can ever offer the same opportunities for progression. Once again, how we buy our food is intersecting with a wider problem in society exacerbating the challenge of progressing to a secure, well paid job.

Those interlinked, conjoined challenges are a constant feature of the food landscape that has evolved over the last 11,000 years since the first Food Revolution. The plates of our ancestors were filled with the produce that reflected the changing nature of their societies and the challenges they posed. The same is true of us today. Our meals are a product of how we live, and they reflect the positive and negative of modern societies. Too often, we fail to acknowledge the wider context of our food, content instead to rejoice in the convenience at hand. However, if we want meaningful change, we need to face into the reality of the food ecosystem that exists today and forms the starting point for any realistic call for change. And to do that, we must examine, in a little more detail, the world as it is today.

2

The world as it is

Reality Check

So, where has all that development, from cave to supermarket, left us? The short answer is in a mess.

We know by now that the world is living through a climate and ecological crisis (and if you don't, this may be the wrong book for you). We, as humans, no longer have the luxury of talking about 'climate change' or 'global warming' as something abstract that may happen in the future. We are living in this planet wide emergency now. Our futures are on the line, not just those of our unborn descendants. Our combined history, including the food we have chosen to eat, has led us to this point. The Anthropocene, born of our love affair with fossil fuels, is presenting the bill for our avarice.

In 2015 the nations of the world came together at an historic climate summit in Paris and signed up to a plan designed to keep average global temperature rises beneath 2°C and ideally limited to 1.5°C[17]. To do this, countries were required to submit voluntary emission reduction targets known as NDC's to gradually reduce the effect humans have on the planet. Follow up COP summits would measure progress with the long-term goal of bringing down the amount of greenhouse gases in the atmosphere so that warming was no longer taking place because of human activity. To reach that point we'd need to hit a target of 'net zero' emissions by 2050 and eventually go beyond that, deep into negative numbers, where we're actively removing historic carbon dioxide build ups.

Net Zero doesn't mean we don't emit any greenhouse gases. That is unrealistic. Instead, it refers to a point of balance. Anything we omit is offset by measures taken to absorb carbon dioxide and other gases such as methane. In reality, this means we need to minimize our emissions footprint as much as possible straight away so that the really difficult stuff to change can genuinely be offset by measures such as tree planting and as yet unproven technologies for carbon capture over the next couple of decades. Current scientific advice suggests we need to hit an approximately 45% reduction in emissions by 2030 to give ourselves a couple of decades to work on the hard bits. COP26, held in Glasgow in late 2021, found us to be collectively falling well short of that target with time ticking away fast.

To be successful we also need to finance ways of mitigating the effects of rising temperatures on less developed nations who have never been large emitters. Reaching net zero means no fossil fuel electricity, no petrol or diesel vehicles, no oil powered heating systems, no single use plastics, greatly reduced numbers of flights each year and plenty more besides. The 'hard to do' list includes finding ways to produce essential products such as steel and cement without large emissions. Farmers would have to use fertilizers that don't use nitrogen created in the way it currently is. And, on top of all that, we would have to change the way we eat and our relationship with food.

The good news is that the technological solutions we need for the first half of our journey towards a net zero world are already in place. We know how to generate electricity from carbon free renewable sources. We know how to create battery powered vehicles. We have all the tools we need to retrofit homes to make them better insulated. The science is clear on why we should reduce our flying immediately. All these actions, if pursued fully, would see us reach 2030 in a position where we can kick on to the goal of net zero by the middle of the century.

So, what is stopping us? What's trapping us in this negative storyline? In the near term, the biggest barriers to tackling the climate emergency we're living through are twofold. The first is a failure of imagination. Information about the dangers we face in the coming decades is more widely available than ever. In early 2022 the Intergovernmental Panel on Climate Change (IPCC) released its latest set of reports detailing likely outcomes and actions we needed to take to prevent the worst climate change predictions become reality. Despite this glut of excellent information, widespread calls for action are not translating into action. Partly this seems to be because our societies have become terrible at imagining how we can affect positive change. As Professor Geoff Mulgan pointed out in an article on the subject for the Joseph Rowntree Foundation; "there are now no media outlets that promote new ideas: magazines and newspapers focus instead on commentary"[18]. This is a visible symptom of wider malaise. We need to find spaces to advocate the case for positive change based on reimagined futures, because once we do, we can work to remove the second of our two barriers: an absence of genuine political action.

In an ideal world we would have far sighted leaders who not only understood the scale of the problem but also possessed the bravery to lead on the subject so that the urgent action we need was driven by widespread engagement. Sadly, back here in the real world, the debate around climate change has become part of the wider culture wars that plague western societies. In the UK this takes the form of backbench groups within the Conservative party disingenuously arguing that the cost of any route to net zero is too expensive and too great a burden for the ordinary voter. In reality co-ordinated, timely action is certain to be less expensive than dealing with a future crisis point. For evidence we can just look at how much it has cost the UK, and other European countries, to subsidise fuel costs of the winter of 2022. Hundreds of billions of pounds will be spent reducing household bills, all of it funded by debt. Yet somehow the same political parties willing to countenance this spending splurge have spent the last decade failing to invest smaller sums on insulating housing, upgrading energy networks, or investing in renewable power. Such attitudes leave our governments falling far short of the required scale of action and the rest of us over reliant on change driven by individuals, and that isn't always realistic or even scientifically possible.

And where does what we eat fit into this pressing planetary catastrophe? What goes on our plate has a massive climate impact. The food we buy is responsible for somewhere between 10 and 30% of the average household's carbon emissions. That figure varies depending on what your diet consists of, but nearly all of us have a sizable footprint associated with our eating habits. The production and transportation of food is estimated to be responsible for more than 30% of total global emissions. On top of that, 30% of the food we produce ends up as food waste here in the UK. Just cutting out what we throw away would make a measurable difference to our impact on the planet, let alone learning to buy and eat in a slightly different way[19].

Unlike some of the other areas that need change, food is a deeply personal thing. Our choice of meal says something about who we are, what our background is and how we learned to interact with food growing up. Our choices are sometimes aspirational and often tied to how we view ourselves. Of all the things we need to change to tackle the climate crisis, this might be the one with the biggest emotional impact. People don't have a deep seated bond with how their concrete is manufactured. But despite all that attachment, the reality is that the food we eat most of time is a convenience, not an active choice.

We need a new relationship and understanding of what eat and we need it quickly. But that is not a simple undertaking. Most of us don't produce our own food and so we need to be able to shop and buy differently in order to change what ends up in our cupboards and on our plates. The whole food industry needs to shift so we can embed different priorities in how we go about feeding ourselves. To do that we would need a food ecosystem with a vastly different mindset from today, one with the concept of sustainability baked into it. The food we eat is killing us and the planet. Changing this would a huge undertaking that would reshape not just where we buy our food, but who makes it and where it comes from. New laws would be needed, and old ones updated. Money would need to flow in different directions and our understanding of the cost of our food and the value we place on it would need to change. To end up with something different on our plate requires huge, systemic adjustments.

Doing it wrong

The need for change in our food ecosystem runs beyond planetary concerns and a desire to reach net zero. Our food is unhealthy, badly priced and helps entrench existing in equalities. The wider case for change is overwhelming. A different tomorrow could save the planet and radically alter the incentives and impacts associated with food.

Doing so will be a deeply emotive and personal process for us all. Some of our most intimate memories are tied up in food. As a child some of my happiest moments revolved around the Sunday dinner table as three generations of family tucked into the most traditional British roast you could imagine. We all sat in the same place each week, were served from the head of the table in the same order and ate the same filling mix of meat and multiple veg. Most weeks it was chicken, on special occasions beef or very rarely, pork. As we sat on the sofa waiting for lunch to arrive a rich aroma, a heady mix of melting butter, homemade gravy, and roasting juices, wafted through from the kitchen where my Grandad would be busy working away. That food was a source of comfort and stimulation to a group of people coming together at the end of the week. It nourished our bodies and nurtured our shared bonds.

For many people food conjures up no such happy recollections, what they eat is a source of anxiety, shortage, or shame. Food prompts illness in far too many people either through diet related ailments or eating disorders. Health conditions, poverty and educational failures create barriers to eating well, compounding other problems. Food, is seems obvious to say, plays a massive part in how we live, and how we view our lives.

Unfortunately, we're doing it really badly.

For evidence of that we can look to the UN Special Rapporteur on extreme poverty and human rights, Philip Alston, who visited the UK in 2018 and produced a report for the UN the following year. This was his lengthy, scathing, summary:

"Although the UK is one the world's largest economies, one fifth of its population (14million people) live in poverty and 1.5 million of them experienced destitution in 2017. Policies of austerity introduced in 2010 continue largely unabated, despite the tragic social consequences. Close to 40 per cent of children are predicted to be living in poverty by 2021. Food banks have proliferated; homelessness and rough sleeping have increased greatly; tens of thousands of poor families must live in accommodation far away from their schools, jobs and community networks; life expectancy is falling for certain groups; and the legal aid system has been decimated. The social safety net has been badly damaged by drastic cuts to local authorities' budgets which have eliminated many social services, reduced policing services, closed public libraries in record numbers, shrunk community and youth centres and sold of public spaces and buildings."[20]

According to the Food Foundation: "The poorest fifth of UK households would need to spend 47% of their disposable income on food to meet the cost of the Governments recommended healthy diet. This compares to just 11% for the richest fifth."[21]

That is all a very, very long way from a happy family lunch and it impacts people in ways far beyond one meal at a time. The unavailability of decent food choices combined with poor information and a loss of knowledge over generations is causing health and social damage that lasts a lifetime. The food we eat comes with an impact that goes way beyond the price at the shelf edge. Poverty doesn't exist in isolation. It frequently sits alongside long-term health issues which act as an additional barrier to people getting the help they need. Our current food landscape causes bad health outcomes, trapping people in what has been called 'the junk food cycle', leading to a huge in rise in obesity and diseases such as diabetes. Any just and fair food system shouldn't be doing this to people who lack access to better options.

Secure in our fabled land

As well as the damage a poor food ecosystem causes individuals, it has a wider impact for us a nation as well. To get a sense of that it helps to head to the pasta shelf of the supermarket. Pasta doesn't seem amongst our biggest issues at first glance. There's always pasta on the shelf, right? And more than one type too. White pasta, wholewheat pasta, linguine, fusilli, penne, lasagne sheets and on and on... Endless availability until one day there isn't any pasta.

For many of us that day arrived during the panic buying of March 2020, bought about by the global Coronavirus pandemic. Suddenly there wasn't always one more bag of pasta. The processes which drive endless availability to our supermarket shelves are a modern miracle and deserve to be acknowledged as such but on this occasion, they failed. The downside of our modern world, illustrated by those empty aisles, is a loss of what would be termed 'food security'. Put simply, by expanding our supply chains around the world we make them more vulnerable to disruption. That might come from war (as we have seen in 2022), economic crisis, freak weather events, failed harvests or something completely unforeseen. Whatever the cause, the net effect is to reduce the probability that there will always be food on our supermarket shelves. Those weaknesses are exacerbated by a very modern dependence on computer programs and internet connections, the existence of bottlenecks at UK ports, an inability to respond nimbly to panic buying due to a reliance on multi-week average purchasing patterns, limited storage capacity particularly for chilled and frozen products and a myriad of other factors as well.

The reality is that it is impossible for the UK to produce all its own food, it is an impractical concept. However,it is not fanciful to think that we can produce a bigger share than we are currently and that we can introduce factors other than merely price into how we decide where to source our food. That would not only make our supply more secure, but it would also lower the greenhouse gas (GHG) footprint associated with food transportation. The UK produced 55% of the food it consumed in 2019.[22] This doesn't sound terrible at first glance, but it hides some large differences once we break that figure down a bit. We produce 62% of our own cereals, 75% of red meat, 77% of dairy, yet only a quarter of the fruit and veg we eat is grown here. We are a green, moist, moderately weathered land on the whole, we should not be so dependent on importing that many of our hypothetical five a day, as a 2022 report from the Sustainable Food Trust showed.[23]

What does the UK grow?

Crop Areas (thousand hectares	2018	2019	2020
Arable crops			
Wheat	4502	4551	4314
Barley	1748	1816	1387
Oats	171	182	210
Rye, mixed corn, and triticale	49	51	53
Oilseed rape	583	530	380
Linseed	25	15	33
Potatoes	140	144	142
Sugar beet	114	108	111
Peas	193	178	233
Maize	221	228	228
Horticultural crops			
Vegetables grown outdoors	116	115	118
Orchard fruits	24	24	23
Soft fruit and wine grapes	11	11	11
Outdoor plants and flowers	12	11	11
Glasshouse crops	3	3	3

Source: Defra. Agriculture in the UK 2020. Table 2.2[24]

It should also be stated clearly that whatever its nebulous, emotional benefits, Brexit left us more food insecure. 26% of our food comes from the EU. Much more of it still comes from non-EU countries and passes through the bloc on its way to us. Increasing friction in that process, caused by erecting trade barriers that previously did not exist, means we leave ourselves more exposed to external events. It was a trade-off barely mentioned during the run up to the 2016 referendum until a cabinet minister belated realised how dependent we are on the Dover crossing and shows how complacent the abundance of supermarkets has made us about our food security. That's not saying Brexit was right or wrong, it's saying our lack of knowledge about how our food gets to our plates left us collectively unable to foresee a problem before it was too late.

And it is not just politics that threatens long term problems. As we move forward, and the climate crisis increasingly impacts our 'normal' supply chains established over the last fifty years, the concept of food security will only become more pressing whether we choose to actively confront it or not. With increasing droughts forecast for all sides of the Mediterranean, which is currently the source for plenty of out of season fresh food, it will take notable change to ensure we can continue to feed ourselves well. We need to actively think about how we are going to keep that pasta shelf full rather than assuming it always will be.

Happy ever after?

Much of what we take for granted about the food we eat is the result of conscious choices. These negative outcomes don't happen by accident, people have chosen the paths that in turn weave stories of poverty, ill health, and planetary decline into our national tale. Whilst we haven't been paying attention, others have been. Decisions have been left in the hands of those with motives more base than the health and wellbeing of a nation. The good news is that this gives us an opportunity. If choices took us here, other choices could take us somewhere else. We (just!) need to place power in the right hands.

Beyond the impact on our bodies, our diets shape the landscape around us and the atmosphere that supports all life. To plot a path to a better future it will be necessary to look at how we farm and produce food and consider how to reduce the negative impacts associated with decisions we've made over the last fifty years that have determined how our agricultural system looks today. We also need to realise that our western consumption habits shape countries on the other side of the globe. Our story frequently dictates the lives of people we'll never meet.

Our food industry, both for producers and retailers is set up to fail the planet and us as consumers. Structural features produce waste, minimise choice, increase food miles and emissions, and damage our health. Such is the concentration of market share that the big retailers now have those negative aspects ingrained in a food ecosystem that could be so much better if power was more dispersed. Our current food culture isn't sustainable and is in no way compatible with the UK's stated desire to be carbon neutral by 2050. This huge tale of failure is our collective story. All of us have lived through it and we live with the consequences on a daily basis. As we think about how to change our food environment we need to hold on to the basics of this tale as a cautionary warning. Our food makes us ill. Our food damages our natural world. The dominance of one flawed system of food retail stymies local networks and small businesses. A lack of genuine choice helps perpetuate existing inequalities by denying people empowering alternatives. The task that faces us is to weave from these strands a whole that shows a better alternative for the future

Idealism

One of the challenges we face in dealing with the broad range of planet wide issues before us is that of scale. How does that huge problem relate to my day to day life? Or, as I have been asked on more than one occasion at the end of long and impassioned rant on such subjects; yes, but what do you want me personally to do about that? It is a challenge particularly applicable to the problem of our food. It covers continent hopping supply chains, global weather patterns, national policy and what we take out the freezer for dinner on a Tuesday evening.

It is a barrier that's not easy to overcome. Humans aren't designed to think on a planet-wide scale. At heart we're still cave dwellers wired to look after our tribe. For most of us, a wider picture than our friends, family and local community is a challenge. Part of the answer lies in small, discrete actions that can help make a difference and allow us to feel a little in control. There are plenty of these throughout the book. Alongside that, we can seek out local examples of change happening already. Doing so removes the burden on our imaginations to conjure up something new from waves of negative news reports and instead take direct inspiration from what is in front of us.

One such force for change exists near to where we call home. It's a small farm called Henbant, and they act as one of our suppliers to the sustainable food shop we now own. When faced with the litany of problems baked into our existing food landscape, they offer an important source of optimism and hope. A reason to believe things can be different and way to make the planetary, personal. They top up my battery of optimism when I feel drained by the size of the challenge. A feeling I think we can all relate too.

My wife and I ended up spending a day there last December. By 6pm in the evening we were sat around an open fire that nestled in a circular, metal pit. Around its beckoning glow hay bales were arranged into a haphazard circle to form seating. They created an amphitheatre focused on a performer with an acoustic guitar. He was on one side of the fire singing folk tales and speaking of mythic histories from this part of the world with a gentle, yet steely passion. In that moment, that barn felt like a magical place to be. The preceding hours had been filled with conversation amongst people who came from a range of nooks, crannies and self-made niches that make up the fringes of our food producing landscape.

The event we attended was formally a Farm Workers Alliance get-together, but it was really just an open house for some of the most interesting food production adjacent people in the area to come together and create bonds that may spin off into something useful. It offered a lesson in how conversation with like-minded souls can nurture you through the hard months of winter. The discussion and the walks drifted from introductions to market gardening, on to Agroforestry and sheep control. After lunch there were informal workshops discussing things like food hubs and storytelling. Despite it being a disparate bunch of people, Matt, the farmer who owns Henbant with his wife Jenny, seemed to find a way to include something for everyone. A key skill on a day like this.

By the time we'd drunk plenty of tea and munched on Bara Brith and mince pies, we were all ready for the shadows to lengthen and Owain to reach for his guitar. In between songs he told us of their origin, of how these tales have shaped the area and its people, and how they continue to influence attitudes to the changing world around today. It was educational, thoughtful, emotional, and beautiful. And we got to sing the chorus of the last tune together before it is time to tear ourselves away from the warmth of the fire and grab some tea. As with everything this farm produces, it was delicious. But then why should it be surprising that food laced with this much love tastes so great? Why should it take such evenings to remind us of the importance links between place, time, story, and food?

Matt finds himself drawn increasingly towards stories and storytelling these days. It is easy to see how that is a natural response to farming the way he does. His farm is regenerative, organic, and filled with ideas such as permaculture, agroforestry and so much more. Together, he and Jenny are trying to build something quite different but also decidedly old-fashioned. A way of producing food that is good for their family, their community, and the land they own. That shouldn't be revolutionary, but sadly it is. Their story is a winding, evolving one and it draws them towards others with interesting tales to tell of their own. Those stories, whether shared around an open fire or in more prosaic settings, contain the seeds of so much we could do differently when it come to the food we eat.

All of that can feel a long way from logistics, supermarkets, war, and famine. An enjoyable time on a small regenerative farm can feel like a jarring contrast whether that's on these pages or in real life. But, if we're serious about finding a better way of feeding ourselves while looking after the world around us, places like Henbant are essential. Part of the wider challenge we face is to find ways to sell a different tomorrow as a positive opportunity rather than a burdensome response to crisis. Too often impassioned individuals can use well-meaning anger as a tool to batter people with. Instead, we need the personal, conversation based, interactions between people to give hope. We need the local to make the global feel manageable.

A revamped food ecosystem can seem like a mirage when we're all surrounded by a food landscape dominated by large scale producers and near-identical retailers. It can feel even further from our grasp when landslides of news stories tell us about ecological destruction and climate change on a scale that is already harming the world that produces our food. However, it is possible to glimpse a happier ending, especially as you peer through the flickering flames of a warming fire with song ringing in your ears. At times like that anything seems possible and even the most ephemeral notions can seem within reach, waiting to be pulled from the darkness and given life. To start that long exhumation, a reconnection with a better way of living and working, we need to understand what we are aiming for. We need to put some flesh on the murky, muddied bones of Sustainability.

3

What is Sustainability?

Tipping, tipping... gone?

One evening, a few years ago, deep into the planning stage for our shop my wife and I were having a discussion on names, missions, visions, and other such nebulous corporate sounding things. That night the shop was conceived as 'The Sustainable Weigh'. It later gained its fabulous Welsh name of 'Siop y Glorian', but at the heart of the idea was sustainability.

In that moment the concept of sustainability meant a whole raft of things we couldn't really define, and in that, I think, we are not alone. It is a word easily used as shorthand for all sorts of things. For us there was a sense that we knew we wanted to sell food you wouldn't necessarily find in a supermarket and in a different way if that was possible. But to be honest, back then, we didn't really know quite what we were groping towards. What is Sustainability?

If we zoom out, far from our homely Welsh hillside, challenging ourselves to see beyond our own hearth and tribe, we can view our planet as a whole. A fragile, beautiful, green and blue ball, suspended, as if by invisible strings, in the darkness of space. When we think about sustainability in layman's terms, I've come to feel it's that image we're thinking of. How do we keep humanity from destroying the equilibrium that keeps the Goldilocks planet balanced there, hosting us all, supporting life?

Tipping points have been a known risk to that equilibrium for quite a while, but they have received less press than some parts of the climate crisis because they are harder to predict or reduce to a snappy soundbite. They are the moment when parts of our planet's ecosystem move into a place of irreversible (at least on a human timescale) damage. For some time our understanding of individual tipping points was limited but with greater research and improved computing power for modelling, our knowledge of the risks posed by these boundaries and potential events are becoming a bit clearer.

The two most talked about tipping points involve the Amazon rainforest and Antarctic ice shelves and the news from both is not positive. The risk in the Amazon is based around evidence that suggests at a certain point of depletion, rainforests lose the ability to maintain their own ecosystems and enter terminal decline resulting in a permanent transition to a savannah style landscape. Put simply, not enough trees means not enough rain generation which in turn means even less tree growth and so on in a deathly spiral until there's not a great deal left. It is thought that more than a third of the Amazon rainforest may already be in a condition where it could be expected to exist as open savannah rather than under tree cover. The actual tipping point depends on the level of climate change that accompanies deforestation. We know that over the last five years Brazilian President and all-round bad guy, Jair Bolsonaro, has been acquiescing in a massive increase in rainforest clearances, halting real progress in protecting the habitat under previous administrations over the preceeding decade or so.

According to the leading Amazon scientist, Carlos Nobre, if the climate conditions remained as they are today, then a 40% deforestation of the Amazon would lead to a tipping point. He goes on to say: "We conclude that with the current rate of global warming, if we exceed 20 to 25 percent deforestation, then we reach the tipping point and 50 to 60 percent of the Amazon forest would become a savanna. That's why we are making this warning — today we already have 15 to 17 percent total deforestation in the Amazon. So, at the current rates of deforestation, we are 20 to 30 years off from reaching this tipping point.[25]"

Now, this is a worst case scenario, but it is not unfeasible. Current climate policies would see us on track for a potential three degree rise in average global temperatures but that doesn't take into account local variations. Carlos Nobre's vision may come to pass if politicians, and the rest of us, fail to heed the warning.

In the depths of the Antarctic the size of challenge is similar. The risk lies in huge ice shelves falling into the ocean and driving up sea levels which in turn would threaten coastal cities with catastrophic flooding all over the globe. The main area of focus is the Pine Island Glacier (and, in turn, the neighbouring Thwaites Glacier) in West Antarctica. This giant, frozen lump is two thirds the size of the whole UK and is melting faster than any other in the vacinity. Studies from March of 2020 confirmed and quantified for the first time the definitive existence of dangerous tipping points in the region. Scientists fear that these large sheets of ice could enter a meltdown loop that could potentially raise sea levels by as much as three metres. Such a rise could displace millions of people in low lying areas and wipe whole Pacific islands from the map permanently.

The science of this is all incredibly complicated but the latest study by the University of Northumbria shows that; "For Pine Island Glacier... the glacier has at least three distinct tipping points. The third and final event, triggered by ocean temperatures increasing by 1.2C, leads to an irreversible retreat of the entire glacier." To put that into perspective, since 1980 global sea temperatures have been rising by 0.18°C per decade. Considering existing temperature rises, we may have as little as 40 years until the last of those three irreversible tipping points is passed for the Pine Island glacier.

All of this seems a long way from how we buy our food and where it is produced, but it is connected. Our current food choices and conveniences are contributing to these problems. Every action that adds to our accumulated planetary warming is part of this issue even if that is sometimes hard to visualise. Swedish scientist Johan Rockström helped lead a 2009 study which came up with a unified model for viewing the tipping points facing the planet. His system consists of nine planetary boundaries which are then graded depending on how close they are to reaching their outer boundary or tipping point.

Planetary Boundaries

(Known tipping points)

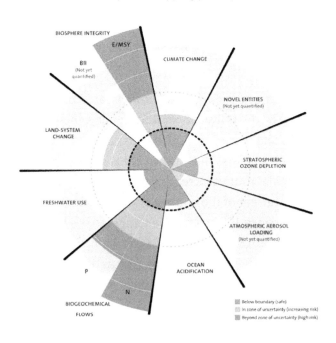

Source: Stockholm Resilience Centre[26]

The diagram on the previous page shows the nine categories and how we're currently doing on each. We've already reached deep into the outer danger zone on two out of nine. These are 'Biogeochemical flows' and' Biosphere Integrity'.

Biogeochemical flows are all about our use of nitrogen and phosphorus, two key parts of modern farming methods. Humans now manufacture copious amounts of nitrogen, which rather than ending up fertilizing crops, is emitted to the atmosphere in various forms due to wasteful processes. In turn this excess goes on to pollutes waterways and coastal areas, having a devastating impact on delicate aquatic ecosystems and causing issues such as huge blooms of algae that starve other species of light and oxygen.

Biosphere integrity refers to the tragic loss of biodiversity the planet has witnessed in recent decades which has been driven by human demand for food and land. So drastic have these changes been that The Millennium Ecosystem Assessment of 2005 concluded that damage to ecosystems caused by human activities were more rapid in the past 50 years than at any time in human history[27].

Beyond these outer triggers, there are two intermediate,, three low, and two we simply don't know as we don't have accurate ways of measuring the state of them.

The idea of this unified system is that it gives a wide ranging view of the state of the planet beyond merely focusing on the single measurement of planetary warming.

If we are looking at long term sustainability, then this is how we need to view our world. We need to restore balance to our fragile planet and the only way to do that is to reduce our resource use, increase our habitat husbandry and take stock of our wider impact so that we find a way back out of the hole we've dug ourselves. And we need to place the food we eat within this context as well.

The question, of course, is can we still stop these tipping points from occurring? Can we stop the ice melt in Antarctica and the loss of the Amazon?

The good news is that we have proved that we can reverse a tipping point. One of the segments; 'Atmospheric Aerosol Loading' shows what we can do when we put our mind to it. During the 1980's it became clear that aerosols such as CFCs were causing huge damage to the ozone layer. Effective regulatory action and behaviour change by consumers combined to reverse the damaging trend and today it sits as one of only two green segments on the model. We did that and we can do it again, but we need to change a lot more of our habits. And that means thinking long and hard about how we consume differently.

Sustainable Consumption

What would the world look like if we stopped consuming? It's a fascinating idea and one that is explored in depth by J.B Mackinnon in his thought provoking book 'The Day the World Stops Shopping'.

We buy too much stuff. In fact, we might end up being the era that reached 'peak stuff' with future generations looking back and shaking their heads at the way we treated shopping as a Saturday afternoon leisure activity rather than something based on need. The Covid pandemic showed what would happen if we stopped shopping. Our western economies would teeter on the brink of disaster. Consumption, in the UK especially, is one of the major economic drivers (the other being finance). If we don't shop, the money doesn't keep moving around. People work in shops and their associated suppliers to earn the wages they spend in other shops. It's a merry-go-round based on actually making very little of any worth in the first place. Minimal genuine value is added, the money (and credit) just keeps on moving in circles. In a time of crisis, our government implored us to keep shopping, a fact that we seemingly don't regard as a sign of the madness we've unleashed upon ourselves.

The goal of continued economic growth is taken for granted as normal. It's the reason for the endless movement of money and goods. Governments set policies to stimulate growth as part of a desire to raise standards for everyone within a given country. The orthodox thinking goes that the more a national economy grows, the better off its people will be. Think of the phrase 'a rising tide lifts all boats', and you'll have the right idea. In many ways this idea is correct. Nothing has lifted more people out of poverty than free market based economic growth. The thing is perpetual economic growth isn't actually the norm through human history. Up until the 1800's the world economy was growing at well under 1% per year on average, and that was mainly due to population increases rather than any desire to grow an economy.[28] The chasing of economic growth as a good in itself is closely correlated with the onset of the industrial revolution and the development of the modern world. In fact, if you took a graph and mapped the moment global temperatures began to increase and the time economic growth rose consistently above 0.1% per year, you'd pretty much have a perfect correlation. Nearly all our historic growth has been powered by our less than 200 year binge on fossil fuels that has wrecked the planet. Virtually all of what we buy has a greenhouse gas footprint associated with it. Growth, as we've known it for last couple of centuries, has a huge cost to pay that we've failed to acknowledge until the planet is sending us urgent warning signs.

But, if we just stopped shopping tomorrow, surely modern society as we know it would collapse? Shops would shut, suppliers would go bankrupt, farmers crops would rot, unemployment would be rampant. We might be able to argue that reducing our purchases would help the planet, but we can't be advocating for that sort of change, can we?

Research conducted by Peter Victor, a Canadian scientist, in his book 'Managing without Growth' shows that cutting consumption doesn't have to lead to an apocalyptic outcome but only if it is a managed reduction. A global catastrophe that causes huge disruption (like a pandemic) would bring about the worst case scenarios if it led to a permanent reduction in consumption by anything approaching 50%, let alone more. Instead, he has created a model showing what he describes as 'Sustainable Prosperity' that reduces growth across a fifty year timespan and avoids huge spikes in unemployment and poverty[29]. However, that's only achievable if governments implement the right policies in the right way. A big If, but an intriguing possibility.

So, how far away from being sustainable levels of consumption are we as a species? How much are we over consuming by? The Global Footprint Network has worked out that our 'ecological footprint' is 170% larger than it should be if it was to be sustained indefinitely. It is their work that gives us the concept of 'Earth Overshoot Day', the moment in the year when we've consumed one year of earth's sustainable resources. In 2021 that fell on July 29th. After that, we're into overshoot, using more than the planet has to give.[30]

J.B Mackinnon has more information on this in his musings on consumption cutting:

"The same calculation can be made for… countries and doing so makes plain how unequally consumption occurs around the globe. Suppose we all lived like the average citizen of Afghanistan, one of the world's poorest countries; we could shrink the Earth by half and still have enough resources to maintain everyone at that standard of living. We'd need a little more than two planets if we all lived the average Chinese, roughly two and a half if were all Spanish, British or New Zealander; three if we lived on Planet Italy, Planet Germany or Planet Netherlands; three and half to live like they do in Russia, Finland or Norway; and four or more to enjoy the way of life in Sweden, South Korea, Australia or Canada. And if we lived on Planet Ecuador, we would need just one Earth."[31]

Which all told, would be handy because we only have one.

Mackinnon goes on to illustrate what such a life looks like. One television per household, a fridge, and a washing machine. Jobs earning an OK wage, a flat to live in, partners, a couple of children. Some people might be able to afford cars, others share. Very few people ever get to fly. Clothes are new but not necessarily highly fashionable. Adults have mobile phones, a family may have one desktop or laptop computer. It is a life we in the western world could recognise whilst still being stripped back of many luxuries we take for granted. Going middle class Ecuadorean isn't stepping back to the stone age but it would definitely be a noticeable change for many in the developed world.

The data, gathered by Global Footprint Network and others, is clear. We are over consuming and that is pushing our planet closer to the tipping points we discussed earlier in the chapter. We need to shift our mindset from consumption as a hobby designed to fill a wet afternoon in a large shopping centre, to one based on genuine need leading to a place where growth is not desired as an end product in itself but is a by-product of making the right choices for us and the planet. The thing is, that's quite a hard idea to get your head around when you're planning on opening a shop. How do we make people buy less but still make enough money to keep a roof over our heads?

A Sustainable Shop

As we pondered on that inherent conflict in the very idea of a sustainable shop, we realised we had more thinking to do around what sustainability really looks like in food retail. We didn't even have a definition for sustainability itself. A little research showed that there was a reason for that. There isn't one straightforward answer and that in itself is a problem. Simple concepts gain traction in our limited attention span, social media addled world. Complex, multi-faceted stuff dies in the gutter of the unseen and unclicked.

The Collins dictionary defines sustainability as "the ability to be maintained at a steady level without exhausting natural resources or causing severe ecological damage."[32] Which seems a reasonable enough, if slightly bland, starting point. The most popularly used description of sustainability is known as the Brundtland Definition[33] and comes from an eponymous report way back in 1987. This is primarily concerned with international development and frames it as "meeting the needs of the present without compromising the ability of future generations to meet their own needs."

The trouble is this is all still a bit vague. How do you define 'needs'? Is a new TV every other year a need? Is one foreign holiday a year a need? Is a new dress for a night out a need? It opens a can of worms and a million interpretations. Our needs are almost certainly different to yours. 7 billion different needs, 7 billion definitions of sustainability. And as we've seen, that leads to mass over consumption in the developed world.

The truth is terms such as 'Sustainability', 'Sustainable Development', 'Sustainable Growth' and many other variants are used pretty much interchangeably. This has a limited advantage in that the inherent vagueness of such an approach allows a wide range of people and organisations to support the broad concept of 'Sustainability' without ever having to define exactly what they mean, and if we're cynical, take the hard choices to bring about such a world.

We felt we needed something more concrete, a set of touchstones to guide us through the many compromises and hard choices associated with the idea of running a sustainable business. After a lot of homework and cherry picking of clever ideas from groups such as Sustain, we came up with what we called our 'Sustainable Seven':

1) Locally sourced

2) Contributes to reducing packaging

3) Offers an alternative to meat or dairy products

4) Offers a Fairtrade or similarly ethically sourced choice

5) Is Palm Oil free

6) Helps reduce food waste

7) Helps you Make It, Bake It, Grow It.

On top of this we had one further goal, to factor in the water use associated with products. The problem is that at the time of writing that sort of information isn't available either to retailers or consumers. We couldn't add an official eighth to our seven because we had no way of bringing it to life. We're confident that as the 2020's pass, water consumption will become part of our shopping decisions and then we can add this to our practical guides to sustainability, but for now our list was limited to seven.

Sustainability in Food

Moving beyond the specifics of our own business we can already see how complicated a seemingly simple notion like sustainability can be. Within a food context it would mean creating new ways of producing, regulating, selling, buying, and eating if our magical list of seven bullet points were to become the norm.

For producers, sustainability involves farming techniques, crop choices, routes to market and much more. A sustainable food ecosystem will need different regulations and a more interventionist government mindset than has been the recent norm for countries like the UK. Consumers will need to make different choices, both in where they shop and what they want to find on the shelves of these new establishments. Such dietary changes will then need to be backed up by education that gives the cooking skills necessary to create healthy meals that have a positive impact on our wellbeing. It affects every part of our food environment.

Sustainability is a mindset that goes far beyond just not taking more than the planet can give. Whilst deep into the editing process that turned this collection of words from an error strewn mess into a meaningful manuscript, one of my customers gave me a book to read in return for the privilege(!) of doing a little proof reading. It was called 'Braiding Sweetgrass' and was written by Robin Wall Kimmerer, a woman of native American descent. Indeed, she would class herself as both a citizen of her tribe and the USA. It's a lovely, beautiful collection, crafted by someone who's life has straddled modern western science and traditional, indigenous teachings and she had a lot to say on the subject of mindset and how we perceive the world around us.

In her book Ms Kimmerer describes a conversation with an ecologist who was also a member of the Algonquin tribe at a meeting on indigenous models of sustainability. The ecologist recalled explaining the standard definition of sustainable development, an idea in line with all we've discussed in the current chapter of this book, at a previous meeting. The response from the tribal elders she was addressing was thoughtful but definite:

"This sustainable development sounds to me like they just want to be able to keep taking like they always have. It's always about taking. You go there and tell them that in our way, our first thoughts are not 'What can we take?' but 'What can we give to Mother Earth?' That's how it's supposed to be."[34]

Upon reading that sentence, I stopped and went back over what I've written in this chapter. How I'd tried to find a definition of sustainability for the shop and the work I do. If I'm honest, the same critique could be labelled at me sometimes. Have I been using the word sustainable to find justifications for stocking certain products? Is that just another way to keep taking? Making it serve my needs, as much as those of the planet. Much of that stems from the inherent conflict in trying to sell stuff in a world in which consumption needs to fall. A lot of the time, I'm selling the least bad option. Indigenous wisdom wouldn't necessarily see that as an appropriate compromise to make.

That doesn't mean all I've written has to be thrown out the window, or that what we're trying to do over the pages of this book is intrinsically wrong. Instead, it shows the need to be on guard against assumptions built deep into how we have been bought up and the structures we exist within. It's a good reminder of the need to keep our minds open to new ideas and ways of thinking because all of us always have things to learn.

The native American cultures described in 'Braiding Sweetgrass' don't say we shouldn't consume or take at all from Mother Earth. Instead, they seek a balance which they call the Honourable Harvest. It's an idea of sustainability based on giving as well as taking. It's a notion that challenges all of us to do better, to find ways to respect a planet which gives us everything we have. A sustainable food future will need to be based on giving as well as taking. We will need to find a new relationship with the world around us, one where we are far more aware of our need for gratitude using the simple, powerful action that is saying thank you for what we do have rather than constantly seeking more. A genuinely sustainable food ecosystem would place reciprocity at its heart, nurturing the planet that gives us life. Unfortunately, that currently feels utopian, especially when we consider the massive inequalities and negative impacts associated with what we eat. Many have far too little to be grateful for right now.

4

Food Beyond the Plate
Health, Wellbeing & Equality

Food Poverty

By February 2021 there were over 2100 Food Banks
operating in the UK, more than half of which were run by
the Trussel Trust[35]. The number of three-day emergency
parcels they hand out has doubled in less than five years.
These stark facts show we are a nation in the grip of a food
poverty crisis where reliance on charity to feed yourself
has become normalised in less than a decade. We should
be far more furious about this than we are. This is not
normal.

However, the societal impacts of our broken food system
go far beyond the immediate challenge of finding dinner.
Even if you do have enough money to buy tea, what sort

of food is readily available and what is it doing to us? How wide are the impacts of what we eat?

Food bank use in the United Kingdom has ballooned in recent years, feeding people who can't afford to feed themselves despite living in the sixth richest country in the world. This, and I'm happy to be accused of repetition here, is not normal. How does a rich country end up with thousands of households needing charity to get a meal?

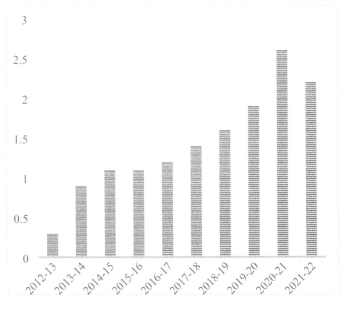

Food Bank Use in the UK

Number of 3 Day Parcels Handed Out (Millions)

Source: House of Commons Research Briefing 2022[36]

The House of Commons library has a research briefing published in April 2021 available for anyone to view. It makes grim reading and starts off with this depressing summary:

"There is no widely accepted definition of 'food poverty', but a household can broadly be defined as experiencing food poverty or 'household food insecurity' if they cannot (or are uncertain about whether they can) acquire 'an adequate quality or sufficient quantity of food in socially acceptable ways'".

The paper went on to note that "In 2019/20, 5 million people (8%) were in food insecure households" and "household food insecurity increased during the coronavirus pandemic. The Food Foundation found that 4.7 million adults and 2.3 million children lived in household which experienced food insecurity in the first 6 months of the pandemic, including 12% of all households with children."

Which is a very dry, bald way of saying a lot of people go very hungry in this well off, massively unequal, nation of ours.

Any realistic attempt to fix our food problems needs to address the issue of food poverty. It is morally unacceptable that millions of people go hungry in 21st century Britain whilst one government minister can waste billions over a career of incompetence. None of us should accept a lazy argument that there is no money to help those who need it. Any move to what would be considered more sustainable types of food needs to be delivered in a way that doesn't exclude large numbers of the population on low incomes. This will, in the short term, at least, it will require government funding. There is no point pretending there is another solution. We should not consider it a waste of our taxes to make sure that everyone can eat regularly and in a way that doesn't damage either themselves or the planet. We need to ask ourselves what sort of society we want to be. At the time of writing UK inflation is running at over 9%[37] and supermarkets are responding to a rising prices by slashing value and budget ranges as highlighted by the anti-poverty campaigner Jack Monroe.[38] The chief executive of supermarket chain Iceland has stated on national TV that his company is losing customers not to competitors but to food banks and charities.[39] Access to food is a key issue facing our society and we need to make sure the solutions are genuinely equitable and sustainable.

It may be that the simplest way to achieve this in the short term is to extend what are now known as Healthy Start vouchers to cover all school age children, set at a level to meet the cost of three meals a day at a given nutritional standard. These vouchers already cover milk, vegetables, and dry staples such as lentils and beans. We aren't a long way from a scheme that includes what is needed. It is an increase in scale rather than scope that is most pressing. If we are looking at the food needs of 5 million people, even a subsidy of £1 a day would equate to what seems like a large sum of money. But the UK spent £213 billion on benefits and tax credits in 2020/21 according to the government's own figures[40]. We are talking about adding another £18 billion to that figure. It's not an inconsiderable sum but it also isn't going to break the bank. And if that £1 a day doesn't seem much, it is £120 a month extra for a family of four to spend on good quality, nutritious food.

In the long term we need to tackle the range of issues that cause poverty and hunger in our affluent western nation. That is no small task, but it's our only choice if we want to be able to use the term 'civilised' to describe ourselves and create a food ecosystem designed for the good of those who eat rather than just those who extract profit. If we look beyond short-term subsidies to prevent food poverty we come up against the challenge of making sure our food represents genuine value rather than lowest price. For that to happen we need a taxation and legislative regime that moves the hidden costs of what we eat away from the less visible corners of our society that they currently reside in, and out into the unobstructed view of the shelf edge.

If such a path were followed, we would over time, create new shopping habits and opportunities along with meaningful shifts in what is consumed in massive quantities. These changes could include shopping more regularly for fresh food, visiting different outlets to gain access to the widest range of products or reducing shopping missions by learning to grown more of our own food as previous generations did. Once that process begins, the cost of these 'new' essentials (our sustainable foods of the future) starts to fall. There is a virtuous cycle waiting to be kickstarted over the medium and long term which can bring foods currently out of reach to many people back to being a realistic choice. That won't happen until we have a joined up program of change to make it a possibility.

Nutrition, what does a good diet even look like?

If cost was no barrier, what should we be eating from a nutritional point of view? It seems like a simple enough question, but I doubt most of us could answer it. Broad swathes of the population have grasped the 'five a day' message even if they get nowhere near achieving it. But what else should we be eating? Is it enough to rely on old truisms such as 'a little of what you like won't kill you'?

In an attempt to answer this, the UK government has produced an 'Eatwell' guide to a balanced diet as well as detailed tables showing what the intake of individual food groups should be for children and adults.[41] This document, available as a colourful download, reinforces the need for 5 portions of fruit and veg a day as well as advice on reducing intake of sugary drinks and sweet treats. It is one page of A4 in size. To be fair, there is an accompanying booklet that goes into more detail. Its summary of advice is as follows:

"Eat at least 5 portions of a variety of fruit and vegetables every day.

Base meals on potatoes, bread, rice, pasta, or other starchy carbohydrates; choosing wholegrain versions where possible

Have some dairy or dairy alternatives (such as soya drinks), choosing lower fat and lower sugar options

Eat some beans, pulses, fish, eggs, meat, and other proteins (including 2 portions of fish every week, one of which should be oily)

Choose unsaturated oils and spreads and eat in small amounts

Drink 6-8 cups/glasses of fluid a day"[42]

That all sounds fine in theory, but it fails to reflect the reality of how large parts of the population eat. There are many interlinking reasons for bad diet, but there can be no doubt that the UK collectively eats badly. And it is a complex thing to get right. Our nutritional needs vary by sex and age. A BBC food report gives a few examples:

"The average consumption of fibre and vitamin D is below the recommended daily intake in every age group. But with some nutrients, people in certain age groups are more at risk than others of missing out. Evidence shows, for example, that females aged 11-49 are more likely to be eating too little iron than other groups, and low calcium intake is a risk for girls aged 11-18."[43] Anecdotal evidence suggests this level of detail is not reaching most of the population.

Further evidence of our failure to give the quality of what eat the attention it deserves come from one of the best independent measures of nutrition available. The Global Nutrition Network is an independent body with a variety of stakeholders including nations, businesses, and the UN. They produce an annual report on the progress of countries towards a series of nutrition goals. In 2021 it found that the UK "is 'off course' to meet all of the global nutrition targets for which there was sufficient data to assess progress."[44] It goes on to state that there is insufficient evidence for a surprisingly considerable number of measures it uses before issuing a damming critique:

"The United Kingdom has shown limited progress towards achieving the diet-related non-communicable disease (NCD) targets. The country has shown no progress towards achieving the target for obesity, with an estimated 31.6% of adult (aged 18 years and over) women and 30.2% of adult men living with obesity." When compared with the rest of Europe the report found "the United Kingdom's obesity prevalence is higher than the regional average of 25.3% for women and 24.9% for men. At the same time, diabetes is estimated to affect 5.1% of adult women and 7.1% of adult men."[45]

Societal pressures also feed into our challenges surrounding nutrition and good food choices. Large swathes of western populations are engaged in a perpetual cycle of unsuccessfully dieting, often based around the notion of calorie control with little thought given to calorie quality. This trend has been reinforced by the actions of those who know better but are acting for their own benefit. An article published as part of the British Medical Journal's 'Food for Thought 2020' series noted that "In 2015 the New York Times revealed that Coca Cola was covertly funding the Global Energy Balance Network based at the University of Colorado, a research network set up to promote the message that all calories are equal. The network's aim was to show that sugar sweetened beverages are no more responsible for the rise in obesity levels than any other foods or a lack of physical activity."[46]

Given those headwinds it is unsurprising that a report by the charity The British Nutrition Foundation, found that less than 1% of the UK population has a diet that meets the Eatwell recommendations.[47] If we follow on from that statistic, what comes next shouldn't seem surprising...

Health – obesity, diabetes and more

The NHS defines obesity as a BMI score of over 30. By 2018 63% of English adults were overweight or obese by that measure.[48] To put that into a little historical perspective, in 1950 almost no one in the country qualified as obese, now 30% of people are. This is one, highly visible, sign of what the food we eat, and the changes that have occurred to it over the last fifty years, is doing to us.

Another, less obviously noticeable, but no less damaging, consequence of our diets is a similarly shocking rise in cases of type 2 diabetes which doubled between 1998 and 2018[49] which was highlighted by the Global Nutrition Network as part of their damming critique. A majority of these cases are linked to obesity and numbers are now growing quickly in young adults and children as the results of poor childhood diets hits home earlier and earlier. All this costs the NHS, and us through our taxes, a fortune each year. Think of how our increased use of Healthy Start vouchers could represent excellent value for money in this context if it got people eating a more nutritious diet that halted the rise in these preventable diseases.

And the impact doesn't stop at making us ill. It reduces our life expectancy as well. Eating this badly is killing us. Having type 2 diabetes potentially knocks ten years off your projected life span. In some parts of the UK, low income households can be expected to live as much as seven years less than more wealthy ones and the correlation between income levels and good diet are well established. Beyond that, bad diet and obesity can cause joint pain and reduced mobility which exaggerate existing problems around accessing decent food. It is no good asking more people to grow a little of their own fruit and veg if their health prevents them bending over without pain. The health implications of bad diets are far reaching and yet faced with limited budgets it's not surprising that people make short term decisions at the till which carry long term consequences.

The 2021 Dimbleby report for the UK government pointed out clearly that sugary, unhealthy calories are cheaper than healthy alternatives. We shouldn't lose sight of the fact that the cheapest way to get 1000 calories in your system is a pack of value custard creams or similar. It's one of the biggest challenges any food revolution faces. [50] How do we feed people in a sustainable, nutritious, *and* affordable way?

When making our food choices we are faced with a myriad of major barriers to healthy eating. These include the addictiveness of sugar, the lack of clear labelling to show what's really in our food and the underrated effectiveness of modern advertising techniques. We might be masters of our own destinies, but addiction is real and messaging works. So pervasive is this problem that Henry Dimbleby devotes a whole chapter in his Food Report to the issue of 'Escaping the Junk Food Trap' as he labels it. At the risk of overloading on the science, it is worth quoting the report at length to explain the problem driving the statistics of just a moment ago:

"The appetite is a classic complex system, controlled by multiple feedback loops. Sophisticated nutrient sensors in our cells and hormones feed information to the hypothalamus in the brain. These hormones include ghrelin, adiponectin, insulin, and glucagon. The release of appetite-inducing or -supressing hormones can be triggered by the level of sugar in your blood, the amount of fat you are already carrying, even how full different parts of your stomach or intestines are. Our responses to flavour, and the pleasure we get from eating, are also part of the appetite system. Numerous studies have shown that most people already know what a healthy diet looks like. More than 90% of us know we should restrict our intake of foods that are high in fat, sugar, and salt (HFSS), and 99% know eating fruit and vegetables is important for a healthy lifestyle. The problem is not information, but implementation. We find it incredibly hard to resist sugary, fatty foods because our appetites keep overriding our good intentions... Our appetite steers us towards calorie-dense foods because these are rare and precious in the wild. We find these kinds of foods particularly delicious... Our hormones take longer to convey satiety signals (the feeling of fullness) when we eat processed foods. And because these products are high in calories, eating just a few extra mouthfuls means consuming a lot more calories. There are hormonal reward mechanisms built into our appetite, which is where poor diet and mental health problems sometimes overlap. You can give yourself a temporary dopamine rush by eating a chocolate bar or a burger. People who are stressed, tired and anxious, often respond by over eating."

We also need to be aware of how our diets have less and less food that isn't highly processed. Ultra-Processed Foods (UPF's) now make up more than half of UK diets[51] and have been linked with a range of health issues including bowel diseases.[52] It is not just how many calories we're consuming that is causing problems. It's what sort of food we are filling our plates with as well. Such evidence gives further weight to information like the UK governments Eatwell guide.

If we're looking at building a sustainable food system, then undoubtedly part of that is reducing the cost of ill-health currently caused by what we eat. It is not sustainable for any health system to continue to grapple with the rising rates of type 2 diabetes. But how would we remove sugar and fat from our diets in sufficient quantities? How do we stop it being cheaper to eat the food that collectively makes us ill? As mentioned before, one solution would be to price food according to is actual cost. The Sustainable Food Trust issued a report on this subject in 2017. In their revised figures they concluded:

"The UK food system generates hidden costs of over £116 billion each year... The report finds that for every pound UK consumers spend on food, an additional hidden cost of 97p is incurred."[53]

By factoring in the hidden costs of mass produced, high sugar, low nutritional value foods which are almost always wrapped in plastic and contain palm oil, we would immediately present a series of different choices to consumers. This a large part of the solution to a lot of the problems faced by our existing food ecosystem but it is highly relevant here. Pricing food according to its genuine impacts would stop high sugar foods looking like the best value at once.

The UK already has what is dubbed a 'sugar tax.' The Soft Drinks Industry Levy came into force in April 2018 and the government claimed that more than 45 million kilograms of sugar was removed from products between the announcement of the policy in March 2016 and its introduction. The law places a levy on all soft drinks sold that contain a certain amount of sugar in them. Any money raised by the levy is meant to be targeted towards education for children. All of this is good, and the evidence does suggest the law has worked within its limited remit. Manufacturers have reformulated their products to avoid the charge and so less sugar is being consumed by those who drink them. However, this is only one sector of the junk food market, we need far wider action to tackle the size of the problem and any regulation needs to consider the substitution of natural sugar for processed sweeteners which may not be a great deal better. The case for further government intervention is clear, the challenge is how to overcome the siren chorus of food industry lobbyists and libertarian politicians who want nothing of the sort to happen.

High sugar products also need to be removed from settings where people are more likely to be in state of anxiety, stress, or poor mental health. It sounds obvious but we shouldn't be selling such items in hospitals for example. It makes no sense to provide a short term hit to people that merely reinforces the long term problems, no matter how harsh that seems at time of distress and potential loss. There is nothing stopping people bringing a chocolate bar with them, we just don't need to be actively providing that option in a health care environment. As an aside, how we sell food in hospitals is ripe for intervention full stop. The idea that we allow private operators to charge a premium for convenience in such settings, making food more expensive for those in a stressful situation, often involving loss, is morally abhorrent.

The same goes for schools. As a nation the UK has recognised that we should not be selling caffeine filled energy drinks to people under sixteen but, again, government intervention can go further. In fairness, rules are being planned for the autumn of 2022 that will move junk food options away from the most eye catching settings in our food shops, but that change will doubtless be countered by innovative and imaginative shelf edge displays including lighting and TV screens paid for by the manufacturers of such products. It is a constant arms race.

Beyond the obvious calls for state intervention in what we can buy and under what level of taxation, there is a need for a wider change in the environment around the food we consume. Good health isn't just about what we pick off the shelf.

Food, social stigma, and mental health

We live in judgemental times. Social media all but guarantees that to be the case but our politicians don't help, and they find handy helpmates in traditional media outlets as well. Over the past decade the UK has seen the concept of the 'undeserving poor' take hold as a mainstream staple for certain outlets and lawmakers.

Accompanying the rise in foodbank use, as detailed earlier in the chapter, we have seen comments from those in power questioning why such usage occurs and seeking to place the blame back on the individual. As an example, the former MP for the Vale of Glamorgan, Alun Cairns was quoted as saying; "It is sad to hear that so many people are needing to use the food bank. This will be for a variety of reasons: inability to manage money and to budget, addiction to alcohol or substance misuse, bullying at home, neglect by the benefit recipient and a range of other reasons." Notice that nowhere in that list is the responsibility due to a government that had been implementing a policy of austerity for a number of years by the time that comment was made. Whilst such deflection is understandable for a ruling party when faced with negative headlines, quotes like that (and there are plenty of others) help create an environment where shame is apportioned to those most in need of help by those most likely to have the power to bring about change.

An excellent report published in the Journal of Poverty and Social Justice, headed; 'Stigma, shame and 'people like us': an ethnographic study of foodbank use in the UK' written by Kayleigh Garthwaite, also draws attention to the wider social context accompanying such political outbursts. She points to rise in TV shows that can be classed as 'poverty porn' which portray a negative image of those dependent on help to survive.[54] All this feeds into an environment where our food choices become the subject of stigma driven by cynical sensationalism.

Garthwaite goes on to explain that research found that whilst foodbank use is free in terms of money, there are other costs associated:

"Shame, embarrassment, and fear can manifest in different ways for foodbank users, worsening existing health problems and creating further stigma. Overall, stigma was produced not from how people were treated at the foodbank, but instead through what other people would think, or through how people using the foodbank perceive themselves."

In short, there are once again hidden costs associated with the food we eat. In this case, those with no choice but to accept the help of food banks are often the lumbered with an unseen and unpriced cost in the form of shame and damaged self-esteem. Stigma doesn't stop at those who need free food. Our supermarket of choice is often loaded with societal connotations and assumptions. All of this impacts our mental health just as much as it does our physical wellbeing. Food is an area of society where we continue to be battered with aspirational advertising messages (just think of Marks & Spencer's TV adverts. 'This isn't just food...) and that has a knock on effect on those unable to access those choices for a variety of reasons.

It is not just a lack of money that can cause shame. People can be excluded from healthier food options because of physical or mental illness. The act of chopping a carrot can be unachievable to those with a physical disability or injury. Likewise, the energy and concentration needed to cook a meal from scratch can be far beyond the capability of someone struggling with mental illness. If you are confined to bed, unable to face social interactions or the noise and light overload that can be a large supermarket, it's no wonder you'll order a takeaway via the app on your phone. Those choices and their cycle of negative impacts lead to further opportunities for shame to be apportioned.

The terrible irony is that stigma often stops people accessing the help they need until they have made other problems or issues in their life worse than they might have been if they had reached out for support earlier. Foodbank users often wait until well after they are entitled to seek an emergency support voucher, which can exacerbate health issues even further. This is particularly true for stress and anxiety based conditions which may have contributed to a loss of earnings in the first place. Those who have never found themselves in that situation often seek to deflect responsibility for actions which may well have driven food bank usage to such record highs. Ultimately it is they who should be feeling the shame, not those most in need of help.

Access to growing opportunities

To consider our wider wellbeing is to step foot firmly into another area where we see the interlinked nature of our food challenges in action. In the UK just two in five adults eat their notional 'five a day' of fresh fruit and vegetables and we've already discussed how little of its own fresh produce the UK grows. If we take these two factors together and combine it with the scientific and anecdotal evidence of the lockdown, then an opportunity exists. We need to encourage more people to grow their own food.

Writing on the Royal Horticultural Society website, Professor Alistair Griffiths enthused about what gardening can bring to people:

"A gardening green revolution has started – with increasing scientific evidence highlighting the critical importance of garden plants, gardens and gardening benefiting our physical, mental, and social wellbeing. There are very few, if any, other activities that can achieve all the things that horticulture and gardening can – in particular, the measurable beneficial impacts on active lifestyles, mental wellbeing, and social interaction."

If one adds in the positive nutritional benefit of producing our own food, fresh and far tastier than the bland, easy to transport varieties that we find in our biggest supermarkets then it's easy to see why this should be encouraged. Local authorities could set targets for expanding access to allotments and developers told to build houses with a minimum size garden to allow for a small veg patch and a 6' x 4' greenhouse. Growing our own food is physical and mental health win. It is time we were proactive about making it as widespread as it was for our grandparents' generation.

Unfortunately, such a positive change will not be easy to bring about. The barriers that stop people cooking their own food or making healthy choices when buying something to eat, are often things that would stop someone growing their own food as well. For there to be a revolution in the ability to grow your own food we would need to tackle disability support, mental health services provision, educational opportunities, ability to access community assets such as minibuses, the wider cost of living crisis, and much more. And all of that before we even discuss where we're going to find the land in urban settings to let all these people grow their own food on. What seems like a simple win from a health, diet and cost perspective is a massive challenge that touches on almost all the intersectional problems rooted in the food we eat today.

As part of our own nascent work on creating a local food hub we've looked at the idea of land access and wondered if we could turn some of our own land into allotments, one of which could be given free of charge to a local charity to use as a base for growing therapy sessions for those who would benefit from it. It is an interesting idea and by the time you're reading this page may well have to come to pass but how many other landowners are willing to parcel off a bit of their land for free? In fact, it will probably cost us money unless we can find another source of funding to bid for. That's not a very realistic scenario except on a highly localised basis. Going forward we need a more joined up, systematic, approach to creating better growing opportunities across the UK, especially as existing allotments are often oversubscribed with lengthy waiting lists.

If we lift our heads beyond allotments and small-scale growing opportunities, we also lack small scale farms, or smallholdings, in the UK. A lot of people don't realise that local authorities in the UK are already owners of small holdings. 1% of the land in Wales is made up of such properties. There is a similar amount in England (The situation in Scotland is very different due to the history of Crofting). Every year the UK (on behalf of England) and Welsh governments are legally required to produce a report detailing the size and economic impact of these assets by the 1970 Countryside Act. One such property in Staffordshire was let to a 21 year old who went on to become the Farmers Weekly Young Farmer of the year in 2019. Without the opportunity to rent a small farm (the term often used is County farm) he wouldn't have had his start in the industry. What's more, as well as creating opportunity, these properties create revenue. The report for 2019 show that local authority owned small holdings in England generated a nearly £9m profit for their owners[55].

Why not have governments own more smallholdings? Owning smallholdings can generate a profit for the government or council which owns them. This is good in a time of austerity and cuts to budgets. Lots of farmers, particularly livestock owners, may well be seeking to leave the industry over the next few years as we transition to a new subsidy regime based on 'public goods' such as soil health and wildlife diversity. Such a move may alter incentives and established practices massively. In such a world, governments at all levels could buy large farms, split them up into smallholdings (building a handful of new rural houses into the bargain) and then lease them out for a profit over the long term. Existing farmers get a dignified exit from the industry and new opportunities for land ownership and stewardship are created alongside the potential for profit for cash strapped councils. We need to think creatively about how we boost access to the opportunities to produce our own food.

Fixing the basics

What goes on our plate doesn't exist in isolation. Our diets shape us as people both physically and mentally. Our food landscape is a mesh of interlocking issues and opportunities. Understanding the full costs of what we eat opens up the chance to make a real impact on the lives of millions of people. Creating more chances for households to produce their own food can have a significant impact on our wellbeing. Currently we are failing to provide people with healthy, nutritious, sustainable food in the UK, a failing which is repeated globally. Giving people the change to grow a proportion themselves can help rectify that.

Beyond that, when we do buy food, we must find ways to make sure the price of what we purchase represents its genuine cost so that our choices are not based on a price that fails to reflect the damage what we eat does to us and our surroundings. Taxation and government support is required to shift the actions of the market towards healthier offerings at a price that does not seem unreasonable when compared with high sugar junk foods that can trap us in a cycle of addiction. The improved long term health outlooks such a policy would create could well offset some of the cost associated with supporting low income families though such a transition.

To return to where this chapter started, it is morally essential that more support (at a cost that is affordable in the big scheme of things) is given so that significant minorities of society are moved away from reliance on charity to a place where it is guaranteed that three nutritious meals a day can be afforded. It is not for those who need help to feel stigma. It for us who do not push for such policies as the minimum any civilised government should be providing, to feel a burning shame and a need for action. No one is undeserving of food that nourishes them and allows them to lead a full and active life. It is a basic right that any future food ecosystem must seek to meet. What sort of nation are we?

5

A Better Support Structure

Rules of Engagement

Fired up by the possibility of creating real change to how our food is produced, how we buy it, and the wellbeing of millions of our fellow citizens, we need to consider of what sort of future we want. What would we scrawl on a mythical blank sheet paper? Where would our imaginations and our stomachs take us?

Unfortunately, we don't have quite that luxury. We are not starting with a clean slate. Our piece of paper is already filled in with the details of the existing food system we've become acquainted with so far. So, we're going to need to set ourselves a couple of boundaries for this exercise, one restricting, one liberating.

First of all, we need to adopt a philosophy stolen from former U.S President, Barack Obama, which suits our needs perfectly. We must acknowledge the world as it is. If we are serious about creating meaningful change and producing solutions which can make real difference to us and our planet, then we need to keep our feet collectively firmly on the floor. There is nothing to be gained from imagining a world with no supermarkets and no commercial farming. We must be harder on ourselves than that and face into the tougher challenge. How do we fix what we have? How do we reshape the system so that the negative actors currently present in our food reality change their behaviours in response to our new choices?

All of which brings us to our second rule. Nothing gets rejected from our blue sky thinking just because it is politically unlikely or unpalatable, providing the idea acknowledges the reality of the present. If there is one thing it is worth bearing mind over the next couple of sections of this exercise, is that it is easier to change which political party is in government in a democratic system than it is to demolish 500 supermarkets.

Political Engagement

And that seems a good place to start for those of us lucky enough to live in a democracy. At the ballot box, where we have the most power.

As mentioned earlier, the biggest barriers to changing the world around us in the short term, are no longer technological or knowledge based. We have the technology we need to reduce emissions by 50% by 2030 which would keep us on track for net zero by 2050. We also have the knowledge. The science is conclusive. The world is heating, a trend caused by rising greenhouse gas (GHG) emissions from a variety of well documented sources and the information is readily available to the public and widely propagated on mainstream media outlets. The largest thing stopping us is political action by our leaders.

That is different from saying we don't need to do anything or that our individual actions don't matter. They do. Massively. However, to drive change at the pace required is going to take big political carrots and sticks which go beyond the power of individual choice. We are going to have to be compelled to do some of these things because we simply do not have time for change to occur organically amongst populations of distracted, time deprived, cash poor, commitment heavy, rich world populations.

Luckily, we may be all those things listed above, but we are also blessed with the power and hope of democracy, even if it doesn't always feel that fabulous when we look at what our elected leaders are up to on a daily basis. The problem is, we are currently not channelling that power where it needs to go. No nation is the world is ruled by a Green party or similar that ran for office on an explicitly environmental platform. That is a shocking indictment of both the way politics runs on entrenched power and of our failure as voters to grasp the influence we have.

According to an Ipsos MORI survey conducted in August 2021 the British public viewed 'Pollution/Environment/Climate Change' as the second most prominent issue facing the nation with 32% of respondents highlighting as important to them.[56] Interestingly that concern cut across traditional political divides with around 30% support across all three of the traditional Westminster parties. The survey also revealed that slightly more older respondents found it a concern compared with 18-24 year olds which maybe counteracts the images of youthful protesters we increasingly see on the television news. It's not just Greta who gets it, Grannies do too.

That headline figure of 32% is up 16% from the previous survey so it seems fair to say that the blizzard of news stories and television programmes, predominantly featuring Sir David Attenborough, which appeared in the run up to the COP26 summit of 2021, held in Glasgow, may well have a had a short term impact of raising awareness. The challenge will be to keep hold of that attention now we have it, because 32%, is quite a substantial number in political terms.

In the last UK general election held in 2019 the Conservative party gained an 80 seat majority in the house of commons and with it virtual impunity to do as they wish for five years, or until another election is held. They achieved this great swathe of power at a key moment in our planets history by winning 43.6% of the vote on a turnout of 67.3%[57]. There were just over 47 and half million registered voters at the time of the election. Crunching those numbers shows us that the Conservative party gained their majority with around 14 million votes out of a total population of just over 66 million. Using those numbers, it only takes about 21% of the people in the country to win an impregnable majority in parliament.

That however is a false figure as babies don't vote (obvious, I know). If instead we use the total registered voters' figure as a proxy for adults (imperfect as it is) that gives us a figure of about 29.5% of the adult population who voted Tory in 2019. Now, remember, according to the most up to date polling information available at the time of writing 32% of those surveyed thought the environment was the second most critical issue facing us. Imagine what would happen if people voted in a way that really reflected that?

Before we get too excited it is important to note that this is an imperfect thought experiment. People are rarely so fixated on a single issue that it reshapes how a nation votes, but it does happen, and the UK has a very recent example of that. The political map was redrawn in 2019 as so called 'red wall' seats crumbled and turned Tory blue for the first time ever in some cases because of the most polarising single issue of our near history, Brexit.

So, all we need to do is get the population of every western style democracy as fired up about saving the planet as 52% of voting Brits were about Brexit. How hard can that be? Well, if we return to where we started this thought experiment, pretty damn hard. No one has managed it yet, nowhere has voted Green in big enough numbers that they are ruling on their own. The world as it is, is telling us we're trying to do something unprecedented.

Resist the urge to get all down heartened again, there is some hope. Green and/or specifically environmental votes are increasing in most countries at all levels, and it is important to remember that we've only had Green parties or their equivalent since the 1970's in Europe and even later in other parts of the world. The traditional parties of power have had sometimes centuries (particularly in the case of the UK Conservative party) to hone the art of winning. And Green parties have had been part of governments over the last thirty years, even if they haven't had sole power. Latvia even had a Green Prime Minister, Indulis Emsis, as part of a coalition in the early 2000's[58].

The most recent, and high profile, success for a Green Party came in the German national elections in October 2021[59]. The German Green Party became part of a tripartite coalition with the Social Democrats and liberal FDP. At one moment over that summer the Greens were leading in the polls, and it was the first time they explicitly campaigned with their leader as a candidate for Chancellor. As part of the government of Europe's most powerful nation this success has created a large opportunity to role model and shape genuinely green policies that set the tone across a continent. The wider world will be watching and hoping for a slice of inspiration, even if it will be pragmatically German in its styling.

While we wait to see if the pace of change quickens in Germany, what would happen if we managed to turn substantial numbers of people into green voters in other countries? What does this power mean? How does it help our goal of creating a better food ecosystem?

Well, first, it would allow us to reorganise central government so that it puts environmental issues at the heart of every decision. Alongside this powerful culture change, Green governments could create a co-ordinated structure that accepts that government has a role to play in food production and consumption to ensure than non-monetary factors are part of the decision making process that puts dinner on our plate. They would start from a position of being more inclined to be interventionist, which as far as our food future goes is a good thing as so much needs changing, and quickly.

On top of that it would create a world where the wider parameters are fixed in a way that would support good choices within our food networks. Green Parties would adopt some form of carbon pricing at a level that really would make an impact on the decisions of producers and consumers. It is also reasonable to expect recycling facilities would be upgraded to make it easier for households to recycle more rather than accidentally cross contaminate separated materials by accident. Waste would be taxed. Environmental damage punished. And so on.

That is not to say Green parties are a panacea to all our problems or that your author specifically endorses one particular green party. It is more that if we are looking for a way of creating a supportive web for our changed food industry to sit in, Green parties generically currently offer the best chance of doing that and we need people to vote accordingly. Green party manifestoes around the world contain policies that would actively move our food reality in a more sustainable direction, something that isn't prevalent in the plans of some other political choices currently.

To help change our political reality there are things that we can all do. Firstly, we need to exercise the soft power we have in our daily lives. Conversations, social media posts, recommendations, articles shared, thoughts discussed. These are the modern equivalent of a nation exporting its culture as a way of shaping the world to its viewpoint. We can shape the discussion for our family, friends, neighbours, and work colleagues. Then, when it is time to vote we can yell when we have done it. Point the way to polling stations, share the links to register to vote (www.gov.uk/register-to-vote), guide new voters to reliable sources of advice and fact checking. It all adds up to helping generate the maximum force for change from our magical power of voting.

It is possible to go beyond this as well. Anyone can become actively engaged, either with a specific political party or with the process of voting itself. Joining a political party involves little more than filling out your details and committing a small sum each month for membership. Just this one act and a small direct debit can help fund political action dedicated to making a difference. There is no requirement to do more than that. You can join and remain a silent member but, if that isn't enough for you then you could always get more involved with the party of your choice. There are never enough people stuffing envelopes or putting flyers through doors. It's not glamorous but this sort of groundwork is especially vital for small parties, which Green and environmentally focused parties tend to be. Raising awareness that they are even an option is often a huge step forward.

Beyond that lies a web of voluntary and sometimes even paid positions within a party as well as the possibility of standing as a candidate yourself. Amazingly, in 2021, we are still in a position in the UK where there isn't a dedicated green candidate available for people to vote for in every constituency when it comes to General Elections. That is not a criticism of those who do the challenging work of spreading the word, more a sign of how much more we still need to do and how big of a difference ordinary people volunteering their time and skills could really make. Imagine if every town council, local authority, and government had at least one Green voice in the room when decisions are made? It's a powerful argument for working to make the choice available to as many people as possible.

The activism doesn't stop with Green orientated parties though. If you are a member of a traditional or mainstream political party that historically hasn't placed that high an importance on issues relating to the environment or climate, then you can use your voice to agitate for more emphasis to be given to the crisis we're experiencing. Use your membership to argue for the inclusion of the sort of policies that can make a difference in the next manifesto or platform. Being a member gives you the right to be part of the discussion.

If committing yourself to one party doesn't sound like the sort of thing you would like to do, how about volunteering to help run elections? Manning polling stations and counting votes is predominantly done by volunteers and this work is crucial in keeping democracy alive. Without the chance to vote it becomes irrelevant what our choices are. This might not seem vital work, but it is. We need flourishing, vibrant democracies with engaged populations to help push the pace of change. Volunteering to help your local authority run elections is a key part of that.

The challenge of saving the planet from anthropological damage is not limited to one country. One of the advantages of social media is its global reach. We can now support the fight for more environmentally aware politicians across the globe. Solidarity with activists fighting for change in more repressive or less forgiving environments can really help boost morale and lift visibility. We've seen that impact with movements such as Black Lives Matters and Friday School Strikes. Working across borders can be effective.

It is always worth remembering that across the world our forebears often fought and died for the right to vote and there was a reason why they deemed it so important. It is up to us to fight against the complacency that exists towards a privilege we take for granted too often. There is no path to saving the planet and creating a sustainable, just, food future unless we use the power of our vote as part of the change needed. Voting matters. In fact, done in big enough numbers, it is not an exaggeration to say that it can save a world.

Government Reform and Structure

Ok, brace yourself. This bit is pretty nerdy, so I'm going to keep it as short as possible.

Let's fast forward a little. The masses have realised the power of their vote and we have a climate orientated party elected to power. What happens then? Government doesn't happen by chance, it is a series of conscious choices, just like most things in life really. And that includes the way governments are structured. In the same way that a boss decides how a company is divided into divisions, groups, and teams, so the way we are ruled is a set of decisions about the most effective means to make things happen. A political party committed to a better food future would be faced with some structural challenges because of choices that have been made previously.

The UK government at Westminster has the Department for Environment, Food and Rural Affairs, known as Defra. That is a choice, food has been linked with the environment and all things rural. Defra, like all modern organisations with a close association to well paid consultants, has a 'Purpose' and set of 'Priority Outcomes'. Included in these is the statement that the department will; "increase the sustainability, productivity and resilience of the agriculture, fishing, food and drink sectors...[60]."

Defra also has an 'Outcome Delivery Plan' which is how they intend to deliver the nice fluffy bits of their Purpose and Priority Outcomes. It is not for the faint hearted. The various parts of the department are broken down into a series of goals with accompanying metrics to measure success. When it comes the part about our food sector it talks of a Food Strategy White Paper (basically how government puts forward a wide range of new ideas on a particular subject) in response to the Henry Dimbleby report which we have quoted previously. It also mentions paying farmers to produce good environmental outcomes and improved opportunities for the fishing industry now that the UK has left the European Union. As metrics for this, we are given Productivity of the UK Agricultural industry, Productivity of the UK Food Industry and Value of UK Food and Drink Exported.[61]

So, just to clarify that. The one part of the UK government that has 'Food' in its job title is only looking at measuring productivity, i.e., how much output (product) is produced for a given number of inputs (wages, costs etc.), and how much food we're selling to other countries. That is why this boring section full of arcane details about how government is run is important, because that is clearly not good enough.

Government Bodies with Responsibility for Food Policy

Source: The Plan. Henry Dimbleby[62]

Unfortunately, it gets worse. The Dimbleby report found that sixteen different government departments play a role in food policy in England in 2020.[63] Responsibility for the governance of what we eat is piecemeal and diffuse, which leads to it being overlooked, either by accident or design. Keep in mind as well that Defra is mostly confined to England. The majority of its remit is the responsibility of the devolved administrations in their respective parts of the UK. The disparate nature of our food governance was recognised during the Brexit negotiations when the post of Parliamentary Under Secretary of State for Food and Animal Welfare was created to oversee any issues involving food supply caused by the intricacies of our departure from the single market. It is a telling admission. Suddenly when the supply of food couldn't be taken for granted or ignored, the value of one person co-ordinating affairs for government was obvious.

Historically the UK has had two periods when it has had a designated 'Food Minister': 1916-1921 and 1939-1958. It is no coincidence that those periods cover the two world wars. Once again, the supply of food was threatened, and central government needed control of what was available and what was eaten. Whilst war analogies are often facile and immature, there is a clear lesson to be drawn here. We are again facing an uncertain future with the potential for large impacts upon our supply of food and what type of food we should be eating. The case for a single 'Minister of Food' type position is clear. This should be a cabinet level position even if it continued to sit within the organisational chart of Defra. The job should be to co-ordinate and lead on all food policy including both the supply (agricultural, fishing, factory production) and sale of (retail, wholesale, catering) food within the UK in appropriate co-ordination with the devolved administrations. To achieve our future food ecosystem, we need to use the powers of central and devolved government to set the boundaries in the right manner.

Talking of the devolved administrations (the Scottish Government, Welsh Senedd and Northern Ireland Assembly), the Welsh have an idea that should be replicated for the whole of the UK to give a long-term voice to all discussions, and in our specific case, food policy.

In 2015 the Welsh Government passed the Well Being of Future Generations (Wales) At which "requires public bodies in Wales to think about the long-term impact of their decisions, to work better with people, communities and each other, and to prevent persistent problems such as poverty, health inequalities and climate change".[64] Well what could be more aligned with the structural food problems of poverty, health inequalities and the impact on climate change than that? The act created the role of Future Generations Commissioner for Wales whose role is to be the public voice of long-term thinking. This is something which is too often absent from our day to day political debate with its fixation on the next confected twitter storm. Creating such a role on a UK wide scale would enshrine into law exactly the sort of thinking we need to fix our food system on a sustainable basis.

These two actions, the creation of a single 'Food Minister' and legislating for a statutory long-term voice in the political system are very much the tip of the iceberg in terms of what can be done to make our political structures more suitable for a sustainable food ecosystem. All levels of government need to understand that policy and law are key parts of steering our existing food system in the right direction and laying the foundations for better outcomes in future. If by some chance you are interested in more detail on the functioning of government and its impact on food policy, then I recommend Tim Lang's book; 'Feeding Britain' which holds a lot of good detail written by someone who has spent a long time interacting with the tentacles of government in various roles.

CAP and Farm

The departure of the United Kingdom from the European Union presents a moment of potentially historic change for the farming industry in this country. For the previous 40 years or so, famers have been granted subsidies based on how much land they farm. (This is a simplistic but fundamentally accurate summary of the hideously complicated Common Agricultural Policy). Upon leaving the EU, the UK government and the devolved administrations have indicated a desire to move to a system whereby farmers are rewarded for delivering 'public goods' such as land management and landscape protection.

This would be a huge change and would reshape the farming industry. Some types of farming are likely to be uneconomical under the new regime with the first indications at the time of writing suggesting large cuts in subsidies for certain types of hill farming. However, it is likely that most types of farms will see reductions or changes to their existing level of subsidy which could severely impact on their profitability.[65]

Into this position of flux and change come deep and fundamental questions about what our farms are for? Are they there to manage hedgerows and soil health? Or they a means to maximise food production? Are they there to provide rural jobs? There are no simple answers to these questions and whole books can, have, and will be written on this subject. For our purposes it's enough to understand that the industry is facing huge change and we need how we want to produce food to be part of that conversation. Later in the book we'll look at some ways that different farming practices might be part of the creation of a healthier food ecosystem, but it is important to understand that the successful implantation of more sustainable practices would flow from a government that understood their value and embedded them within the framework of future subsidy regimes for farming. It's another demonstration that who we vote for and how they choose to structure the power of government really matters.

The introduction of new subsidy regimes between 2022 and 2025 in the individual nations that make up the UK is a key moment in our food production story. Currently we are in a world where government(s) are beginning to understand the need to shape a financial support regime that values biodiversity, landscape management and soil health. This is all brilliant. However, food production is slightly missing from the conversation. What we need is a balance with schemes that reward good land management practices *and* sustainable food production techniques such as regenerative agriculture. Writers such as James Rebanks, based in the Lake District, have shown that there is a path that can be plotted which satisfies both those aims, even if it is hard and not yet financially rewarding. Rebanks has looked to heed the lessons of the previous generations of his family who farmed the land before him. By learning of the pressures and pitfalls that befell his father as commercial scale agriculture became the norm and marrying that awareness to a passion for the older, less intrusive or intensive methods of his grandfather, he gives us a sense of how we can both learn from the past and avoid its worst excesses.

If we fail to embed sustainable food production in this round of reforms there is a danger we will endure a lost decade as we wait to see the impact of the new subsidies before realising the damage done to our ability to feed ourselves well, and in a way that increases our resilience in the face of external events.

Beyond those questions, the discussions around a better food industry touches on issues such as immigration and skills. Do we want to allow seasonal workers into the country to help boost the fruit industry in particular? Do we want to make those jobs more attractive for existing residents of these isles? Is food important enough to partially shape something as big as who we want to live in this country. There is a need to acknowledge that in the short term at least, we probably don't have the skills and experience to grow industries dependent on seasonal pickers on our own. It is another area where government needs to recognise the reality of our food industry and the importance of keeping it economically viable and ethically sound.

Education and Opportunity

All of which leads us onto education. Change only occurs if we arm people with the knowledge to make great decisions. Political engagement takes knowledge. Activism takes knowledge. Growing stuff takes knowledge. And a way to minimise damage done by slugs. But mainly, knowledge. The inter-generational hand-me-down of information that formed the backbone of families growing a bit of their own fruit and veg has been lost over the last forty years. The rise of the supermarkets and their ridiculously cheap, all year round produce sections has prompted the decline of the back garden veg patch. To reverse this trend, we need to reintroduce that knowledge. That can be through gardening clubs, YouTube tutorials, evening college classes, formal qualifications and more. All these means are part of the solution and will bring health benefits, physical and mental.

At University level, agriculture and forestry degrees are well established and there are a variety of NVQ course available at all four levels of qualification. However, there are no educational opportunities at A level or GCSE in such topics and basic gardening skills are not included on any curriculum that we have seen, even if individual schools do still do some bits on their own initiative. An attempt to teach a short primer on basic cooking, growing and food knowledge could be a way forward, but it must be acknowledged that timetables are always under pressure to cram more content in, and budgets are not generous for most schools. Even so, it can't be right that one of the biggest barriers to eating in a more sustainable fashion (according to informal conversations we've had with those working in the sector) remains a lack of skills to prepare and cook food from scratch. If we view schools as a tool to arm people with the life skills they require, then this is an obvious failing of current curriculums. The much maligned and under equipped 'food tech' could become something far more meaningful. Food, ecology, and sustainability education could be a powerful tool in our better future. Add it to the list of structural changes a well-intentioned government could make.

NVQ's also exist within food retail though they are underutilised in a world where staffing levels are so tight that room for people development is limited. Increasing the incentives for large retailers to make use of these courses would be a relatively low cost way of creating more opportunities to develop in a world where opportunities are scarcer.

There is also a need to find a way to make jobs such as fruit picking more inviting to British workers. As we noted previously, our departure from the EU has raised questions around how we staff these industries. Whilst mechanisation has replaced some jobs, we still need seasonal workers to make sure our harvests don't go to waste. Creating a system where summer spent picking fruit counts towards other qualifications or earns credits towards enjoying a gap year seem like ideas which might be worth considering to attract student aged workers to a type of work, which at the moment is unattractive to them. Three months on the land before heading off to university could become something of a norm if linked to the right incentives.

Failing that, the government is going to have to put considerable effort into creating a long term seasonal worker scheme that makes the British fruit growing industry, in particular, viable. The Office of National Statistics reported that a National Farmers Union survey found that 99% of seasonal workers were from the EU in 2018[66]. To replace this work force entirely with UK nationals would require large investments in equipment and mechanisation which would need a level of government subsidy or support, alongside a cultural change in how such jobs are viewed. This combination of events seems unlikely in the short term at least and may well lead to prices rising if wage increases are not matched by productivity gains. It is that old conundrum of making better food affordable, all over again. It may be that the benefits system needs to recognise the nature of seasonal work to allow such employees to be supported during the off seasons effectively. In the immediate future though, seasonal immigration is unavoidable.

Through the pandemic increasing numbers of people turned to growing their own food for both their well mental and physical health, and as result of facing the threat of food shortages in the near term. By improving access to formal and informal educational tools, that moment can be made into a long term transformation which can bring real benefits to wellbeing and may well bring about a change in how agricultural jobs are perceived.

Growing a bit of veg, along with structural reform, tackling health issues and nagging our friends and families to vote doesn't necessarily sound all that sexy but nuts and bolts issues like these are key to creating an environment where different food choices can flourish. Without better legislative support for healthy options, encouragement for fruit and veg production at all scales and a government that views the food we eat as a priority for its attention, any reforms we want to see in how our food is produced, where it is sourced from or where it is sold, are likely to end up failing. Wider reforms such as carbon pricing and immigration policy may not seem immediately relevant to the dinner that ends up on our plates tonight, but they really are. Food touches so many parts of our lives that the laying of the right groundwork for real change will need to be widespread and impact on many aspects of policy and decision making. To make the required impact these ideas need embedding deep into our education system to arm our next generation with better skills and choices.

Better Food

Part 2
The Producers of Tomorrow
Locally Sourced
Reduce Packaging
Meat/Dairy Alternative
Fairly Traded
Palm Oil Free
Reduced Food Waste
Sustainable Water Consumption

The Foodifesto

Better Food

- Legally binding targets for local government provision of allotments and other growing spaces.
- Government scheme to purchase existing commercial scale farms to be converted into smallholdings. Providing a dignified exit from the industry for existing farmers, more growing opportunities for others and additional rural housing.
- Updated Planning regulations to enforce provision of growing space both privately and collectively for all new builds.
- Sustainable Farming practices to be embedded alongside landscape management in all replacements for the Common Agricultural Policy.
- Creation of a permanent seasonal worker's scheme at a scale capable of supporting, and growing, agricultural production with emphasis on fruit picking etc.
- Report into the provision of farming support services such as abattoirs with a view to filling any gaps in provision and specialist skills to ensure

small scale farming is economically viable in all parts of the UK.

➤ Security of food supply and production to be enshrined in UK government resilience planning with the attitude of 'we'll always be able to import what we need' made redundant.

➤ Taxation of all non-sustainable palm oil.

➤ Creation of a Minister for Food at national level.

➤ Establishment of a UK Future Generations Commissioner in line with existing Welsh government provision.

➤ Legal standards for 'sustainable' packaging information to avoid misleading claims.

➤ 10 year plan to introduce robust water consumption labelling on all fresh and single origin products.

➤ Completion and publication of promised UK government White Paper in response to Henry Dimbleby's Food Plan.

➤ Competition authorities to include measures of local and sustainable food supply when considering any further mergers in the food retail industry.

➤ Tax on internet sales equivalent to business rates for all companies with turnover above £250,000 per annum.

6

The Producers of tomorrow

Biodiversity and Farming Practices

So, we've set finding fixes for some of the structural problems that hold back meaningful change in what we eat, trying to create a wider context where better food outcomes are possible. What next? Well, we need to think about who is going to supply our more sustainable food and from where. Who are our producers of tomorrow and what is holding them back in the present?

Farming is an emotive topic, and this book doesn't seek to be the definitive answer on the future on British farming. There are a plethora of great writers out there talking about what our farms could look like. However, we can say that any future farming sector needs to have its values and financial incentives aligned with the goal of a sustainable food industry. To achieve these goals, it is vital we take advantage of the window of opportunity granted by the need to replace the Common Agricultural Policy with something better and more effective at producing a farming sector that safeguards habitats and provides affordable, sustainable food.

Alongside modern, just-in-time, supply chains, increases in farming productivity since the second world war are the other unsung hero of the food that currently ends up on our plates. Yields of staple crops have increased dramatically over the last eighty years, beginning with the work of American agronomist Norman Borlaug in the 1940's. As an example, the UK yields of barley, wheat and oats nearly tripled between the 1950's and 1990's[67]. That progress, based around the use of artificial, nitrogen based fertilisers, has helped saved the planet from starvation as the population of humans exploded. It has also contributed to the global environmental issues we face today.

The costs of this modern miracle must be tackled if we are to create a balanced future that respects the planet as well as feeds us. Borlaug himself recognised some of these risks. His eponymous 'Hypothesis' saw clearly that increasing human populations would lead to one of three outcomes, starvation, increasing amounts of land dedicated to food production or increased food yields on existing farmland. In the end, we've got a bad combination of the latter two with added side effects as the price for avoiding the first.

Despite his work, and foresight, we therefore have some of the worst of all possible outcomes embedded in our existing farming industry. Higher yields continue to deliver huge qualities of staples but at the cost of developing large scale monoculture farming practices. Much of this food then goes to feed animals that humans will eat, a fundamentally inefficient way of using the calories produced which uses up more land for farming and shrinks the amount of genuine wilderness available for wildlife. All the while, people continue to go without food as we saw when discussing food poverty earlier in this book.

Partly because of these large scale farming practices biodiversity has plummeted over the last half century. In research conducted jointly by the Natural History Museum and the RSPB, the UK was ranked lowest amongst the G7 nations and third lowest of all countries within Europe on thier Biodiversity Intact Index. In practical terms they found that the UK had retained only 50% of its natural biodiversity. For comparison, Canada still nurtures 89% of its natural abundance.[68]

Once again, these negative forces within our food ecosystem are interlinked. Reducing biodiversity not only harms the natural world, it also increases our food insecurity. Declining populations of insects now pose a risk to the pollination of the plants we depend on for food. Bee numbers have dropped to such an extent that tech companies are experimenting with tiny bee replacement drones to do the job of pollination instead. This is truly a case of insanity piling upon madness. Maybe we should just stop the practices that lead to the decimation of insect numbers and let nature do her job, as she has for millennia? Or is the problem that, unlike a drone, the humble bee does not provide a steady stream of data ready to be monetised? It is hard not to be cynical in the face of such stupidity.

When we think of the work done by Norman Borlaug and his successors in growing yields, it is the part played by the pervasive use of nitrogen based fertilizers that troubles many. Nitrogen occurs naturally and is part of the lifecycle of all plants but a way to produce it synthetically was discovered in the early part of the twentieth century in a process that became known as the Haber-Bosch technique. As of 2018 230 million tonnes of ammonia were produced this way, the bulk of which ended up as nitrogen based fertilizer. Its production used 1-2% of the world's energy supply alone.[69] The carbon footprint of this manufacture is a significant reason by itself to seek to reduce our dependence upon it.

However, that is not the only problem with such large scale nitrogen use. Estimates suggest that as much as 50% of the nitrogen based fertilizer applied to crops ends up as run off. That means it does nothing to help feed us or our livestock, instead it merely pollutes our rivers, streams, and seas, warping delicate marine ecosystems as it passes through. The problem is so severe that in Wales that an 'All Wales Nitrate zone' was established in 2021 with strict rules on any potential run off being applied to all farmers, not just the heaviest polluters. This has proved controversial and unpopular with the farming community at large, but is a good indicator of the scale of the problem and the difficulty of tackling it on a piecemeal basis. When seeking a balanced food production system that values biodiversity alongside other factors, it's hard to see how such widespread use of nitrogen based fertilizers can continue. That in turn would lead to radical change in how farmers grow what we eat.

Down on the Farm

Henbant is a vision of another, better future. It is a small scale, family owned farm dedicated to holistic and regenerative farming practices. And, happily for us, they are one of the suppliers for our own shop. They are also the place we sat round the fire, drinking in the magic of song and conversation, pondering on the stories associated with our food.

18 months or more before that night, when we first found about what Matt and Jenny were trying to achieve just a few short miles from where we live and work, we dropped them a message and suggested popping over for a chat with a view to stocking their eggs straight away. That initial hello ended up stretching to over two hours of their precious time soaked up as they walked us around the farm and explained what they were doing and what they hoped to create. It was all, without exception, fabulous. A little higgledy piggledy perhaps, but fabulous all the same.

Even better were the two steaks we left with as a hello gift; the product of their pasture fed cows. When cooked they were like nothing either of us had ever eaten. The meat was tender and full of taste, the cream coloured fat separating into soft, wave like, ripples. They were exceptional. They were also not cheap and if I am honest I'm not sure we'd have bought them for ourselves if we hadn't tried them and realised how good they were. Matt and Jenny aren't daft, they understand as well as anyone the challenges around access to local food and they work hard to build connections within their community to ensure that locals are benefiting from what is on their doorstep whenever possible. It's also easy to see why people would keep going back once they tried their meat. We have subsequently had a mutton freezer pack from them as well which was just as delicious even if the punchy aroma did leave parts of the house a little sheepy for a while afterwards. It is good to still smell dinner three days later, isn't it?

For all that, when we consider our food future, something becomes obvious immediately. Henbant, and others like it, are oases. Islands of sustainable ideas, in this case bought to life by a couple of fabulous famers and gaggle of ever changing volunteers. Their veg box scheme is growing and is well- regarded locally, but it isn't always as profitable as it might be. The meat is amazing but beyond the price of some. The courses they host are excellent and informative. Matt does consultancy work as well. The whole just about keeps going in a way that would be

133

familiar to farmers of all shapes and sizes who have learned that diversification is the only real survival strategy for most. But as a blueprint for a different way of producing food it struggles with the realities of the world just like most dreams do. It's an old maxim, but if it was easy, everyone would be doing it. It is an equally obvious truth that the universe contains a lot of sharp edges when you are existing in a beautiful bubble. That's why we dealt with those boring structural changes first, it was all about creating a world when farms like this could become normal. Finding a way to blunt those who would puncture the dream.

To understand more of what Henbant are trying to do and why it is so hard, we need to step back and have a look at what some farming related terms mean, and why they are relevant to creating a better food future. What is permaculture? How does one rewild? Can you mow a silvopasture? Is agroforestry a tree you can eat? Are any of those concepts essential to our new food universe?

Before we wade into this, it is important to note that many of these terms overlap significantly and some of the descriptions may seem to cover similar ground. That isn't by accident, these ideas are all working towards similar goals and are often used in conjunction with each other as complementary tools creating a broadly sustainable (or 'holistic') whole.

Rewilding

Rewilding has been, in its own way, a bit of a controversial idea. In Sussex, the first large scale project featuring this idea had to fight to be taken seriously by DEFRA and other government bodies, and convince their neighbours that they were not intent on destroying a well-liked 'traditional' English estate and farm. Since then, opponents of the idea have grown more vocal, particularly animated by the belief that rewilding is about eliminating farmers and their historic role on the land. In one well publicised case in Wales, the advocating body, Rewilding Britain, has had to step back and let other agencies take the project forward such was the animosity generated.[70] Despite this, the same organisation found that 81% of Britons surveyed supported the concept of rewilding within existing National Parks[71].

Despite this mixed reaction, the basic idea is simple. Rewilding is a concept based around returning land to a more natural condition. It seeks to create a functioning ecosystem based around minimal human activity that promotes biodiversity and healthy animal populations. The idea being that this is a state closer to that which would have existed before widespread human intervention. However, it doesn't rule out farming in different ways alongside that or from culling animals as a source of income. It is, however, dramatically different in approach from mainstream, large scale agriculture.

The most visible pioneers of the idea in the UK are based at Knepp Estate in the south of England. It was they who had to reassure their neighbours and the relevant authorities when looking to introduce the idea. The owners of Knepp took a loss making farm and turned it on its head. Rewilding there involved introducing new species, creating and restoring waterways, and stepping back from attempting to hold back the spread of scrub and seemingly non-productive plant species. In short, neat ploughed and grazed fields became something far less pleasing to our pampered eye but far more conducive to animal health and growth. Species of birds, barely seen across the whole of the country returned to Knepp within the space of a few years. As they themselves explain; "Since the project began, the Estate has seen extraordinary increases in wildlife. Extremely rare species like turtle doves, nightingales, peregrine falcons, and purple emperor butterflies are now breeding here; and populations of more common species are rocketing."[72] Exmoor ponies, foraging pigs and deer were introduced to replicate the churn of the land that would have been common before enclosures and modern farming. The farm went from losing money year after year to profitability, albeit it on a lower turnover. Instead of chucking an endless number of high cost inputs in for a variable or falling return, the owners stepped back and found a way to work with nature.

In terms of food production, the outcomes of these changes are a mixed bag. Per acre, a rewilded estate like

Knepp now produces less food than it did 30 years ago. However, that food was being produced in an unsustainable way. The owners are quite clear, either they changed what they were doing, or they were headed to bankruptcy and nothing would have been grown or raised. If rewilding projects are to spread across the UK as campaigners would like, then there is a balance to be struck. We all need to find ways to encourage more insect populations back to health or we will struggle to pollinate what we want to eat (or end up reliant on bee drones), but we also need to have enough food being produced that we minimise our reliance on food imports where possible. This example shows the balance we need to strike. Luckily, when we look at fruit production in particular, concepts such as regenerative agriculture and rewilding can dovetail really well with increased production if the transition is managed carefully, and the right incentives are created.

Regenerative Agriculture

To further their own transition, Knepp is embarking on a regenerative farming project in 2022 adjacent to the land they've been rewilding over the past couple of decades. Regenerative farming is also what Matt and Jenny do at Henbant. So, what is it?

Regenerative farming is an umbrella term based around six core principles; understand the context of your farming operation, minimise soil disturbance, maximise crop diversity, keep the soil covered, maintain living root year round and integrate livestock.[73]

The practical application of those concepts involves enriching the soil, increasing biodiversity, and protecting water sources whilst working with nature. It has a lot of common ground with the ethos of rewilding. Indeed, it might be helpful to think of rewilding as one end of a spectrum of sustainability with complete land break down and soil loss at the other end. Regenerative farming seeks to sit somewhere in the middle, aiming to use the land primarily for food production but in a way that also improves biodiversity and minimises impacts on nature.

In terms of the themes we've looked to address across this book, regenerative agriculture has a couple more important points in its favour. The practices of soil management and ground cover, which are a key part of this approach, also increase carbon capture. The website regenerativefarming.co.uk explains the scale of the problem that has developed over time; "Over the years our cultivated soils have lost 50-70 percent of their original carbon content, due to cultivation, erosion, weathering, the use of chemicals and converting mixed species grasslands and forestland to cropland and mono species grazing land. Soil should contain around 28% organic matter, currently most of our soil contains less than 2%! Modern agriculture unintentionally, tends to take more carbon out than it puts back in."[74] Regenerative soil practices seek to reverse this trend and reduce the carbon impact of the way we farm.

Regenerative agriculture also seeks to improve food resilience and security. By seeking to widen the varieties of crops grown whilst protecting soil health and access to water, our food supply could be made more able to cope with changes to climate or extreme weather events. This is something that should concern us all over the next few decades. As areas that we in the UK have traditionally relied on to produce food for us, such as the whole of the Mediterranean coastline, both African and European, become unsuitable for such crop growth, it will be ever more important for us to find ways of diversifying what we grow at home. If sustainability can be seen as the drive to create an equilibrium that can be maintained indefinitely, regenerative practices seek to actively create a state that was better than that which previously existed.

Permaculture

The UK Permaculture association defines permaculture in the following way:

"Permaculture is a design approach based on understandings of how nature works. At its heart permaculture has three ethics: Earth Care, People Care, Fair Shares.

This makes permaculture a unique toolkit that is used to design regenerative systems at all scales - from home and garden to community, farms, and bioregions around the world.

With permaculture, people are treading lightly on our planet, in harmony with nature. Taking care of people and fellow creatures. Making sure that we can sustain human activities for many generations to come.[75]"

Now, as is often the way with these things, that is a little wordy but at heart permaculture is about designing a way of managing the world around us whilst respecting nature, ourselves and others. That design ethos is not limited to farming, it has applications in all sorts of settings, but for us, its importance lies in its use as a tool to create a different way of producing food. In this context permaculture covers topics such as soil management, animal husbandry and waste minimisation. All of these are areas which directly relate to our food future.

To many of you reading, these ideas might not seem that revolutionary. Surely, we want healthy soil, thriving environments and animal centric herd management? But think back to earlier in the chapter and how we looked at the revolution in agriculture that followed the second world war. Think of Norman Borlaug and the explosion in yields that drove large scale farms and massive changes to our traditional landscape. Calling for a system that doesn't view the size of yield as the sole measure of success is pretty radical for a lot of farmers who have only survived by a ruthless focus on driving productivity on their land. Many such landowners would argue passionately and correctly that they were only doing what they were asked to do in the face of a tide of food insecurity that was left behind as direct memories of war and rationing faded away.

Within the farming community there is a deep sense of loss and internal conflict when they reflect on how they have operated, amplified by a feeling they had no choice if they wanted to survive economically. When we speak of adopting a permacultural approach to farming we are looking at the chance of a reset. A redesign of how we farm, what process we use, how different crops and animals work together and interact with the world around them. By adopting such ideas there is an opportunity to give farmers an alternative way of operating that many may welcome given the chance.

Agroforesty

Next on our list of terms that we might have heard but are not sure exactly what they mean, is Agroforestry. The Soil Association says that "Agroforestry is the practice of combining agricultural crops or livestock with trees and shrubs. It is a great example of agroecology in action."[76]

Unlike some aspects of permaculture which can seem a little abstract, this is pretty simple. Trees + Crop = Agroforestry. Silvopasture, a type of agroforestry, is similar; Tree + Animal. You might have rows of nut trees with goats foraging between them or you could have well-spaced rows of fruits trees with cereals being grown in between. The idea is you move away from the reductive nature of a single species and towards a mixed system that maintains a good output of food but does so in a way that nurtures both biodiversity and the interlinked relationship between plants and animals.

The Ellen MacArthur foundation is an organisation set up to promote the idea of the circular economy and they have produced an excellent report titled 'The Big Food Redesign' which looks at a lot of the subjects covered in this book and is available online from their website as a free download[77]. When talking about the idea of Silvopasture they imagine a new fictional product bought to market that is a triumph of the idea. The authors conjure up a new range of cheese products produced from a system that sees Walnuts grown alongside cattle.[78] They explain how such a system could produce "a Roquefort made from walnuts, Comte made from dairy milk, and a Caseum made from a blend of dairy milk and walnuts."[79] This is a great practical example of Agroforestry and Silvopasture in particular. Who wouldn't want a future filled with walnut cheese?

No Dig

This one should be the friend of all gardeners as far as I can see. No Dig does exactly what it says on the tin. You can put you spade away and rest your weary back. The future lies not in frustrating toil but in disturbing the soil as little as possible.

The No Dig approach is definitely catching on amongst gardeners and small holders and a lot of that has been driven by the popularity of champions such as Charles Dowding and his YouTube channel. It's a great way of seeing how big scale ideas such as regenerative farming can effectively trickle down to smaller scales. When talking

142

about protecting soil health, No Dig is a practical path you can take in your own back garden based on the principle of digging into the ground as little as possible. The aim being to preserve the structures within the soil whist not disturbing the worms and bacteria that are vital to good growing. Unless you have heavily compacted soil, it should work for anyone.

In practical terms a No Dig bed is created by mulching (laying cardboard of the ground usually) and then adding manure or compost on top. It really is that simple and advocates such as Mr Dowding are adamant that crop yields are higher as well as the soil healthier. You can check out his many online videos where he details the way he tests and weighs his output in a given year as evidence of that. Maybe less work really is the future...

Back to the Farm (again)

Hopefully that whistlestop glossary has given a little familiarity with what a few of these future farming terms mean. Ultimately, the answers lie in a combination of all of the above and more. We need a locally sensitive patchwork of solutions that takes the best of all these ideas and implements them in the optimum way possible for each location. Rewilding was the right solution for Knepp with its large estate and ground breaking owners. That doesn't mean it's the right solution for a small farm or a commercial dairy operation. What we require is a legislative framework and subsidy system flexible enough to recognise the value in what works within a given landscape.

For Henbant, the vision is very much based around regenerative farming. If we think back to those six basic principles, the local context is unavoidable up here. The weather is unescapable and, by UK standards, pretty brutal at times. Your choices are shaped by the opportunities the climate allows. But equally, as the climate changes, new ideas could flourish.

To look after their soil, Matt and Jenny keep their animals on the move more than traditional farmers might do. The mobile chicken house is a particular joy. The flock heads to bed in one location and then wakes, stretches, pecks expectantly and then wanders down, moderately bemused, to a different patch of land than the one that was there when they went to sleep. It stops the ground being over grazed and protects the cover of that all important soil.

The confused chickens are following a few days behind the dairy and meat herds of cattle that keep moving regularly through the outlines of what will be agroforestry areas. That's something we've put into practice at home as well. Up on our hillside the two, moderately chunky, little ponies are shuttled around the acreage in reasonable sharp fashion as we seek that balance of small hooves creating some churn without totally grazing the ground bare. Felipé follows them. It's a good, if slightly ridiculous looking, example of how these practices can work on large estates, moderate size farms and modest small holdings. The principles remain the same, the execution of them lies in the hands of the individual. By following that path change can become empowering rather than prescriptive.

Back at Henbant a wide range of crops has been introduced, a thriving market garden sits alongside an orchard and some nut trees. Hedgerows are slowly being planted and Matt talks with his usual exuberance about green corridors across the land. Again, this is a concept directly transferable no matter what the size of land available. As for us, we've planted mixed hedgerows at home full of hawthorns and various berries including the delicious but painstakingly harvested Sea Buckthorn. Instead of the three of four tree varieties that were present when we bought the place, there's now more than a dozen with more on the way as I write. But it scales down further. On a patio not much wider than a garden path we know people who are growing veg, fruit and flowers in a glorious mix of the productive and the pollinator friendly. The only difference in all these examples is the scale. These ideas are open to everyone.

Smaller can be better

If we think about these changes in practical terms, just how small scale can these ideas go?

As part of the process of writing this book, we took stock of what we were achieving at our shop and how we could put to life the ideas that we hoped would appear on these pages. As part of that discussion, we concluded that we weren't doing enough community engagement. With our ethos and beliefs surely we could be part of a spider's web of interconnected food producers, retailers and consumers that becomes more than the sum of our individual parts? Could we play a little part in bringing the area together?

Following on from that we stuck up a few social media posts and had a chat with a handful of our more interesting customers. Before we knew it, new connections were being made, often in unexpected places. Very quickly it felt like we were pushing at a series of open doors.

Our nearest leisure centre is best described as functional. It's a grey pebble dashed slab of box, tinged with acrylic red. It's never going to win any design awards but, like many such municipal buildings up and down the land, it does what it says on the tin. I must have driven past it hundreds of times over the years but it wasn't until one of our new connections sparked into life that I stumbled across something beautiful happening in unpromising circumstances.

Nestled against the unprepossessing walls, beneath the ramp that leads to the first floor entrance sits a handful of raised beds and a community sensory garden. Here individuals who need exercise or therapy can be referred by their doctor to take part in growing sessions as part of their health care. These are people for whom going to the gym might not be appropriate, but some form of exercise is necessary. Talking to the team charged with bringing this idea to life a lot of the interlinked issues we've discussed earlier in the book came to the fore. There was a lack of training in basic gardening for those running the sessions, as most of them came from a physical fitness background. Impressively they had overcome that challenge and they were keen to show me pictures of beds full of successfully grown produce. The kicker was that no one had eaten it.

All the effort had gone into getting the raised beds built, finding patients to attend the sessions, scraping together some growing skills and getting seeds planted. Only months later did everyone involved realise that, such is the intersectional nature of so many of these food related problems, the people growing the food either didn't want to, or couldn't, cook their own fresh vegetables. Such a thought might seem staggering, but this is the real life manifestation of all we talked about in our chapter on food and health. There are real physical, mental and educational barriers to people consuming great, locally grown food. And in this case, although people had managed to bring a small community space to life and offer a growing opportunity to people otherwise deprived of it, that wasn't enough. There was more work that needed doing.

The answer is to build more of those ad hoc spiderwebs we spoke of a moment ago, so that our food systems are flexible enough to take a small one off crop of surplus from tiny growers. That's tricky, and we'll talk more about that in our section on how the food retail industry needs to change, but it's an important part of the story of our new look food producers. Micro growing is key, from multiple perspectives. It brings health, wellbeing, resilience and diversity benefits that are sorely needed. In our vision of tomorrow, small can never be too small.

Stunting Imbalances

For all the positives associated with them, there are limitations linked with enterprises such as Henbant and all the others like them. Food produced this way is more expensive compared to mass grown monocrops which make heavy use of nitrogen based fertilisers. It is, as is so often the case in the food industry, an unequal fight. So, whilst it is right to say that these ideas are open to all, the ability to put them into practice successfully is constrained by the wider problems of the UK food and farming industries.

Let's start with carbon. By now we all know that we need to reduce the amount of carbon dioxide and its equivalents, in the atmosphere. Large scale agriculture practices are considerable sources of carbon emissions and yet that is not taken into account when the price of the product is determined because the requisite carbon taxes and legislation don't exist. The flip side of that is that the beneficial effect on carbon emissions that comes from regenerative farming and other such practices are also not taken into account. If they were, the price of 'cheap' veg would rise and the additional cost to the consumer of buying locally sourced, organically grown, sustainably produced produce would fall. Such moves might not make up the whole gap, but they would bring them an awful lot closer together. As it is, carbon polluters go unpunished and those doing the right thing are unrewarded. That has to change. When we waded our way through the detail of governance reform and law changes earlier in this book, this was exactly the sort of thing we had in mind.

But the structural imbalances go beyond carbon accounting. Small scale producing means higher cost per unit by its very nature and that can be exacerbated by a lack of infrastructure. For example, pigs can be a really valued part of a rewilding project or agroforestry system. They are natural ground browsers and land churners. They're brilliant for rooting around underneath trees, it's what they did historically. We'd quite like pigs, other small farmers in the area would too, but the nearest abattoir that can handle pork is in Wrexham, more than 90 minutes' drive away. That's just not practical for one or two pigs at a time. The fuel costs alone would render the resultant chops and bacon totally unaffordable. Any government serious about creating a world where small producers are valued and supported needs to address such gaps in our basic food production infrastructure.

Further inequalities exist in access to training, finance, and data. The last one of these is particularly prevalent in modern farming. Large agro-businesses are, like so much of the world, increasingly data driven. Multinational seed and fertiliser companies increasingly offer farmers access to data, whether that's historical, or up to the minute based on machinery movements or weather patterns. Such detailed information help reinforce the advantages that large scale growers already have. To be clear, they can't be blamed for using what is available to them, any business would. Yet it's another area where help is needed to ensure that, because our food future is the very definition of a public good, such data isn't exclusively locked away behind price walls in private hands.

Without the systemic changes we're exploring, we can't shift to a better food future because better food producers won't stand a chance. We need to put a price on emissions and environmental damage, we need to assign a monetary value to the health implications of what is currently cheap food and we need to support those on low incomes whilst we transition from our current food reality to our better ecosystem of tomorrow so that those with least are not punished for historic failings that treated food as little more than the number of calories we were shovelling into ourselves. Different ways of growing food and safeguarding the environment do exist, we just need to give them a space to flourish.

All those hungry mouths...

As much as regenerative agriculture and all those other ideas we've touched on sound great, there is a reason large scale, intensive farming exists; it produces a lot of food. How would lots of little farms doing their own thing replicate that total output? How do you feed everyone if we stop supersizing yields through artificial fertilizer use?

The simple answer is, they can't. Not directly. Changes in the way we produce food have to sit alongside changes in what we eat. If these two things happen in unison then there is no reason we can't produce food in the ways outlined in this chapter.

In June 2022 the Sustainable Food Trust released a report called 'Feeding Britain from the Ground Up'[80]. The document breaks down the type of land the UK has and shows the most effective use of each category. In practical terms that means there is some great quality farmland that we can grow anything on and some lumpy bits that are only fit for grazing. Whilst that sounds like common sense, by placing numerical values on each sort of land and assigning hypothetical farm models accordingly, the Sustainable Food Trust we able to produce estimates of outputs that could be possible in a future food system.

The Executive summary of the report found that; "… modelling suggests that a nationwide shift to sustainable farming would result in an increased availability of seasonal vegetables, fruit and pulses; slightly less beef and lamb and about a third less dairy, produced from high-welfare, mainly pasture-based systems; significantly less chicken, eggs and pork – with the remaining produce coming from free-range systems with high standards of welfare; and roughly the same amount of grain-based foods, but from a greater variety of cereals including more oats and rye."

Such a future scenario would see us eating less meat, but a wider range of cereals and other crops suited to our land and climate. The report makes clear the argument for such as shift. "By aligning our diets to what the UK could sustainably produce and eating according to the recommended intake of calories and key nutrients, we would be able to maintain or potentially even improve on current levels of self-sufficiency."

All of this is a powerful argument for change and a strong case that we do not need to fear a move away from large scale commercial farming, no matter how dependent we seem on it currently. Building on the work of the Sustainable Food Trust and others, it's easy to see how farms such as Henbant are a definite part of this improved vision for the future, no matter what their size. We need a world filled with Regenerative agriculture, holistic management practices, growers working with nature to produce more resilient outcomes and the sharing of knowledge that allows these things to trickle down to growers of all shapes and sizes.

The widespread propagation of these ideas is essential to improving how we eat. As we saw in the second chapter of this book, opportunities exist for us to be growing more of our fruit and vegetables as well as things like nuts but it's not enough to simply do more of the same and chase high yields from ever more diminished soils. We need to rethink how we farm and for what purpose. There has never been a better moment to have that discussion as the UK seeks to replace the common agricultural policy with something more suited to our individual circumstances and a better food future.

It's also true that those steaks we tried, with their delicious, melted waves of fat, are the future of the meat we should be eating. Part of our transition to a better food future involves moving to a world where we eat less meat, but what we do have is of a higher quality. Pasture grazed beef is one answer, as is high welfare poultry and relationships with local farmers and butchers. The future needs cows, just not as many and not ones that are sensitive, highly selected breeds that rely on soy based feeds, intensive farming practices and eye-watering amounts of medication to keep them healthy. At the risk of sounding like an old romantic, we need traditional breeds managed in a holistic way producing high quality meat that we regard as a treat amongst a diet which contains a variety of other protein sources.

An emphasis on quality should inform much of our thinking on farming as we move forward. Instead of focusing on yield, which is just how productive a field is by weigh of crops harvested, we should be looking a nutritional value produced per hectare instead. A shift from mass producing cheap calories as simply as possible to valuing the quality of the calories we're growing would lead us to a place where we can feed the world by using different farming practices and different diets in unison.

Just think of how different the choices on the shelves of our local shops would look in such a reality.

7

Locally sourced

Local Food Availability

As delicious as freshly grown fruit and veg are, they are not a complete diet. Our food future will be filled with other products. But what do we need those products to look like? What sort of standards do they need to achieve to make a positive impact on us and the planet?

In our shop, the answers to those questions come from our 'Sustainable Seven', the list of rules that determine what we stock. It's now time to take a look at most of those concepts in closer detail because it is those ideas that define what sort of food should fill our vision of a better tomorrow. Having laid out the systemic changes needed to support our new ecosystem and the types of growers and producers needed, it's time to set out some aspirations for what we could all eat. Doing so will illustrate how those choices can positively impact the wider planet, the places we live and our health and wellbeing. Within these solutions also lie another raft of positive differences we can make to how our food future looks. Even better, many of them are things we're able to influence directly as consumers and they dovetail neatly with some of the concepts we met in the previous chapter such as permaculture, rewilding, no dig, agroforestry and so on.

To start this off we'll begin where many of us are most comfortable, close to home...

We touched on global supply chains and their impact on our food resilience when looking at the concept of food security and we've seen how globalised soy feed production fattens cows in one country whilst deforesting another. These disparate strands of our failing food ecosystem show the need for us to shop for food produced far closer to home than we currently do. But there are two other main reasons to shop locally as well.

The first of these is the carbon footprint that comes with the Herculean task of shipping all this food around the world. The greenhouse gas (GHG) emissions currently associated with the transportation of our food currently amount to 12% of the total sector quantity. (This is dwarfed by the 40% caused by agriculture but still the joint second highest contributor to the total). [81] The worst thing about this is that as consumers we have very little way of knowing what is contributing to the problem as we make our purchases. How we transport our fruit and veg, for example, should make a massive difference to what we buy but we are not readily given that information. Bananas are shipped on boats across the world, asparagus, eaten out of season, is air freighted a similar distance. The disparity in carbon footprint is huge and yet you wouldn't know it unless you went specifically looking for the information.

This information gap is brilliantly addressed by Tim Berners-Lee in his fabulous book 'How Bad are Bananas'. In it he delves into the minutiae that makes up the carbon footprint of everything with consistently surprising and informative results. His work found that a typical banana has a footprint of 80g of CO_2. In comparison Peruvian asparagus came in at a whopping 3.5kg of CO_2 for a 250g pack.[82] We'd have no way of putting a number to that massive difference without the dedicated work of people like Berners-Lee, certainly our food retailers aren't going to volunteer such information, if they even have it in the first place.

To follow its work through to its end, 'How Bad are Banana's' details the footprint associated with UK grown, in season asparagus. It's just 125g of CO_2, not that different to our original banana. It's a graphic illustration of how damaging the supermarket culture of all year round availability really is and how it's warped our expectations totally. It is not normal to eat asparagus 12 months of the year. If we stopped and reacquainted ourselves with this simple, intuitive fact, we could make a real difference to the planetary impact of our food. Regaining our understanding and acceptance of seasonality is key.

The second reason to shop locally is less easily defined in statistics but no less real for it. By producing food closer to home we can build a connection with what ends up on our plates and the people who are responsible for it. Such ties form one of the strands that make up the often discussed, less rarely spotted, sense of community that many public figures are so keen to pontificate about on a regular basis.

This connection to real people and their lives has been one of the joys of owning our own sustainable food shop. We talk to the people who make a lot of what we sell. I know who grows our local veg. I chat to the woman who keeps the chickens for eggs we sell. I've had good conversations with a number of local brewers and cider makers, and so on. These bonds aren't measurable on the balance sheet, but they add to the fabric and heft of our business. They give it a sense of place that is something online shopping or large supermarkets can't replicate.

Despite the undeniable emotional pull to the idea of shopping locally, most people don't get the choice to do so on a regular basis. The vast majority of the UK public does its weekly food shop in supermarket chains whose idea of 'local' involves a beer brewed four hours away in Cardiff being relevant to the customers of North Wales. Whilst the big retailers bring many miracles of standardised availability to our shelves, they are all really bad at genuinely local choice. For them it's complicated, inconsistent and hard to push through their systems which are set up for huge quantities. Such relatively niche products also lack a sales history that makes their computerised ordering systems happy. The loss of these regional differences deprives shoppers of genuine choice and local growers and producers of large scale outlets for their products.

The persuasive case for shopping for locally produced food is wider than just what we pick off the shelf. It can support local employment, create strong links within communities and reduces the food miles and GHG footprint associated with the product in a wider sense than just transportation of the finished item. Local food is a good thing, we just need to be aware as consumers of the full picture associated with what we eat. Never forget that we live in a world where if we type 'what is local food?' into an internet search engine, the first item that comes up is an advert for pizza delivery.

So, as consumers we need to be hyper aware of what really is local food and take an interest in the little details that make a big difference. As we seem to say repeatedly when it comes to what we eat, that isn't easy. Products can be labelled as 'local' despite being processed, packaged, or manufactured some distance away from where a given company is actually based. In our area we know of regional beers that travel hundreds of miles for bottling, reducing massively the footprint benefits associated with drinking a local product. The same goes for some chilled products labelled with Welsh language information that were packaged up a long way from home. It's not easy to be an ethical consumer and straight forward good choices are hard to find. So, when we go beyond local farmers, what should we be looking for in our local producers of tomorrow?

Genuinely Local

Sometimes the obvious needs stating. Is your favourite local product really that beneficial to the area? There are cases when this is going to be clear cut. The local bakery that produces fresh bread every morning. The cheese maker who farms the animals that produces the milk that goes into their award winning Cheddar. But how about your favourite cake shop? They are right there on that characterful side street just off the remains of the main shopping precinct in town. They employ a couple of local girls and you know the owner from when you were at school together, even if you were a couple of years apart. Surely that's better than mass produced cake?

And of course, the answer is… Probably.

The devil, as always is in the detail. Where does our hypothetical baker source her ingredients? Does she use locally produced flour or at least a UK based mill? Do they use the cheapest available plastic packaging for their cakes, or do they use cardboard boxes or compostable wrap? Are the paying those couple of assistants the living wage? As a consumer it's really hard to know the answers to these questions. How many of us walk into a local bakery and ask if the nuts in their almond slice are contributing to the desertification of parts of California? (I wouldn't necessarily recommend this as a good opening gambit by the way, you might not get allowed back in unless the business owner in question is exceptionally environmentally aware or very forgiving).

In this example, your local cakes are almost certainly better than a mass produced, cheaply priced, palm oil stuffed, widely available product. But it can't be taken for granted that they are automatically a lot better. As always, we need to do our homework to find the people genuinely offering a real and substantive alternative.

To us a really local product is one that uses local ingredients wherever possible and minimises the distance and impact of all the stage of production, be that the raw ingredients, the packaging and bottling or the actual manufacture. When it comes to ingredients it's quite simple to work on the basis of 'local first, national second, everything else last' when looking at the supply of goods or the ingredients for a product. Flour from a mill ten miles away is great. If you're a food producer and your area doesn't have a flour mill (very likely in this day and age) then source what you need from a UK supplier who uses sustainable packaging. If you need a specialist product that is only manufactured abroad then use that only as a last resort and consider alternatives first. Sounds simple but it needs to happen more widely, and the information needs to be visible.

To illustrate this point even further, last Christmas we looked to stock a tin of biscuits as part of our seasonal range in the shop. Tins are reusable, particularly if you bring them back to us and fill them with pasta or something else. When we went looking, we found that the nearest tin of biscuits we could find to us was produced in Lancashire. We ordered some in and made a point of labelling up why we chose them. They might have come from more than 100 miles away (and outside of Wales), but they were still the best choice in terms of transport footprint. For us they were the most 'local' biscuit option available.

There isn't one definition of what local food is. As with so much of what we're discussing through the pages, it's another amorphous, slippery concept. What seems local to you, might not seem so to someone else. The definition will vary on where on you live. On whether your setting is urban or rural. The idea of local also speaks to how communities define themselves, particularly in the less densely populated parts of the UK. Local can mean something very specific. My village, my valley, my tribe. In trying to place a finger on what local food is, we run into not only geographical definitions, but also cultural boundaries which can be will-o-the-wisp like at the best of times.

Research by Kantar carried out through the global pandemic highlighted a growing trend in what they define as 'localism'. According to their work: "localism continues to be important. Half (52%) of all respondents pay more attention to product origins than they did pre-pandemic. 68% prefer supermarkets close to home while 64% think local stores are important for the community". Whilst this seems promising and is a good indicator that people have become more aware of the need to support their local area, it's important to note that in this context it could mean that consumers were just having a short term reaction to lockdowns and pandemic regulations. It will take more time to know if a genuine upswing in support for local businesses is under way. A more unambiguously upbeat note was sounded in research carried out by Statista. Their survey found that number of consumers intending to shop locally rose from 40% in 2019 to 60% a year later.[83] A positive trend that would be great to see continue.

In 2020 the UK government issued a press release in support of 'Shop Local Week', highlighting 8 reasons why it was important to support your local community. They ranged from saving jobs to helping the environment. The list is all fairly valid although it does beg the question why it's worth supporting these aims for one week a year when for the other 51 weeks government policy does so much to work against small scale and local producers. Number 4 on the list was 'A safe way to shop', highlighting something we found during the pandemic in our day to day work. When faced with the unknown, the idea of being served by someone who you could trust to take your safety seriously, and that you were able to have a meaningful interaction with had never been more important or more valued. Shopping local build connections not just via the food we eat but by the chats we have along the way. If it wasn't for those conversations this book probably wouldn't exist. Humans, after all, are highly sociable animals that thrive on the stimulation of interaction. Amazon can't satisfy that need in us no matter how much it trims delivery times. Under the harsh glare of the pandemic, it turned out that our idea of local and what it can bring to us is another concept of high value that eludes the simple idea of price.

Decision Circles

So, how do we go about picking our way through the various sources of information (and lack thereof) out there to make good choices about what really is local and worth our hard earned pennies?

For a practical exercise that can help, let's start with simple geography. If we accept that everyone's idea of local is different, then it follows that everyone can draw their own inner circle of distance. How far from home are you willing to call local? Ten miles? Twenty? Your town and the next one over? Maybe it's less if you live in a really strong community that still has a butcher and a baker. Maybe it's closer to fifty if you know you eat a wide range of foods and you want to maintain that diet. Whatever it is, take a map, real or imaginary and draw a circle around the area that means local to you.

Now you've done that, move outwards. Is there a second ring of options that is meaningful to you, or would you go straight to a circle covering the whole of the UK? For people in the Celtic nations for example, you might well have a local circle and then a second one covering the whole of either Scotland or Wales before then having a third circle covering the rest of the UK. However you do it, the point is to make how you define local a conscious choice based around a series of concentric circles with the innermost one being your top priority.

Before drawing your circle, you might want to do some homework about what is available within your given area. Is it realistic to draw a line five miles from home? Are the producers and retailers there to make that something you can really bring to life via your choices? We're looking for a balance between reducing food miles and emissions, and practicality. Remember, this is the real world. Good intentions don't give us more time or money. Once you've done that piece of work, why not set yourself a target to see if you can meet a certain percentage of your food needs from within you first circle. Can you buy 50% of what you eat from local suppliers and retailers from within 5 miles of home? As always with targets, resolutions and goals, don't set yourself up to fail. You're not going to eat 100% locally in year one of making changes (if ever). Find that balance between stretching yourself and being realistic. Creating goals that are just sticks to beat yourself with is no more sustainable than eating processed food every night.

Value Judgements

Devising a well thought out plan to reduce the footprint associated with the distance your food travels is great, but it's only part of the challenge. The next bit is harder, but also in keeping with our goal of realistic choices that acknowledge the realities of the world we live in. ▨

Very often two worthwhile, sustainable aims will be in conflict and, as consumers there won't be an easy answer as to what to do for the best. This is unfortunate. It can put people off even trying to do the right thing, especially if they feel they can't win no matter what they do. In circumstances such as this we always advise our customers to pause and think about their intent. Are they trying to do the right thing? Are they making a small positive step in the right direction? If they can say yes to those questions, then they should avoid being too self-critical. To use a well-worn phrase, we don't need 1 person doing sustainability perfectly, we need millions doing it imperfectly. And that means compromise.

Let's take a real world example to illustrate the problem. Cow's milk bought from most supermarkets comes in a type of plastic bottle that is widely recycled right around the UK. If you put that bottle in the recycling tub you can be pretty sure that it will end up being processed correctly. The problem is dairy, especially commercially farmed dairy, tends to have a high emissions footprint. So, while the plastic isn't the worst problem, at least it will get properly recycled, the milk itself isn't great from a sustainability viewpoint.

Armed with this knowledge you think to yourself, I'm going to make a change. I'm going to move to a dairy free alternative. You're an intelligent, diligent sort of individual (of course you are, you're reading this book), so you do some more homework and realise that of all the alternative milks out there, Oat or Hemp milk are the lowest in footprint. Because its most widely available you decide to switch to Oat Milk.

Well done you. A good, sensible decision based on facts. I only have one question; what are you going to do with that Tetrapak carton your new oat milk comes in?

Tetrapak cartons (or any composite material packaging) are not widely recycled. You may have a drop off point somewhere near you for a scheme that does take them back, but you often can't put them in your recycling tubs at home. So now you've swapped the footprint associated with dairy for the waste related to packaging. How is a person meant to win?

The truth is that very often you can't. Not 100%. This is where value judgements come in. You're going to have compromise and pick the best of a set of imperfect solutions unless you can find Oat milk in a glass bottle (possible but rare) or good recycling facilities for awkward packaging. This doesn't mean the change isn't worth making or that the research was wasted, it's just a reflection of the world we live in. It's worth remembering that climate change isn't a zero sum game as we've mentioned before. Every small positive step forward makes the eventually worst case scenario less bad than it would have been, even if that step is based on compromise.

Very often when shopping locally we're dealing with small scale food producers who themselves may lack the resources to be as sustainable as they'd like to be. This increases the chance that we'll need to compromise and accept the least bad option in our shopping basket. Rather than treating that as a reason not to shop locally, we should turn that thought process around. By supporting the small producer, we can help them grow and become more sustainable and aligned with our beliefs. In this way our spending power can help create the future we desire. Speaking of which...

The Power of our Pound

High streets across the UK have a had tough time of it in recent years. A BBC report in September 2021 found that on average, 50 high street shops a day were closing down across the UK.[84] This continued a trend that has been going on for a decade or more as the rise of online shopping, combined with large amounts of out of town retail space, dealt repeated blows to the traditional town centre.

The upshot is a landscape that is dramatically different from even twenty years ago for many towns and cities across the UK. Large retailers don't want to own as many stores as they did before internet shopping became widespread. Most now want a physical presence in what they would dub a 'regional hub' and then rely on online orders for the rest of their trade. Such a strategy might keep their costs down and be more efficient, but it does nothing to make our local high streets vibrant places to be.

As a result of this strategy of retrenchment, many of our town centres now have high numbers of empty shop units and the brutal truth is that very few national retailers are going to be looking to fill them. Realistically they are only going to be occupied by local businesses starting up or expanding. There are no white knights coming over the hill to save us, it is up to us to create the thriving independent operators who can repopulate our towns. This unescapable logic throws into context the power of our spending decisions. Do we want our villages, towns and cities to feel like nice places to live? Do we want bustling town centres? Well then, we need to spend our money locally. There is no other choice.

If we combine this harsh economic reality with the other benefits of shopping locally, including the ability to support ethical minded local food producers then we can see how it can be possible to bring life back to our high streets, but only if we place a value on doing so. Shopping online or in supermarkets is extremely time efficient and price conscious. There is no escaping that reality. But as consumers we can use our spending power to send a signal that once more, we place value on things other than pounds and pence. We can shop locally and make a statement that we want locally grown food, sold by local people with whom it is possible to build decent, resilient, relationships. It is our choice.

Life is one long (difficult) choice

Shopping local is an admirable, impactful goal, but that doesn't mean it's straightforward as we've seen throughout this chapter. If we consider our ambitions for creating a future full of regeneratively farmed produce, we could very easily find a situation where we're forced to choose between local veg which has been intensively grown or a permaculture produced crop with a higher transportation footprint. The compromises dictated by such choices are real and shouldn't be ignored. They are part of the challenge that faces us. It's are job to pick our way through such decisions in the best way we can, using good intent as a guide.

There are, however, easy places to start. Do you have a local milkman or veg box scheme? Not sure? Well now is the time to go and find out. Go on, put this book down for five minutes and see if you can find a local, convenient delivery option to start making a difference. If you don't have those choices, is there a butcher you could start using once a month as an alternative to always buying from the supermarket? Is there a local farmers market once a month? Could you get a birthday cake made by someone in your town instead of buying a mass produced one? Maybe you have a food festival once a year?

Whatever it is, there are ways almost all of us can find to shop locally in some small way. Of course, such actions are budget dependent, and we always have to be realistic about that. But where possible we need to widen our concept of value to include the things that matter to us. Shopping locally creates vibrant places to live and work. We can bring to life the areas we live by taking simple small steps to support local businesses. And don't forget, by supporting local small producers you're keeping employment opportunities and skills within your area as well. This increases economic resilience and can help communities to withstand shock events such as pandemics. Who wouldn't have wanted a great local pasta maker on their doorsteps at the height of the panic buying we saw in the first lockdowns of 2020?

8

Reduce Packaging

Plastic, plastic, everywhere...

I love a good statistic, so let's start this chapter with a couple. A report produced for the UK government in January 2022 found that we get through about five million tonnes of plastic packaging per year.[85] The not-for-profit group WRAP found that about 572,000 tonnes of plastic was recycled from homes in the latest set of figures available. Which does beg the question, where is the rest of it going?

The same Westminster report also highlights a few damning issues. Firstly, we don't necessarily know how much plastic waste we produce and how much is sent for recycling. The National Audit Office found the government's own figures "not sufficiently robust". Independent assessments suggest the real figures on plastic waste might be as much as 50% higher.

On top of that the report shows that the UK is still exporting a lot of our rubbish overseas each year. They state: "In 2020 the UK exported 0.54 million tonnes of plastic waste. The amount exported increased rapidly in the decade to its 2011 peak of almost 0.9 million tonnes... it has generally fallen since then. The 2019 level was the lowest for a decade."[86]

The amount might be slowly falling but it's still true that we're shipping abroad as much plastic waste as we're managing to recycle at home. Historically much of that waste went to China but they stopped taking it in 2018. This has led to a rebalancing of where we send our rubbish so that it's out of sight and mind. Now, the highest percentage of plastic sent to other countries ends up in Malaysia and Turkey. I'm not sure they're very grateful.

Once there some of this waste ends up illegally dumped and burned, causing environmental damage far from where the product was actually used. Such action also encourages criminality and insecure informal employment for local people. The rules on this behaviour are clear, countries should not be exporting their waste unless it is going to be recycled. The UK has consistently failed in this. Various charities and organisations have found UK plastics waste (particularly easily identifiable supermarket carrier bags) in illegal rubbish dumps in a number of countries around the world. The charity Greenpeace conducted an investigation and found "British plastic dumped by the side of the road, abandoned in illegal dumps or even set on fire in Turkey and Malaysia."[87] Their 'Unearthed' investigation spoke to CK Lee, a local solicitor who works with the Kuala Langat Environmental Association, who said: "Local residents were having breathing difficulties, having difficulty to sleep, feeling nausea, [and] feeling unwell."[88]

Keep in mind, all those stories are of plastic that the UK counts as 'recycled'. No wonder the National Audit Office felt UK government figures weren't as good as they might be and that's just the situation with 'controlled' rubbish, the stuff that enters a recognised stream of disposal (landfill, recycling etc.). A lot of our rubbish never ends up in such process. For traces of what happens to all of that you have to look away from far off lands to blue and murky depths instead.

Much of our uncontrolled plastic waste ends up in the ocean where it wreaks untold damage to fragile ecosystems and species. You may have heard of something called The Great Pacific garbage patch. In popular imagination (in so far as people are conscious of it) this is a giant island of plastic debris floating in the ocean that stretches for huge distances and is an ugly, putrid scar that serves as a visible rebuke to our unthinking plastic habit. It's a sort of reverse pin up for the pollution of our oceans. The U.S National Ocean Service points out the reality is less clear cut but actually worse in its impact: "The name "Pacific Garbage Patch" has led many to believe that this area is a large and continuous patch of easily visible marine debris items such as bottles and other litter—akin to a literal island of trash that should be visible with satellite or aerial photographs. This is not the case. While higher concentrations of litter items can be found in this area, much of the debris is actually small pieces of floating plastic that are not immediately evident to the naked eye."[89]

This tiny, floating, waste, breaks down into the smaller pieces described by the Ocean Service and then either ends up consumed by marine animals or drifting down to the bottom of the ocean where it accumulates and ends up wrecking ocean floor habitats. And this is what happens in all our oceans, seas, large rivers, estuaries and so on. The Great Pacific Garbage patch may catch whatever limited mainstream attention is shone on this issue but terrifyingly it's a tiny part of the problem. Microplastics are everywhere in our marine environments. The end result of all this is that some of our plastic waste is ending up in the guts of fish. And then, we eat those fish ourselves, thereby ingesting the micro plastics we as a society created through our wasteful, short-sighted ways. I suppose some might call that karma, but it doesn't' seem a good way to function, for us or the innocent animals caught up in the unnatural ecosystem of a product that refuses to go away.

This avalanche of waste accumulating in our oceans really caught public attention when it was highlighted by the BBC's Blue Planet II series, fronted by David Attenborough. Scenes of animals caught up in beer packaging or plastic sacks created a minor tipping point in awareness. For the first time many people were forced to consider what happened to the waste they threw away each week. The zero waste shopping sector grew massively (from a tiny starting point) after that series was broadcast.

175

Clearly, disposing of our plastic waste is a huge problem, whether formally, informally or in some legal limbo grey area that consists of a fire by the side of a road halfway around the globe. But it isn't the only issue associated with our use of the stuff. According to the Ellen MacArthur foundation 6% of global fossil fuel production is used to produce plastics. That's an awful lot of GHG emissions associated with something we use unthinkingly on a daily basis.[90] Amongst the outcry over the disposal of the stuff, it's easy to lose sight of the fact that its production involves the extraction of fossil fuels from the ground and large amounts of (normally) fossil fuel powered energy to break that initial product down into polymers that become our bottles, tubs and bags. Plastic is environmentally unsound to produce and dispose of and ends up shipped around the globe leaving poor nations to get rid of a problem caused by more affluent nations. It's a mess in every sense.

Kicking the habit?

Clearly, having waded our way through all that bad news, we need to cut the amount of plastic we use. Much of that waste is generated by the food we buy and so comes within the remit of improving our future food ecosystem. Food that is more sustainable will need to come in less packaging. However, as with so much of what we as a society consume, it's not just the product that's the problem, it's our use of it.

First up, the unambiguous bit. We need to eliminate single use plastics. Using fossil fuels (which is what plastics are made of) to create something that is only used once and doesn't degrade for hundreds of years is madness. Please, stop it. In practice that means refilling household liquid bottles and buying packaging free food at your local zero waste shop, giving up the plastic cotton buds and finding a way to reuse all those other tubs and pots that come into the house on a weekly basis. On top of this we collectively need to give up the bottled water habit that has sprung from almost nowhere over the last twenty years (and which we'll touch on again later in the book) plus we need to purchase fruit and veg that isn't swathed in pointless wrapping. Oh, buy some beeswax wraps so you can give up clingfilm too.

Great, once you've tackled that list of changes, I have some good news. You don't need to give up plastic totally. In fact, I'm going to go further. Sometimes, plastic is the right solution to a problem.

That might seem like a crazy thing to say after all these words I've thrown at you explaining why plastic is bad for planet in a whole host of ways. But that only applies to what we throw away. If we keep using a plastic product indefinitely it may well be the most sustainable solution to a problem. There is a reason why plastics are ubiquitous in modern society. The very same qualities that make them such a problem to dispose are also those that make it so useful in a whole host of contexts. Take a plastic lunchbox that's used every day for three years. If we take off four weeks holiday a year that's potentially 720 lunches kept safe and edible by that plastic. What else would do that job? And let's be honest, your average tub can last far longer than three years. How much 1970's 'vintage' Tupperware type stuff is still kicking around in households today? I know we've got some in our wider family and so do many others. I'm not convinced my Grandad hasn't still got 1980's Vitalite pots in the cupboard under the sink. This stuff lasts and if we reuse it time and time again, we can turn that from a weakness to a strength as it cuts our need to buy and consume in the present.

Understanding the alternatives

So, what's next? We reused as much as we can, but we still need to cut how much new, hard to recycle, plastic we're buying. We now have to navigate another minefield placed in front of the well intentioned consumer. We need to understand what we're actually picking up when we see a positive sounding label that seems to offer an ethical alternative. Let's have a look at some of the most common options out there:

Degradable

Sounds positive but isn't really. Degradable means the product is still plastic and will just break up into smaller pieces of plastic. That isn't really getting us anywhere as those small pieces linger around and get everywhere as we saw at the start of the chapter. By all means buy a product that says it's wrapped in degradable packaging but be aware that you're still going to need to find a way to recycle it properly.

Biodegradable

Better. Lots better actually, but still a small caveat. Biodegradable means it breaks down into organic materials without leaving anything else behind. Just be aware that some products labelled biodegradable only do this under certain commercial processes which may not be widely available where you live.

Compostable

These products break down into nutrients or substances that enhance the soil. This is really good. However (I know, there's always a bloody however) some products labelled compostable need really high temperatures in commercial composting facilities to achieve this end result. Again, there may not be that many places where that happens in your area so you might have to check you're getting the outcome you want.

Home Compostable

This is good. Very good. Mostly. (Sighs). Home compostable products are the best of the alternatives we've looked at so far. Like standard compostable products they break down into nutrients good for the soil and they do so at lower temperatures so they don't need commercial processing, they can just be dealt with as part of your compost pile at home. (If you don't have one, you really should, it doesn't take much space).

Bioplastics

These are part of the future. The best Bioplastics are made from things like potato starch and break down really easily with no nasties left behind. You might have noticed magazines starting to come wrapped in them amongst other applications. These are only going to get more common, and we absolutely need to be supporting their use. However, there are problems associated with them. Just like all other crops there are costs associated with their production due to the harmful nature of modern farming practices. To be a truly sustainable option we'd need to confident that their source material is grown in a way that isn't causing run off of pollutants into rivers or habitat destruction and biodiversity loss. As is often the case, we just don't have that information when picking up a compostable bag or wrapped product in a shop.

Beeswax (and plant wax) wraps

We mentioned them briefly earlier in the chapter. These are a great way of cutting out clingfilm or other wraps in the home and lunchbox. There are loads of small, artisan makers of beeswax wraps located all around the UK so by choosing to use them you're not only cutting waste, but you can also probably help support your local economy too. What's not to like?

The good news with these positive options is that they are becoming far more common. In the three or so years we've been seeking out stuff not wrapped in conventional plastic for the shop we've noticed a real increase in what is available. Even better, we're noticing these options appear in mainstream supermarkets sometimes as well.

It's getting better all the time. (Sort of)

Now for some more good news. The UK is making progress on cutting the amount of packaging and plastic associated with our shopping. Let's start with those carrier bags lying on the side of a far off field in a foreign land. According to figures gathered by the UK Government, the number of single use carrier bags given out by supermarkets has dropped by 95% since 2015 when the single use bag levy was introduced.[91] If ever you wanted a poster child for how effective government intervention and taxation can make a difference to established patterns of behaviour, then this is surely it. For the cost of 10p per bag, we've wiped out a pattern of wasteful single use consumption that had been going on decades. This is a real plastic success story. Well done you and your bags for life.

Supermarkets are making progress on the wider issue of plastic use as well. In February 2022 the consumer organisation Which released a ranking of the Sustainability credentials of each major food retailer. We'll touch on this more later but in terms of plastic impact, the report had this to say:

"The supermarkets all plan to make their plastic packaging 100% reusable, recyclable or compostable by 2025 at the latest. By weight, 94% of Co-op own-brand plastic is already recyclable at home, with the remainder recyclable in-store. Ocado has further to go: less than 40% of its own-brand plastic is recyclable at kerbside. M&S told us it aimed to make all food packaging recyclable by the end of this year. Using less plastic is better for the environment than recycling, so we compared how many tonnes of plastic each supermarket puts onto the market annually, per 100,000 items sold. We found that Iceland's plastic intensity was the worst, while Waitrose does the best. We found buying a basket of 20 items at Iceland could result in 73% more plastic packaging than buying 20 typical items at Waitrose."[92]

This is a sign that the concept of reducing plastic has cut through as a mainstream idea. Supermarkets now view it as in their interests commercially to be seen on the right side of this argument. It's another positive example and lesson in how creating the right sort of awareness and pressure can lead even monoliths like giant food retailers to change their behaviour. Whilst there is a long way to go and these figures only represent a start, it's important to keep this in mind when we look at how we could reshape the food retail industry itself later in the book.

As part of that change, 2018 saw the launch of the UK Plastic Pact. This scheme, organised by WRAP and facilitated by the ever excellent Ellen MacArthur Foundation, brings together business and other bodies from right across the broad cycle of plastic creation and use. All signatories to the pact pledge to "eliminate problematic, plastics reducing the total amount of packaging on supermarket shelves, stimulate innovation and new business models and help build a stronger recycling system in the UK... (and) we will ensure that plastic packaging is designed so it can be easily recycled and made into new products and packaging and, with the support of governments, ensure consistent UK recycling is met."[93] Almost all UK supermarkets have joined up to this promise, as have a whole range of food producers including a lot of big brands you'll have heard of from Birdseye frozen foods to Kettle Chips snacks. Three years after its conception the Plastic Pact is making a difference according to the annual review competed by WRAP. They found that in 2020 there had been a 46% reduction in problematic and unnecessary plastic items compared to 2018. They also concluded that recycling rates for packaging had risen from 44% to 52% across the same time period amongst their members.[94] This is all progress in the right direction, albeit incomplete.

Let's just take a moment to reflect that the launch date of this pact was not a coincidence. It began in 2018, less than a year after Blue Planet II was screened creating an increased awareness of the problem. Public education and pressure can work if aided by powerful messages delivered by trusted figures.

There are other positive developments on the horizon as well. Scotland is to introduce a Deposit Return scheme for plastic bottles in 2023, with the rest of the UK promising to join in (ok, a bit vaguely but you have to live in hope) at some date after that.[95] The aim is that the introduction of this option in Scotland will lead to a 90% collection rate within a year of launch. If that seems a little ambitious, keep in mind that schemes such as these in Nordic nations reach above a 95% return rate so it is possible.[96]

These slivers of positivity have made this a slightly odd chapter to write in some ways. Humankind's use of plastic is still growing and the quantities of waste littering our lands and oceans is causing damage that we still don't understand fully. The cost of unthinking use of a substance that can stick around for centuries has been truly staggering for all the other species we share the planet with. We have to change our behaviour, eliminate single use plastics entirely and find solutions where possible and practical to minimise our reliance on the stuff more widely.

All of this is true and a pressing threat to our planet's biodiversity and well-being.

And yet, tackling plastic waste is one of the areas where we've seen some progress, including amongst the biggest and most powerful players in the food industry. If we're trying to show how change is possible and that hope is not a futile gesture, then we have to look at signs of positive improvement as a stepping stone towards a better future despite the size of the challenge that still faces us. If we don't, we'll fail to find the positive narrative that can guide us towards our sustainable food future. In the face of mounting pile of waste dumped in far off countries and micro plastics filling our seas, we can take hope both from the work being done by groups such as WRAP and the

184

MacArthur foundation and from the fact that our awareness of the problem and desire for change has prompted movement from big companies. That is a small change right now, but it offers up big opportunities for the future if we find further cultural tipping points to drive sustainable outcomes.

9

Meat/Dairy alternatives

Meat and Dairy production

Many of the separate challenges facing our food ecosystem overlap. Rarely does a food issue exists in isolation. The Dimbleby food report called its chapter on our animal heavy diets, 'the complexities of meat'. Our choices and options aren't straightforward, often because they are so entwined with other issues associated with what we eat.

Any discussion on farming and our future food choices has to tackle our appetite for meat. The National Food Strategy, written for the government calls for a 30% reduction in meat consumption over the course of a decade. It points to the fact that ruminants farting and pooping contribute two thirds of the GHG footprint associated with UK agriculture.[97] Those cows are producing way too much methane to be considered a sustainable option in their current form. However, that is not the same as saying we shouldn't eat any red meat or that all cattle farming needs to disappear.

A 2021 study by the Lancet found the UK was cutting its consumption of red meat, but at the same time increasing how much white meat it eats. The net effect was a 17% total reduction over the course of the 2010's.[98] This is a step in the right direction but clearly not enough if we're going to hit the target laid out by Henry Dimbleby in his food plan. Even if the progress isn't all that we'd like, it still has multiple positives. Not only does it reduce our methane emissions which are one of the more damaging greenhouse gases in the short term, it also ties into the health problems associated with our current diets as eating red meat is linked to various health issues including our type 2 diabetes crisis and some types of cancer.

If we stay on the subject of emissions, the Dimbleby food report gives this important long term perspective on methane, animals and our consumption patterns:

"The methane produced by ruminants is estimated to have caused a third of total global warming since the industrial revolution. And... there are currently more animals being reared for food than ever before. The combined mass of agricultural livestock is now 1.8 times bigger than all the humans on Earth. Every year, around the world, around 1.3 billion ruminants are slaughtered for food".

Methane makes a great case study to highlight one of the dangers of just grouping all greenhouse gases into one amorphous lump. Different gases behave differently. Not every gas released into the atmosphere has the same effect over the same time span. Methane causes more of a heating effect in the short term, but crucially, stops having much impact after about a decade. That is much shorter than carbon dioxide which can linger for half a century. Cutting methane emissions is therefore a quick way to help the challenge of climate change. Which, I guess, is unfortunate chemistry if you're a cow minding its own business on hillside somewhere.

Reducing these emissions is currently taxing the minds of scientists and others across the globe. Feeding ruminants red seaweed as part of their diet might reduce methane production by as much as 80% although that seems a stretch and is yet to verified on a wide scale[99]. Feed giants Cargill claim a 10% reduction for a 200g dose of its new feed additive, and other products are appearing as well.[100] And it's not only big industry working on this. A small Sydney microbrewery is working with a local university to see if a by-product of the brewing process can be turned into a methane reduction product for cattle which would give good ecological reasons for having a pint if nothing else.[101]

Unfortunately, even if we can significantly reduce the methane emissions associated with ruminants reared for human food, there is another challenge associated with their farming. Feed. To put it at its most simple, a lot of cows are fed soy based feeds. Soy is often (but not exclusively) grown in South American areas associated with widespread deforestation including the Amazon rainforest. Having more and more people on the planet eating a diet rich in red meat leads to the loss of precious natural habitat as demand for feed increases. This drives our biodiversity crisis and pushes the planet closer to the brink as we lose what should be natural store of carbon dioxide. None of this process is sustainable and it has to change if we're going to limit the worst effects of the climate crisis we're living through.

Production of Soya Beans 2021

(Million Metric Tonnes)

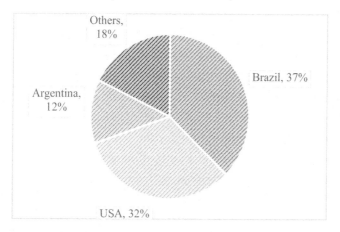

Source: Statista.com[102]

According to Greenpeace, soy production in Brazil has quadrupled in the twenty years since 1996 and 90% of that is used to feed animals rather than being eaten by humans directly.[103] Statistics published by World in Data show that since 1980 soy yields have doubled in Brazil. They go on to say; "This is impressive but not enough to keep up with demand: soy production increased by 680%. Instead, Brazil has had to devote more and more land to soy production: land use has tripled since 1980."[104]

Those statistics are bad enough and there is a whole load more that we could quote at you, but they still don't capture the entwined nature of the challenge we face when it comes to solving the climate crisis. Into this heady mix we need to add the negative impact of our political choices.

Deforestation in Brazil was actually declining before the election of Jair Bolsonaro in 2019. He was elected as a political outsider. A former army officer who claimed to speak the truth to power and stand up the ordinary, working Brazilian whist being part of a global wave of right wing authoritarians who have come to power in countries as disparate as India, Hungary and, of course, the USA. Bolsonaro has no more time for the science of climate change than he does the science of pandemics. Brazil has recorded shocking death figures from the Covid pandemic at the same time as gutting legislation and regulatory bodies that protect the Amazon. To Bolsonaro, the economic gain of deforestation and increased farming outweigh any concerns about the damage done to the planet.

In 2021, the Financial Times had this to say about his wanton destruction of an irreplaceable natural wonder:

"The country is home to 40 per cent of the world's tropical forests, 20 per cent of freshwater reserves and 10 per cent of its biodiversity. Yet during this administration, deforestation rates have surged by 50 per cent, and invasions of protected land more than doubled. A group of indigenous leaders and human rights activists have even asked the International Criminal Court to investigate Bolsonaro for "ecocide". It need not be like this. In fact, it should not. Instead, Brazil could become a green superpower. It is already one of the biggest producers of soyabean, sugar, corn and beef. But it needs to do so based on a shift towards sustainable agriculture, a thriving bioeconomy and responsible eco-tourism. This is not an impossible dream. About two-thirds of already-cleared Amazonian land is underused, degraded or abandoned. So, Brazil doesn't need to clear more; it needs to increase the productivity of existing land. It also needs to crack down on environmental crime — such as illegal logging, illicit mining and the financial flows that sustain them — and empower scientists rather than fire them as this government has done."[105]

We've talked about the power of politics and why it is an important part of any meaningful change we want to bring about but the election of Bolsonaro and the impact he has had in such a short space of time shows again the importance of how people vote globally and how that interacts with the market forces that drive our consumption patterns to devastating effect. If the global demand for soya wasn't there, Bolsonaro would not be encouraging the deforestation of the Amazon. That's not saying it's all our fault, but the reality of free market economics is that the supply would not exist without the demand.

It is possible to raise cattle on feed other than soy based products and in alternative ways to the large scale farming practices we see globally. We can see hints of how those alternatives might impact the planet in figures set out by Tim Lang in his book, Feeding Britain. He baldly states both the scale of the challenge involved in meat consumption but also how widely farming practices vary based on a study by Joseph Poore and Thomas Memeckek:

"High impact beef producers, for instance, created 105kg of CO_2 and used 370m² of land per 100g of protein which was 12-50 times greater than low impact beef producers. Meanwhile low impact beans, peas and other plant based proteins can create just 0.3kg of CO_2 (including all processing, packaging and transport) and use just 1m² of land per 100g of protein.[106]"

His point is that it's not enough to just label meat production bad, bean production good. Outputs vary considerably depending on what farming practices, packaging and transportation types are used in producing the food we eat. And within that detail lies a possible future for red meat production for our friends at Henbant, and all the others like them. We need to scale back industrial beef herds and promote pasture grazed, small scale, regenerative cattle rearing. This will produce smaller quantities of higher quality meat that can be seen as an occasional treat by consumers.

All of these numbers form an empirical truth, but they are only part of the wider picture. We have to find ways to manage our landscapes in harmony with producing food. Cows and other ruminants are part of that holistic whole, as are the farmers who keep them. We need cows and we need meat alternatives being produced in Silicon Valley laboratories. This is not a binary choice. We cannot berate a generation of famers for being in thrall to little more than total yields and then commit the same error ourselves. There is more to this argument than an equation based on calories produced per bubble of methane.

James Rebanks, a writer and farmer from the Lake District, has been on journey of discovery on his own family farm. Working with various experts he's come to realise the science behind the truths handed down by previous generations that were based on a different kind a wisdom. The sort forged by long days on unforgiving slopes and fells. The type that keeps your head just above water when the bank manager comes to visit. Just as we saw when we looked at the practices underlying regenerative farming, James (and his family) have learned that soil health is the foundation of a farm, and essential for food production. And for healthy soil you need animals. As he writes in his stunningly beautiful book 'English Pastoral" the secret to soil wellbeing is:

"... to mimic wild herbivore behaviour with sudden bursts of mob grazing, that tramples the grass and dots it with shit, piss and saliva. It looks trashed with wasted grass trampled down, but it is soil heaven. Dung beetles, worms and countless other creatures start to take the leaves and the herbivore muck (which is also full of condensed and partly digested plant matter) back into the ground. A giant feast ensues, a soil based feeding frenzy, which we can encourage further by having more trees and hedges that litter the ground with leaf matter and rotting wood. Together they all play a valuable role in soil formation, and over time new soil gets created and carbon gets trapped in the ground."[107]

In short, we need cows and their like to play their part in creating soil and trapping carbon. The future is balanced, nuanced, and complicated. Much like the best of life itself. We can't do without cows, but we can seriously reduce our dependence on commercial, large scale farming techniques with all the damage they bring. When choosing beef in particular the benefits of eating UK reared meat of any sort are huge as we're not clearing prime forest or other habitat to create large scale cattle ranches as it often the case with cheap South American options. There is a hierarchy of choice here with high quality, pasture grassed British beef at the top and low quality imports at the bottom. We don't have to give up meat, we do need to make better decisions. Doing so can help the small scale, regeneratively managed mob herds of happy cows become the norm.

But it's not just meat we need to cut back on. Cow's milk, associated with methane emissions and soya feed, has come under scrutiny as well. Henry Dimbleby's food report found that 40% of the total emissions associated with our food comes from agriculture.[108] Part of the answer to that problem lies in shifting our habits and embracing the alternatives. There's an ever increasing range of different choices out there, however, not all of them are equal.

Oat Mad

Does Oatly annoy you?

I ask that because Oatly has made a lot of people really quite angry over the last few years and it's not the sort of people you're imagining. I'm not referring to those who consider oat milk some sort of coffee adulterating manifestation of woke cultural gone crazy. No, I'm talking about Oatly customers. Or, maybe more accurately, ex-customers.

Oatly is a Scandinavian producer of oat milk. They're in the vanguard of the booming milk alternative sector (the fact we can even say that is a sign of progress) and their products have spread far beyond their Nordic beginnings. But such growth takes money. And more growth takes even more money. So, Oatly took some investment from an American financial company called Blackrock. They didn't sell the company or the brand, they just took some cash in return for a share of the business. Blackrock isn't a specialist green firm, they've invested in pretty much everything over the years, including an awful lot of things that have contributed to the amount of carbon in the atmosphere. To put it succinctly, they aren't the good guys. Their chief exec admits that he doesn't invest in green products to save planet but because they're likely to make his company a good return.[109] Their actions have been the subject of protest and criticism. Many owners and customers in the zero waste sector have voiced their unhappiness at Oatly being involved with such people. Some have made the decision to stop stocking their products.

In summary, such a move makes a lot of people upset. I think it's fabulous news.

The reason for this happiness spreads beyond any naturally argumentative nature I might possess. To me this investment is excellent for two reasons. Firstly, we need large scale, global, sustainable food producers. We need millions of people switching to dairy alternatives and that only happens if the products are widely available at a competitive price. That takes scale and money. Oatly now have access to a little more of both. This is good.

Secondly, the investing logic of Larry Fink, our Blackrock realist is proof that the tide is turning in the favour of environmentally sound and ethical products. As a hard headed market analyst he has understood that the path towards lowering greenhouse gas emissions is now a reality even if we don't reach net zero by 2050. As a result, any country or business not committed to that journey risks being left behind and, by definition, will be less profitable from the perspective of an investor. The flip side of that is the understanding that growth will come from those who embrace the lower footprint reality. For him Oatly makes sense in cold hard business terms and that's exactly where we need to be. We need the power of global finance on our side in the battle for a better food future. And it's not just in the food industry that we see this trend towards understanding the true value of planet friendly businesses. For example, Tesla and NextGen have higher market values than General Motors and Exxon respectively.

Oat milk also provides us with another great case study of the challenges involved in doing the right thing. Not all milk replacements are equally good. Coconuts are associated with low pay and workforce exploitation as global demand soars, almonds produced in California (which most are) soak up huge amounts of scarce water and their pollination kills 30% of the bees involved each year, rice milk is again massively water intensive and has few nutritional benefits and soy milk can have the same problems of deforestation as is associated with South American beef production. In reality, hemp and oat milks have the lowest carbon footprints, nut milks have a higher impact.

Greenhouse Gas Emissions of Milk Alternatives

(Kg of Gas Emitted per Unit of Production)

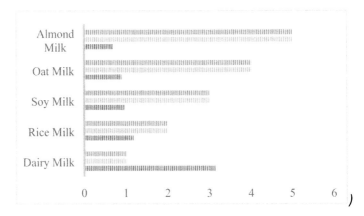

Freshwater Use by Milk Alternatives

(Litres per Unit of Production)

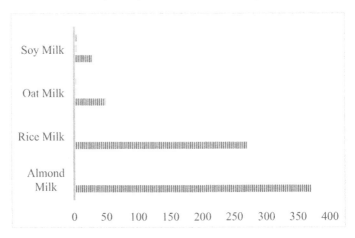

Source: ourworldindata.org[110]

All these alternatives are lower in footprint than intensively farmed, mass produced cow's milk though. Mike Berners-Lee estimates that a household getting through two pints of cow's milk a day would be racking up a carbon footprint equivalent to a return flight from London to Madrid over the course of a year.[111] Producing a pint of milk causes around 720g of GHG emissions, that's three times more than any of the non-dairy alternatives. More than 80% of that total comes from the farm, with packaging and transportation making up the rest. Milk has the same ruminant related issues as beef does. Cows burp while being milked too. The case for loving those capitalists at Oatly is clear.

Show me the growth

So, what are people going to eat if they aren't eating meat? It may well be that the answer is already in a supermarket aisle near you and taking up an ever increasing amount of shelf space. Sales of meat replacement products are growing fast. Brands such as Beyond Meat and Impossible Foods are driving forward technological innovation that is leading to meat free products almost indistinguishable from their carnivorous cousins. In a sure fire sign that the future is made of greenery, even McDonalds are now getting in on the act with the inventively named McPlant and Burger King have meat free nuggets in the pipeline.

Such choices form a big part of our vision for the future. If we're looking to use our land sustainably, in order to find a balance between our needs and those of every other animal on the planet, then we can't keep growing huge quantities of food to feed animals which we in turn eat for less calorific gain than the original crop contained. We need to reduce the demand at source, and this is a global challenge. The rise of middle class consumers in previously less wealthy nations has created new waves of high meat eating shoppers. If we need proof of that look no further than China. Their meat consumption has exploded over the last twenty years as improved economic prosperity has created a middle class. As a result their GHG emissions associated with food production has grown by more than 50% to nearly 2.5bn tonnes per year.[112] To give some context the equivalent figure for Europe has actually declined slightly over the same period.

When the Economist magazine devoted its Technology Quarterly briefing to the Future of Food in October 2021, meat replacement products were the first thing they tackled after the introduction. They detailed the rise of Beyond Meat from its beginnings in 2009 to a company which now "sells its products in more than 80 countries, with net revenues in 2020 of $406.8m, up more than 36% from the previous year."[113] It listed the company's value at $7bn

The darkly named research organisation Mordor Intelligence predicts that growth in meat replacement products will average nearly 8% per annum over the next five years[114] and a visit to any supermarket will show why. Choice is booming as more people become aware of the need to substitute at least some meat based meals with a non-meat alternative (with a caveat around our consumption of ultra processed foods which also needs to fall). KBV Research are even more bullish predicting that "The Global Plant-based Meat Market size is expected to reach $12.32 billion by 2027, rising at a market growth of 18.3%".[115]

Nearly all the large food producers are hedging their bets by taking stakes in this fast growing market, the profit potential is too big to miss out on. The Economist Future of Food report note that "major meat producers such as Cargill, JBS and Tyson Foods have their own plant based lines, just as Danone and Chobani are getting into plant based milks."[116] That is another significant sign that change in consumer behaviour forces even the largest of corporations to re-evaluate what they do. Once again, we see that our pound has power.

In his latest book, Regenesis, the journalist and environmentalist George Monbiot argues strongly that all meat consumption is bad for the planet and that we should embrace lab produced meat alternatives as the sustainable protein source of the future. However, such an absolutist view should make us pause. As we've already seen, pasture grazed cattle can provide important landscape management benefits, particularly to soil health (a fact measured empirically by regenerative agriculture pioneers like Gabe Brown). A future filled with diets dependent on meat alternative proteins would leave us with many of the same structural flaws we already have. If only a handful of privately owned, highly profitable companies hold the patents and designs for the food that feeds billions is that ethical or sustainable? Does that bring people closer to the food they eat? Are we merely substituting one form of arm's length, mass produced calories for another?

Choices, choices

So, with all these new choices out there, what should we as consumers be doing about all this?

First of all, we need some honesty with ourselves about what we're eating. When we eat meat, we're eating animals. Those animals have a backstory which is longer than just their lifespan and journey to our plates. Mass reared, commercially successful animals are highly bred for the traits needed to make them most profitable. I knew this but hadn't fully comprehended the scale of the reality until I read in the aforementioned 'English Pastoral'. For some types of cow only the first female calf is kept because by the time the second has come along she's probably genetically out of date. Just ponder on that particular slice of madness for a minute.

As a result we need to be aware that cheap meat, whilst providing a good source of protein that is within the budget of most (but not all) households, is often hugely dependent on medication and incapable of being healthy in what we think of as a 'natural' outdoor environment. The highly selective breeding has created animals only suited to being kept mostly indoors so that they can pile on mass, or milking potential as quickly as possible. Is this what we want to be eating if we have the luxury of a choice?

We also need to be aware that the cheapest types of meat, particularly that found in processed products such as 'dippers' and the like, normally don't come from UK reared animals. In fact, the country of origin is rarely specified on this type of meal. Because of this we have no idea of the welfare standards associated with these breadcrumbed and battered delights. The same goes for a lot of low priced sausages. Are these sustainable choices to pick off the shelf? I'm not stupid when it comes to this sort of thing. We're often dragging ourselves home tired at the end of a long day wanting to do nothing more complicated than pull an easy option out the freezer and bang it in the oven for twenty minutes with some potato wedges and beans. Very few people are eating lovely, fully cooked from scratch meals every day of the week. But that doesn't mean we have no choice but to support these low sustainability options.

In many ways this is where the rise of plant based options really has the highest impact. We can replace the highest negative impact choices in our diets with meat free replacements. Seriously, you can't tell a plant based nugget from a chicken one if you chose sensibly these days and there are some lovely veggie sausages out there. Their prices are coming down (and nearly always on some sort of offer in the supermarkets) and their quality is comparable to the meat based option. If you've had a negative taste experience with products like this in the past, give them another go, they're improving all the time from this perspective, even if that doesn't change their fundamentally processed nature. Changing you frozen easy dinner options to plant based alternatives is one the easiest wins out there. There is almost no excuse not to do it from the next time you go shopping.

Before anyone gets too agitated out there. Eating an ultra processed, soya based meat alternative is not ideal. but it should still be better option than eating intensively reared meat fed on a soya based feed. You'll need less soya to make you full than it will take to fatten up an animal to be ready for you to eat. Don't get me wrong, it would be great if we were all devouring home cooked meals stuffed with fresh vegetables five or six days a week in order to help the planet but we need to be realistic and avoid reasons to make ourselves feel guilty when we're acting with good intent or making small steps in the right direction. Our diets of heavily processed foods have played a major role in the health problems associated with how we eat. However, this book is all about trying to deal with the world as it is. People have busy lives and need easy dinners. Best to make the least impactful choice within that setting whilst working on changing routines in the long run to make room for more homecooked meals.

To achieve that long term goal we come again to the subject of our food knowledge and the need to educate ourselves. We've had to do it in our household. A few years ago pretty much 100% of our meals contained meat and to change that we have had to learn some new recipes and how to cook with some different ingredients. Now we have vegetable curries cooked from scratch, an amazing lentil wellington and an equally good veggie shepherd's pie. These are dinners most of us would recognise, but we learned to use beans, lentils and fruit instead of meat. Neither of us would proclaim to be world class chef's so our experience would suggest this is possible for a lot of people. We all just need to be motivated to make these changes, understanding why they are important, from a planetary and health perspective. By these small steps of education and change we can avoid the trap of swapping one processed meal of unknown origin for another, irrespective of whether it's derived from a cow, soya beans or a lab. Next up on our list is perfecting a nut roast option for our Sunday dinner. We sell at nut roast mix at the shop, but I don't think we've quite got the seasoning and bulking out of it quite right. Beyond that, I need to follow in my wife's footsteps and embrace vegan cheese for basic things like spreading on top of a pasta bake and so on. I'm sure there's plenty of other little changes beyond that, it's an ongoing bit of work, but that's ok. Little changes, made over time, one after the other, are far more likely to stick in the long run. At least that's what I tell myself as I guiltily pick up another cheap pack of cheddar. None of us is perfect, I guess.

The subject of meat eating is an emotive, complex one. Alongside the benefits to rearing herds of ruminants as part of land management practices that seek to improve soil health and capture more carbon, it's fair to say that if we stopped farming cows and sheep, our 'traditional' farming landscape, which so many of us take pleasure in, would cease to exist. Our land has been shaped by our carnivorous diets over the centuries. Indeed, if we take on board the work of the Sustainable Food Trust regarding land use within the UK, removing all animal farming would make no sense as some of our land isn't suitable for anything else.

Despite all of that, there is a clear environmental need for us to rethink how much meat we eat and how it is produced. In that sense, it acts as a microcosm of the wider arguments in this book. Agricultural emissions account for a large chunk of the GHG footprint associated with our food and there are plenty of other negative impacts from large scale commercial farming including fertilizer and pesticide run off, plus the widespread use of anti-biotics. On top of all that we have the human cost of losing the relationships between farmers and the herds as farms expand in the quest for ever more 'efficiency'.

It's not just famers who need to reconnect with something lost. In forgoing our connection with where our food comes from, we have insulated ourselves from the reality of food production. Reconsidering how dinner gets to our plate might well cause more people to value the moral argument for an animal product free lifestyle. In short, if you can't handle the idea your dinner was once running around a field, should you really be eating it? A better food future needs more food honesty to underpin it which in turn may create more sustainable levels of demand for meat.

Whatever our logic or moral perspective, we need to embrace a different balance to our diet. Veganism and vegetarianism are positive lifestyle changes for some, but everyone can start to choose meat free meal options at least 50% of the time. The rise of plant based options, fuelled by huge investments and technological know-how mean that our choices are appetising and nutritious, something that wasn't always the case in the past. We don't need to feel like we're missing out, instead we can frame this a positive way of making a difference while acknowledging the end goal of diets based on locally produced, low impact, minimally processed food.

10

Fairly traded

Is that Fair?

Warrington. A town perched between Liverpool and Manchester in the north west of England. It's the home of a pretty decent rugby league team and boasts a history of making wire. Beyond that I didn't know as much about the place as maybe I should have done. My wife and I first visited Warrington because it had the nearest IKEA to where we live. It's a good site. Great motorway connections, easy to get to from a couple of different directions. You really can't fault the Swedish property spotters who came up with this find. We've being popping to it for years now. All our shelving in the shop comes from there, as do plenty of other bits and bobs, both for home and work.

A couple of years ago we changed our route through the town, I can't think why, it might have been an accident or bad traffic. Instead of circling round to the north and then dropping in on those excellent road links to hit the distinctive blue blob of a building we were aiming for, we drove through the centre of Warrington. Boy, was it a shock. Now, we don't get out much and I spend a lot of time cocooned in our nice little zero waste shop chatting to people who pretty much think the same as me, a dangerous state of affairs. Maybe I'd started to forget that's not how most people live. Warrington gave a definite reminder. Since we last drove that way, it'd had been on a retail park building extravaganza. Seriously, there's miles of them. It's a neon bright, warehouse filled vision of a consumption driven nirvana. Or a planet wrecking, cheap plastic tat filled, sign of the impending apocalypse. All depends on your perspective, I guess.

I don't say that to criticise Warrington, it's no more consumerist than any other town in the UK and all those shops provide jobs which are much needed. Instead, it was surprising because back on our normal route there's an unobtrusive sign by the side of the road just before the first Costa drive-thru that tells you something interesting; Warrington is a Fairtrade Town.

Fairtrade products first hit our shelves in 1994. Their aim is simple, to make sure the benefits of global trade are distributed more equitably with particular emphasis on giving the small scale producers of crops a bigger slice of the pie. By doing this they help communities stand on their own two feet and create lasting improvements to their lives. In a climate crisis context, such increases in profitability can lead to better resilience in the future, something that in turn would help safeguard the supply of the foods we in the western world like to eat. Once again, it is a positive story that can benefit all if adopted widely enough and presents a clear case for supporting Fairtrade products in our better food future. It's important to remember that sustainability doesn't stop at national borders. There is no sustainable future for the planet unless it spans the whole of the globe.

According to the Fairtrade Foundation there are now more than 1.9 million farmers and workers in Fairtrade certified organisations. Altogether they received £169 million in Fairtrade premium (I.e. what they earned extra from being part of the Fairtrade family instead of signing standard commercial deals) in 2020. That's making a real difference particularly in the coffee and flower industries where the bulk of Fairtrade suppliers exist.[117] The scheme works by guaranteeing a 'Fairtrade premium' to producer to help ensure they're receiving a fair price for what they have grown. It's a simple idea that has been effective.

Global Fairtrade Production by Category

(As a percentage of Fairtrade output)

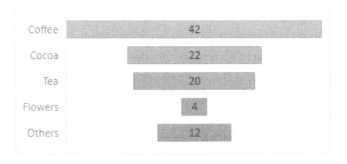

Source: Fairtrade.org.uk[118]

Every year in the UK we have a 'Fairtrade Fortnight' which seeks to highlight the products available to consumers who would like to support this important work. Traditionally the Co-op has been very good at both getting behind the two week promotion and stocking Fairtrade products in general. In the distant past (and dear reader, you can be grateful here for the lack of pictures in this book), I dressed as a giant banana and toured around some local schools as part of the work done promoting Fairtrade fortnight by them. It was, by some considerable distance, the closest I will ever come to feeling like a rock star. Those audiences loved me... even if they were only nine years old.

Far more important than the image of me as a banana, is the impact buying Fairtrade has on the lives of real people. When buying a Fairtrade or even 'beyond Fairtrade' product what we're actually doing is investing in people and our relationship with them. Personal connections, food producers dealing directly with their suppliers of extended period of time, customers having confidence that those links are fostering better outcomes. This is what we're signing up for when we support Fairtrade.

Bird Brains

Of course, we stock Fairtrade products in our shop, and we need to find more. If I'm honest, I think it's something we don't do well enough yet. There's plenty of room for growing our support.

Back when we opened our shop, some decisions took a little more time than others. One of those that took longest was which coffee to sell. We knew we needed to sell great ethically sourced coffee and we've plenty of great roasters locally so in our mind that was half the equation. But at the same time, we were looking for something a little different. Something that really showed how making the right choices when we buy our staples can really help us trade with the world in a way that enforces great decisions half a globe away from our morning cuppa. This is where we stumbled across Bird & Wild which is a shade grown, Fairtrade coffee. For those of you who haven't come across the phrase before (and I hadn't) 'shade grown' means the coffee is planted around the edge of, or mixed within, fields full of other crops. This helps to increase diversity and is great for local wildlife, plus Bird & Wild also donate a percentage of their profits to the RSPB.

We, as a nation, are not going to give up drinking coffee and nor should we. Equally, the UK is never going to be a major coffee growing nation. (Or if we are, things have gone very, very wrong and coffee is the least of our worries). It's a long life product (in transportation terms) and so can be shipped on boats instead of planes, thereby reducing its carbon footprint compared to some other products. What's needed to complete that picture is ethical trade that fosters sustainable behaviours at home and where it is produced. Bird & Wild is a splendid example of how we do that and acts as a perfect complement to our locally roasted products which support jobs in our area. By making such careful choice we can align the interests of producers, retailers and consumers and create a slightly better world.

Even better, we are now seeing products, particularly in the coffee and cocoa sectors that claim to go 'beyond Fairtrade'. These businesses are looking at ways of moving past the Fairtrade model of an improved premium for small scale producers to find even more inclusive and fair ways of selling products on the global market. One example of this is the Banyan Alliance, a chocolate producer that has partnered with the Swiss organisation Equal Profit. Together they're seeking to implement a model that assigns a share of the profit made on each product according to each stakeholders share of production costs. This is a radical change from how things usually work, and it will be interesting to see if ideas like this are able to grow from the small beginnings they have currently. Imagine a world where Fairtrade was just the start...

Trading Better

There are now more than six hundred Fairtrade Communities across the UK, plus another couple of thousand globally, covering villages, towns and cities. Garstang, in Lancashire was the first in the world back in 2001 and since then they've mushroomed in number. They are a testament to ordinary people coming together to make a positive difference to the place they live. Those activists and communities have engaged with more than 14000 business according to the Fairtrade Foundation. If you visit their website (fairtrade.org.uk) you can find some useful tools on how you could make where you live a champion of Fairtrade as well.[119]

To become a Fairtrade community you need to meet five goals (which are set out on the Fairtrade Foundation website) and work to gain real community awareness of why Fairtrade can make a difference. It's what Warrington, home of our local IKEA, did back in 2006 and they have managed to renew their certification ever since with the support of the local council, newspaper and community groups. It doesn't mean the end of normal retail in a town, as we saw with Warrington's myriad out of town retail units, it just means there is a genuine alternative available. When we look at how we reshape food retail in the next part of the book, that's one of the key things. Making the option readily accessible to as many people as possible. Fairtrade communities help to do that for ethically sourced products. Maybe you're reading this thinking it is something you could bring to life in your community as well?

If we needed further motivation to consider the terms under which we source what we eat, and the ethical implications of those choices, then all we need to do is consider our biggest weakness as a nation. Chocolate.

Fairtrade chocolate has been available for nearly thirty years in the UK an ever increasing variety out there.

Unfortunately, the bulk of the chocolate we consume is not covered by the scheme. Instead, a misleading mismatch of different labels and standards have appeared, each one set up and policed by the largest individual manufacturers in the sector[120]. This has two main consequences. It muddies the water, sowing confusion, leaving the consumer less able to make a good choice, and it saves the largest producers money as they don't pay the full Fairtrade premium or invest in high enough monitoring through their supply chains to ensure their lofty words are backed up with real action.

This matters because cocoa production is rife with child labour. April 2022 saw the broadcast of a Channel 4 Dispatches programme which found evidence of underage labour in poor working conditions on farms that supply Mondelez, the owner of Cadbury[121]. Children as young as ten were wielding large machetes and sharp knives with little or no footwear to protect them from accidents. Their parents, the cocoa farmers themselves, were often open about their reasons for choosing labour instead of schooling for their offspring. The price they received for their crop was too low to afford adult staff. They could only survive by using free child workers.

This is the story of the Fairtrade premium in action. This is how directly our choices matter. If we all ate only genuinely Fairtrade and beyond Fairtrade chocolate we could improve the lives of families in countries such as Ghana which featured in this particular documentary. According to the evidence found by the Channel 4 team, our choice of a £1 bar of Cadbury's chocolate is contributing to children missing out on their schooling. Is that a fair price to pay?

No man is an island

As we have seen throughout this book, the UK does not feed itself. We don't grow as much as we could and so we are reliant on importing produce from around the world. This creates an imbalance known as the 'Food Trade Gap'. According to Tim Lang in his book 'Feeding Britain', the gap between how much food we sell to the world and how much we import was a record breaking £24.3bn in 2018[122]. Even if we adopted regenerative farming practices, reshaped our diets, and fixed out structural deficiencies, we're still going to need to import some food. It makes sense that if we are to buy in some of what we need, we should be doing that on terms that are fair to all parts of the supply chain, including the initial growers of the crops themselves. This is where Fairtrade as a tool to build resilience becomes a positive influence on our food supply.

This need for fairness becomes even more clear when we lift our heads up from the food landscape here in the UK and consider briefly what happens globally. The Food and Agriculture Organisation, a UN body, produced a report in 2021 titled 'The State of Food Security and Nutrition in the World'. Some of the report's findings stated:

- "World hunger increased in 2020 under the shadow of the COVID-19 pandemic. After remaining virtually unchanged for five years, the prevalence of undernourishment (PoU) increased from 8.4 to around 9.9 percent in just one year, heightening the challenge of achieving the Zero Hunger target by 2030.
- While the global prevalence of moderate or severe food insecurity (measured using the Food Insecurity Experience Scale) has been slowly on the rise since 2014, the estimated increase in 2020 was equal to that of the previous five years combined. Nearly one in three people in the world (2.37 billion) did not have access to adequate food in 2020 – an increase of almost 320 million people in just one year.
- The sharpest increases in moderate or severe food insecurity in 2020 occurred in Latin America and the Caribbean and in Africa. In Northern America and Europe, food insecurity increased for the first time since the beginning of FIES data collection in 2014.
- Of the 2.37 billion people facing moderate or severe food insecurity, half (1.2 billion) are found in Asia, one-third (799 million) in Africa, and 11 percent (267 million) in Latin America and the Caribbean.
- Close to 12 percent of the global population was severely food insecure in 2020, representing 928 million people – 148 million more than in 2019.

- The high cost of healthy diets coupled with persistent high levels of income inequality put healthy diets out of reach for around 3 billion people, especially the poor, in every region of the world in 2019 – slightly less than in 2017."[123]

Food poverty is on the rise globally. Yes, many of the sharpest increases in the data recorded between 2019 and 2022 are related to the covid pandemic but that is no reason to dismiss them. On the contrary, it shows how vulnerable to external shocks the food supplies of millions of people are. Globally our food systems lack the strength to respond to crisis.

When we consider food as global commodity and take into account the levels of food insecurity around the world, the need for us to trade in a fair and equitable manner become even clearer. If we are choosing to grow less food than we might and indulge in diets that rely on out of season products grown on continents other than ours, then we have a responsibility to make sure we are not making a fragile, insecure situation worse. This is where Fairtrade and its counterparts are crucial. It is how we use our position within a planet wide web of food as a force for good.

Fair enough?

Fairtrade accreditation is not without its critics. Becoming a 'Fairtrade' supplier costs money. It is not free for a small scale coffee producer to gain access to that little blue and black logo that opens up slightly higher profits. Those costs can function as a barrier to some of those who could really do with the benefits Fairtrade brings.

It is also true that all schemes which rely on self-accreditation can be open to abuse. We see this in other areas such as sustainable fisheries schemes as well. Yet despite these drawbacks, Fairtrade needs to become the norm in sectors where it's already strong. Coffee, chocolate, bananas, and flowers. Whilst keeping up pressure for improvement, Fairtrade is a clear example of not letting great be the enemy of the good. Fairtrade isn't perfect but it is better than the commercially normal alternative.

As consumers we need to be cautious about individual companies introducing their own schemes that fragment our understanding of what is being achieved. This is a particular problem with some large, international chocolate retailers who've opted out of Fairtrade in favour of their own in-house schemes. Beyond the existing success stories, Fairtrade needs to expand to other global crops, reaching out and spreading the positive impact of the choices we can make at home. It's another way we can encourage the growth of sustainable networks and ecosystems across a wide distance, far bigger than maybe we sometime realise. Our choices matter far beyond the shelf edge. Wouldn't it be a great starting point if Fairtrade chocolate became the norm so that it sat at the tills in all those retail parks clustered around Warrington, bringing to life that humble sign we drive past so easily on our visits.

11

Palm oil free

Once up a time

Alfred Russel Wallace is one of those unfortunate figures that history has tried its best to forgot despite their stellar achievements. He should be genuinely famous, but you've probably only heard of him in passing at best. Wallace was the man who came up with theory of evolution independently of Charles Darwin at pretty much the same time. If there was any justice, school children down the ages would have learned all about him.

His career started slowly. After less than successful voyages to South America, the undeterred but still unknown Wallace sailed for the East in 1854. By the time he returned, his reputation was made, widely acknowledged as the foremost authority on tropical botany in the world. Today, his adventures are marked by the 'Wallace line', the place the animal species of Asia give way to those of Australia. His journey around what was then known as 'Malay' allowed up him a small piece of one-up-manship in the eye of the historical gaze. He, unlike Darwin, made it to Borneo.

Our intrepid Welshman spent eight years touring the archipelago of islands that today make up Indonesia and Malaysia collecting thousands of samples and recording in detail the habits and habitats of the native wildlife. The book he wrote on his return home, 'The Malay Archipelago' was lavishly illustrated with scenes of what one inscription described as "A forest in Borneo, with characteristic Mammalia."[124]

It's a great read. Right from the first chapter of the book it is clear that Wallace has a keen eye for detail but little patience for boring the reader with what he considers insignificant. On occasions he passes up months of his journey in little more than a sentence if he considers the topic well covered in other contemporary publications.

By the time he reaches the Island of Borneo he's well into his task. Determined not to waste time, he strikes for areas 'seldom visited by Europeans.'[125] That doesn't mean the modern world hadn't arrived. At the Simunjon Coalworks the Chinese are busy creating the infrastructure needed for extraction, cutting two miles through the forest to lay a railroad to the nearest river. And yet, from this vantage point Wallace could see "for hundreds of miles in each direction a magnificent forest extended over plain and mountain, rock and morass."[126] He goes on to demonstrate the abundance of the Eden he's stumbled into:

"When I arrived at the mines, on the 14th of March, I had collected in the proceeding four months, 320 different kinds of beetles. In less than a fortnight I had doubled this number, an average of about 24 new species a day. On one day I collected 76 different kinds, of which 34 were new to me. By the end of April I had more than a thousand species, and then they went on increasing at a slower rate; so that I obtained altogether in Borneo about two thousand distinct kinds, of which all but about a hundred were collected at this place, and on scarcely more than a square mile of ground."[127]

It is an astonishing rate of discovery and collection, although amongst the ridiculous success I particularly like the peeved note that after a blistering start, the rate of cataloguing only managed to keep going 'at a slower rate'. Truly man was spoilt in such surroundings.

Wallace also found fault with his collection of mammals, regretting his lack of an accompanying hunter to make up for his preoccupation with the never ending stream of insects. Despite this he lists; "five squirrels, two tiger-cats, the Gymnurus Rafflesii, which looks like a cross between a pig and polecat, and the Cynogale Bennetti – a rare, otter like animal"[128] He also made extensive record of a flying frog bought to him by a man who swore he had seen it descending from a tree nearby. Wallace was so intrigued that he includes one of his lavish illustrations of this find in the book, determining that its webbed feet were proof of what became Darwinian theories.

And all of this was before he reaches the real reason for his trip deep into the forests of Borneo. Wallace wanted to see the Orang-utans. Here, with the knowledge of what is to come, the book becomes more difficult reading. Pleasing illustrations of young female 'Mias,' as the locals call them, can't make up for the detailed descriptions and pure veracity with which Wallace hunts and shoots Orang-utans. His only regrets are linked to his own inability to be more lethal: "On May 2nd, I again found one on a very high tree, when I had only a small 80-bore gun with me. However, I fired at it, and on seeing me it began howling in a strange voice like a cough, and seemed in a great rage."[129]

One can't imagine why the Orang was quite so annoyed.

Wallace goes on undeterred by such unsuccessful shots: "On the 12th of May I found another, which behaved in a very similar manner, howling and hooting with rage, and throwing down branches. I shot at it five times."[130]

Despite being no nearer to an insight into why men with guns were so annoying to the inhabitants of the forest he was traipsing through, Wallace did recognise the link between humans and one of its closest relatives. He ended up with an orphan baby Orang in his care (after he had shot the mother) and tries his best to feed it. He notes the similarity in behaviour between his hungry young charge and human baby, suckling on a finger desperate for milk and screaming when none was available. He details, with a great deal of affection, the trials and tribulations of this young orphan until the inevitable happens and his best attempts at care fail. The infant succumbing to symptoms that seemed to Wallace to be just like those of an intermittent fever in a human. The Welshman had mused on taking the Orang home with him and watching its development with a paternal eye. Instead, he had to make do with preserving the skin and skeleton.

Modern sensibilities aside, Wallace's trip to Borneo was a staggering success. He documented hundreds of new species and bought back cases upon cases of prized specimens, including, it must be said, a range of deceased Orang-utans. His book is an astounding record of a time and place, each page stuffed with fine detail of his work and adventures. It is a time capsule, beautifully illustrated and lavishly filled with wonders that Wallace had taken the care to understand as best he could. To the modern reader it's a captivating assault on the imagination even if it ruffles our 21st century distaste for shooting at animals merely for the sake of collecting them. Through Wallace's eyes comes a Borneo that is a magical place. A stuffed cornucopia of wildlife you couldn't help but trip over.

This is the Modern Way

Today Borneo is, in many places, a biodiversity desert. The characteristic Mammalia of Wallace's time, severely denuded by intensive farming has transformed the island and Wallace wouldn't recognise the place if his less rational spiritual beliefs deposited his soul back where he'd seen forests and animals aplenty in the 1850's. The cause of this dramatic transformation is the subject of this chapter, the modern world's lust for palm oil.

Palm oil is genuinely ubiquitous. It's bloody everywhere and nowhere is that truer than in almost all of the processed food we now consume in such vast quantities. Feel free to go and check your cupboards if you haven't already. You'll find palm oil in biscuits, crisps, sweets, sauces, ready meals and more. It is yet another reason to cut back on ultra processed foods and the effect on the landscape of Borneo has been horrific. When considering all the topics we have dipped our toe into across this book, it's hard to think of a hidden cost of our food that is so visible, if we cared to look. It's an ugly scar trackable from high above the surface of the earth. The deforestation isn't subtle or gradual. It is rapacious and grasping.

The WWF lays out the scale of the problem in clear language, worth quoting in full:

"Satellite studies show that some 56% of protected lowland tropical rainforests in Kalimantan were cut down between 1985 and 2001 to supply global timber demand – that's more than 29,000 km² (almost the size of Belgium).

Protection laws are in effect throughout Borneo, but are often inadequate or are flagrantly violated, usually without any consequences.

One of the biggest drivers of deforestation in the HoB (Heart of Borneo) and Kalimantan is the growth of oil palm plantations in response to global demand for palm oil, the most important tropical vegetable oil in the global oils and fats industry. Within Indonesia, oil palm production expanded from 600,000 hectares in 1985 to over 6 million hectares by 2007.

Oil palm development contributes to deforestation - directly and indirectly. About half of all presently productive plantations... were established in secondary forest and bush areas in Malaysia and Indonesia.

Without the maintenance of very large blocks of inter-connected forest, there is a clear risk that hundreds of species could become extinct. Large mammals such as orang-utans and elephants are particularly affected because of the vast areas they require to survive. For example, the Borneo elephant has increasingly come into conflict with the expansion of human agriculture activities in its natural habitat.

Other smaller species, especially small mammals, may not be able to re-colonize isolated patches of suitable habitat and thus will become locally extinct. Road construction through protected areas leads to further separation of habitat ranges and provides easy access for poachers to some of the more remote and diverse tracts of remaining virgin forest."[131]

It is hard to know where to start with that avalanche of interconnected bad news. Many communities in Borneo have become economically dependent on either selling timber which has been cut as a result of illegal clearing or on the palm oil industry itself. This happens because of an absence of alternatives. It's important to recognise, as always, the systemic failures that have to be in place for such terrible outcomes to occur. Rural villagers are not going to turn down the only opportunity to put food on their plate in the name of nebulous concepts such as 'conservation' and it is unfair to ask them to do so. The lack of economic alternatives i.e., good jobs, is key factor in the spread of deforestation.

And what of the wonders that Alfred Russel Wallace saw? What is left? With the massive reduction in widespread forest cover has come the loss of habitat for many species. Wallace noted upon lengthy observation of the Orang-Utan that 'a wide extent of unbroken and equally lofty virgin forest is necessary to the comfortable existence of these animals'[132] That coverage no longer exists. Writing in the journal 'Current Biology' a team from Liverpool John Moores university found staggering declines in Orang-Utan numbers. They estimated that nearly 150,000 of these precious primates were lost between 1999 and 2015. That is half the population in 16 years.[133]

And it's not just Orang's that are impacted. Take the very distinctive looking Nasalis Larvatus, a long nosed type of monkey. Wallace records an abundance of these and other similar species on the river banks as he journeyed deeper into the forest. Today the species is listed as endangered by the Convention on International Trade in Endangered Species (CITES) and by the International Trade in Endangered Species of Wild Fauna and Flora (IUCN).[134] Such designation is increasingly common.

Charities working in Borneo are keen to stress the numbers still in existence. The Borneo Nature Foundation found 65 species of mammal, 172 bird types, 66 different butterflies and 57 separate types of reptiles and amphibians in the areas they cover.[135] That is good and the work documenting what is left of Borneo's biodiversity is vital but let's not forget, Wallace was capturing thousands of different species in a couple of months.

Making the Change

By now it should be clear why cutting our palm oil consumption is so important. Our love of processed food has driven the spread of this easy to use ingredient at the cost of huge swathes of habitat vital to some of our nearest relatives in the animal kingdom and plenty of other species as well.

When considering how to move to a better palm oil future it is worth remembering there are two options (as there are with products like soya as well). We can either cut the palm oil out completely or we can move our consumption to certified sustainable sources that shouldn't have the problems of deforestation and habitat destruction associated with them. Sustainably sourced options are possible because of one simple fact that it's wise to keep in mind when considering our choices. Palm oil (or soya or any other plant species we eat) isn't the problem. How humans have chosen to use it is. By following this logic more environmentally friendly choices can come from the better use of a product as well as switching to alternatives.

Currently, sustainable palm oil remains a relatively niche product compared to the standard type but that is changing slowly as awareness spreads. Happily, there are beacons of positive activity and change happening that show what is possible with concerted action. Even more usefully for this author, one of the best examples of this in the UK is happening less than a couple of hours away from our hillside home.

Chester, a roman city perched across the English and Welsh border is fun combination of the historic and the newly monied (allayed of course with the unavoidable scar of poverty present in every British city these days). The city centre, still laid out on the classic cross shaped road plan of Roman times and home to rows of uneven looking timber framed buildings, bustles with Cheshire's nouveau cash creating a pleasant environment to be in.

On our numerous visits it is not a somewhere I'd ever really associated with conservation or climate change awareness, but it turns out we'd been underestimating the place. Chester is the world's first Sustainable Palm Oil city. The idea was driven by Chester Zoo who modelled the idea on the Sustainable Fish Cities project which is run by the group Sustain. Working in partnership with a number of independent organisations and involving local businesses across multiple sectors including restaurants and school dinner providers, Chester has worked hard to convince as many people as possible to switch all the palm oil they use to products sourced from sustainable suppliers.

Commenting on the success they've had, Cat Barton, Field Programmes manager at the zoo emphasised why such action is so important: "A vast array of species are under threat and on the brink of being lost forever, because oil palm plantations are wiping out rainforests to produce the food and household items we all consume every day. But it is not too late. By embracing a more sustainable future, we can stop this crisis. The fact that more than fifty organisations in one city alone have made changes to the products they use – and committed to a 100% sustainable future – shows that the tide is turning. We are already seeing the wider impact of the campaign. More cities are now engaging in talks to follow this model and major large companies nationwide are working with us to make the switch to sustainable palm oil."

Hopefully other cities and regions will get onboard with the scheme quickly and over the next couple of years visibility will increase and consumers will be able to get used to looking out for signs that they are consuming products made with sustainably sourced palm oil when they're out and about.

The other option is reducing our palm oil consumption altogether. Alternatives do exist and include products such as coconut or rapeseed oil (depending on the type of final product). Unfortunately, these aren't always as cheap as palm oil or produced in such huge quantities. Because of this the most realistic way to reduce our palm oil consumption is by reducing our processed food intake. As previously stated, this can be a win on multiple fronts including for our health. Any sustainable food future needs to wean itself off palm oil grown in ways that cause habitat destruction and biodiversity loss and If we learn once again to use fresh ingredients, cooked from scratch we'll have the happy effect of making us healthier and less dependent on a product that has devastated the population numbers of one of our closest relatives, the Orang Utan.

Whilst we can't recapture what explorers such as Wallace saw in the 19th century, we can preserve what we still have by backing voluntary schemes like the Sustainable Palm Oil City project which has had such a positive start in Chester. However, as so often in this book, taxation which demonstrates the real hidden cost of palm oil, may be the only solution to drive change quickly enough. Can we afford to wait another ten years and find we've driven yet more species to the brink of extinction?

12

Reduce food waste

Waste-full

Food waste accounts for 30% of all the food produced globally[136]. Just think about that for a moment. We could radically reduce the planetary impact of the food we eat just by throwing away less. Add to that the moral imperative of not wasting food in a nation that is home to more than three thousand foodbanks and it becomes clear that reducing waste is a big part of any future solution.

Food Waste in the UK

(Percentage of total waste, post farm gate)

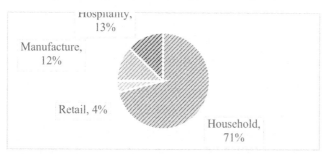

Source: Wrap[137]

Currently more than 70% of UK food waste results from households as opposed to other parts of the supply chain according to WRAP, the leading UK charity on waste and sustainability. That figure, at first glance, places a heavy burden on responsibility on individuals to change their behaviour but that is not the full story. It is fair to say that zero food waste is unrealistic, products will always get damaged or go off slightly quicker than expected and families will never totally eliminate that even if we could all be doing more to bring that figure down. However, whilst taking on our own fair share of responsibility for the problem we also need to realise that our current food ecosystem produces waste by its very nature. But, there is another way of doing things.

Meet the team

Food waste is a challenge when you run your own shop selling fresh fruit and veg. It's great to support local growers and offer packaging free produce to our customers but it is inevitable that we'll generate some waste along the way. A case of peppers isn't all going to go mouldy on the same day. Some will perish before others are sold. Luckily, our little personal ecosystem is getting more and more adept at handling this issue.

It starts at the shop. Good rotation of products helps the shortest life products sell first and careful ordering prevents as much unnecessary stock as possible coming in the door in the first place. Once we've done what we can to get the right items in the right place on the right days, then it's down to the mercurial gods of customer flow and weather to dictate how much gets sold. Once we lock the door on a Saturday ready for our two days off, our five stage veg disposal system kicks in.

Step 1 – we eat as much of what we haven't sold as possible. Fruit and veg might not look pretty enough to sell but it's still very edible. We tend to have six different vegetables with our Sunday dinner. A ridiculous luxury for most people, our glut is driven by slightly wonky looking things that haven't sold.

Step 2 – Once we've eaten what we can it's on to the first of our organic waste disposal teams. Or as you may more commonly know them, ducks. Seriously, they love greens and cucumbers. Our three ducks get through a surprising amount of veg in a week (plus frozen peas weirdly. Seriously, they love them).

Step 3 – Organic waste disposal team 2, chickens. Got something a bit soft and squidgy? Give it to the chickens to peck at. They're particularly useful for getting rid of most members of the squash family and cauliflowers.

Step 4 – Compost. I mean there's not a great deal left once the disposal teams have had their fill but what there is goes into the compost pile, theoretically balanced by cardboard also from the shop (Handy tip: your compost should be equal mixes of green and brown waste).

Step 5 – Closing the circle. After an appropriate period of time our decomposed veg, cardboard and a bit of organic waste becomes compost. That is then used to grow more vegetables, some of which are then sold in the shop.

By this moderately haphazard process of squawks, quacks and shovels we end up with no 'waste' at all. Everything should have a use if we have done our bit correctly. We've managed to bring to life our own system that doesn't recognise the term waste. What we're describing, is the makings of a circular system.

Waste is a feature, not a bug

Obviously not everyone has ducks and chickens to help with their food waste, but it does show that the very idea of food as 'waste' can be challenged. Unfortunately, our shop/home is an outlier. We in western societies live in a world where waste is baked into the systems that deliver such seeming abundance to us on a daily basis.

To repeat again that statistic from the start of the chapter, as much as 30% of food that is produced ends up as waste. When we live on a planet where globally and at home food poverty is an ongoing issue, this is unacceptable. When we combine that with awareness of the need to reduce the carbon footprint and land use associated with growing what we eat, this status quo becomes clearly untenable. We cannot keep emitting greenhouse gases, destroying habitats and throwing stuff in the bin whilst people go hungry. We need fundamental change in how we think about food waste.

When we think about waste, we tend to visualise something going mouldy in the fridge or out of date on our shelves. And yes, that is part of the problem, but it ignores the bigger, structural problems which make it so hard not to waste food. We should be asking ourselves why are there too many carrots in the fridge in the first place?

When customers come into our shop for the first time, the initial conversation with them is illuminating. We try and start people off with a basic staple, for example pasta. The interaction generally goes something like this; I ask how much pasta they need, they look at me confused and say they have no idea how much pasta their family gets through beyond just buying another bag from the supermarket when the cupboard is running low.

And then the lightbulb moment happens.

How many of us know how much pasta we eat in a week? How many of us know how big a portion of pasta should be in grams for a healthy amount? The answer, if we are honest, is very few of us. I certainly didn't know before we opened the shop. I just went to the supermarket and bought another pack without knowing what size that was. Suddenly in that first interaction our mythical new customer has that realisation. I don't know how much I am buying or how much I'm eating. In such a world it is inevitable that people end up over cooking and throwing some in the bin, it is a natural outcome of the convenience of buying our food prepacked. We don't have to think, just pick another pack off the shelf. Keep buying and nothing needs to change. There will always be more pasta.

Now transfer that mindset to the fruit and veg section of large supermarket. We're not buying based on our need, but on what we are presented with. Most people don't buy how many carrots they need for the week, they buy the bag of carrots that represents the best (price based) value in the moment. And then they go home, use as many as they can before they go off and throw away the rest. These are systemic flaws and constitute madness. Food waste, and its associated footprint, will always occur in any such system. By continuing this way, we are simply allowing supermarkets to push the waste (and financial risk) onto households instead of taking responsibility for it themselves.

Large supermarkets run to incredibly tight budgets for waste generated within their shops and warehouses. To give an idea of this, 15 years ago I was running a fresh section in a large supermarket for one of the big four retailers. My section was generating sales in excess of £100,000 per week and I was allocated a waste budget of around £1000 per week. That £1000 had to cover any damages in store, anything dumped by a customer in a non-chilled environment, and stuff we missed as we checked the sell-by dates on a daily basis. That is a staggeringly small number, but it is the norm for those operations.

How do they hit those targets? Well party by being ruthless with suppliers. If there is any possibility at all, the supermarket will claim the loss against a delivery from a specific firm. For example, if some bread is found with a split bag, instead of marking that down as waste in store, the supermarket employee will be encouraged to claim that money back from the bread supplier whoever that might be. In this way, some of the value of the waste created by the supply of food is transferred from the supermarkets, back to the suppliers who take the financial hit. There is also pressure placed on employees within store not to miss anything when date checking fresh sections. For those of you who have no experience of working in a food retail environment, fresh products must be checked daily for anything going out of date so that they can be reduced and not become waste. This is a time consuming process that can be aided by technology but ultimately boils down to someone, often on not much more than the minimum wage, paying enough attention to spot items needing a reduction. Failure to spot something leads to waste budgets being missed, which in turn hits profitability. I can clearly recall being told by an irate Store Manager that although he liked me personally, he would not hesitate to sack me if I didn't clear all evidence of some waste products away instantly. It's not an easy environment sometimes.

But the truth is, the way supermarkets sell food guarantees there will be waste somewhere. If you only sell carrots in bags of six or eight and Doris only needs two, then the other six are going to end up going off. That shows up in Doris' waste bin at home but is the result of supermarkets selling easy to handle fixed pack sizes rather than customer and planet friendly loose produce. And as cost pressures rise that same logic applies to the disappearance of delicatessen, butchers, and fishmonger counters where items can be bought by weight. It drives greater waste at home whilst leaving supermarkets more profitable. In the drive for cheap food and amidst cut throat price competition our biggest retailers are actually just creating another hidden cost.

It is important to note that large food retailers have got much, much better over the last decade in finding a home for food that has been deemed waste in store. Ten years ago it was very unusual for an individual supermarket to have a direct link with a local foodbank or charity as an outlet for each days wasted products. It is slowly becoming more normal but there is still a long way to go. An investigation by the Independent in 2021 found that only 9% of supermarket waste was making its way to food banks.[138] To put that in context, that is around 25,000 tonnes going to help those in need out of a total ten times that size. WRAP, suggest that food redistribution has tripled in the five years from 2015 and as of 2020 equated to 220 million meals[139]. Whilst that is definite improvement, it is hard not to feel that's still a failure with the massive rise in food bank use over the same period.

I am going to leave you with one last anecdote before we get more number driven for a bit. Another family member of mine works for a national retailer which specialises in small, community sized stores. They have waste collections by a local food charity most evenings but not all. On the nights nothing is collected, the food waste ends up in the fenced and gated yard at the rear of the shop waiting to return to the distribution warehouse in the morning. One night, someone broke into the yard and stole the bag of waste. It happened again a few nights later. A couple of colleagues, including my family member left a note pinned to the locked gate asking the person responsible to get in touch with the local food charity directly as they could help. They put the contact number on the note. This isn't an isolated incident. If you have worked in food retail over the last few years you've been on the sharp end of watching people, often in low paid work, unable to pay for food or scrabbling around for change to get what they need. It is now normal to see a couple come to the till and nervously watch the total add up before breathing a sigh of relief that they have enough on their card to pay. Our society, so casually accepting of food poverty whilst happily enabling the systems that make waste a reality, are complicit in this unseen human disaster. The unusual has become normalised.

The size of the crime

Let's have some more of those hard numbers we saw in the chart at the start of this chapter, as a counteract to all that emotional outrage. The ever informative Tim Lang and his oft quoted book 'Feeding Britain' gives a good summary:

"According to the Waste and Resources Action Programme (WRAP) the UK wastes of 10mt (metric tonnes) of food after the farmgate or an average of 156 kg per person per year. Household food waste is 7.3mt, estimated by WRAP as worth £15bn and emitting 22mt of CO2e. Industry wastes 1.7mt (worth £1.4bn), the hospitality sector wastes 0.9mt and retailers 0.25mt."[140]

This is the definite proof of how, despite handling the bulk of the food we eat, the retail sector has proved very adept at shifting waste away from its own balance sheets. That 71% of food waste is attributable to households is wrong. As we've seen, the structural forces of limited choice and price promotions that lead to over purchasing are far more to blame than care free shoppers who happily throw money in the bin by buying too much food for fun. And on top of that, as pointed out in the excellent National Food Plan by Henry Dimbleby, amongst others, food accounts for 19% of the UK's greenhouse gas emissions.[141] If we weren't wasting as much as 30% of that, we'd reduce our national emissions by 6% and leave no one hungrier than they are now.

If we shift our focus outwards to the global impact of this problem, we can look to the UN Food and Agriculture Organisation who "calculate(d) that if food waste was a country, it would be the third-largest CO^2 emitting country in the world, after China and the USA."

Again, Tim Lang, in 'Feeding Britain,' states that: "In 2019, the global carbon footprint of food waste was 44 gigatonnes CO_2e per year; that's equivalent to 87% of all global road transport. If the target for the UN's Sustainable Development Goal 12 to reduce food waste by 50% by 2030 was met, 1.4 gigatonnes of CO_2e/year, equivalent to the greenhouse gas emissions of Japan would be cut. EU food waste according to the INHERIT project is 88mt of food at different levels of the food chain: 53% is at the household level, 19% in the processing sector, 12% in food service and 5% in the wholesale-retail sector."[142]

It is interesting to note that the UK manages to combine higher than EU average levels of household food waste as a percentage of the total, and lower than average waste in the retail sector. This is another sign of how the UK's highly developed and price competitive food industry is better at pushing the consequences of systemic waste producing practices onto consumers than even its counterparts in other western nations, let alone those in less developed parts of the globe.

Solutions, not outrage 1 – societal change

Enough of the heavy detail. How do we go about fixing this problem?

To find the long term solutions to the problem of food waste we need to return to the concept highlighted by our organic processing teams at the beginning of the chapter:

circular systems. The idea of circular economies and systems is amazingly simple. Nothing is wasted and resources are used and reused at the highest value possible. In the UK the Ellen MacArthur foundation is one of the leading proponents of such systems. They explain the idea in the following way:

"In our current economy, we take materials from the Earth, make products from them, and eventually throw them away as waste – the process is linear. In a circular economy, by contrast, we stop waste being produced in the first place.

The circular economy is based on three principles, driven by design:

Eliminate waste and pollution, Circulate products and materials (at their highest value), Regenerate nature.

It is underpinned by a transition to renewable energy and materials. A circular economy decouples economic activity from the consumption of finite resources. It is a resilient system that is good for business, people and the environment."[143]

In a future populated by circular systems, waste is removed at the point of design. A product that results in unusable waste wouldn't hit the shelves in the first place. Instead, solutions which use finite resources in a careful manner, seeking to reuse them repeatedly, would eliminate much of what we think of as rubbish today. That might seem highly utopian, but it is possible in many areas of our lives, including food. Indeed, our existing supplier of refillable liquids for the shop works on the principle. The containers are sent back and used time and again. There is no waste to dispose of, just a loop that keeps turning.

As the MacArthur Foundation has shown through their work, such principles are applicable at all stages of the food chain and in almost every type of location. They have examples of insects being grown as animal food, new products made from existing urban waste streams, and highly developed edible coatings that can protect fruit in transit instead of plastic wrapping as well as many more ground breaking ideas. One particular favourite of ours is their case study of a circular economy one acre farm in Uganda. It is a miracle of intelligence and working with what nature has given you. The farmer, Dr Emma Naluyima, has woven together her own ecosystem of integrated supports and resource management. Water and animal waste are treated as valuable inputs to be used carefully rather than problematic waste to dispose of. Natural relationships between animal species are harnessed in service of the goal of food production. It just goes to show what can be done if we approach growing our food with a different mindset. And it's entirely fitting, that "In 2019, she was awarded the prestigious Africa Food Prize, for demonstrating to hundreds of millions of smallholder farmers in Africa, the multiple benefits of shifting to circular agriculture."[144]

It is not just famers in Africa who could learn a lot from her work.

Solutions, not outrage 2 – individual change

Tackling food waste is a prime example of an area of our food ecosystem where there are plenty of small individual actions that we can take to make a real difference. Once again, there is a positive story to weave based around a changed attitude to the food we buy which places the principles of the circular economy right inside our own houses.

As so often, these actions start with education. Collectively we need to make sure we have a grip on a couple of important parts of our food knowledge.

First up is the distinction between the Use By dates and Best Before dates that we find on our food. This might seem like a really small detail when we are trying to prevent billions of pounds of waste, but it makes a big difference. Use By is a hard deadline. Food eaten beyond a Use By date may not be safe for consumption and you should be very cautious about eating anything that has gone past these dates. In contrast, Best Before is a guide. As the name suggests, food may well be at its best before this date but that does not mean it's inedible after it. Instead, we need to use our common sense and judgement to reduce unnecessary waste. In essence, it boils down to a good old fashioned sniff and taste test. If it doesn't smell off, doesn't taste funny and is not visibly mouldy then it may well be safe to eat. Understanding the difference between these two date systems can really help reduce what we throw away, particularly if we develop the skills needed to use up leftovers effectively. There's a myriad of slightly past their best vegetables and dried goods that by chucked quite happily into a stir-fry, pasta sauce or curry dish causing no harm whatsoever. We have a particularly tasty butternut squash curry in our house that is often home to some produce that doesn't look great but is still able to form part of a tasty, nutritious dinner.

The second key area of education for us is portion sizes. As remarked before, this is often the 'lightbulb' conversation we have with customers when they visit the shop for the first time. By knowing how much rice/pasta/potato to cook, we remove the risk of throwing away a surplus that wasn't needed once we're dishing up. It is a really simple win.

Alongside portion sizes sits meal planning as a key tool for household waste reduction. Again, I'm well aware that in our busy lives such an idea can seem a bit utopian, but it can save you hassle over the course of the week and it's a great way of counteracting the need to buy in bigger packs sizes than you might ideally want to. If you don't have a packaging free produce option near you then meal planning can help you make sure you use up those extra carrots before they go off. If you need some of them for something on a Monday, plan in a Bolognese or stir fry towards the end of the week to clear the rest out before it is too late. By planning you can also make use of inexpensive options such as dried beans and pulses which may need soaking for eight hours before use.

We had customers at the shop who took the idea of meal planning to the next level. The wrote all their commonly eaten meals onto blank lollipop sticks and at the start of each week pulled them out of a bag at random to decide what they would have each night. Not only did they avoid falling into the trap of having the same old routine each week, but they also had some fun in the name of saving money and waste.

Next up, if at all possible, start composting. I know it is not an option for everyone and that in a world of crazy property prices having access to green space is a luxury a lot of people can't afford, but if you've got a little patch of ground, you can compost. Home composters are available to buy, and they take up no more space than a large external dustbin. If you've got more room, well the world is your oyster, and you can create a fabulous source of nutritious goodness for your existing soil form the food you don't manage to eat in time. It is worth producing compost from your waste, even if you can't make use of it yourself. There is always someone who wants some and would be prepared to take it off your hands. Theoretically you could actually turn the food you didn't eat into a small amount of money with the help of little time and brown waste and even if you only give it away, you're helping your area become less wasteful and more capable of producing its own food.

Beyond the immediacy of the meals we eat and the food we buy, we can use our time and influence to shape a more sustainable system. Ask the staff at your local supermarket if they have a link with a local foodbank or charity and harass them very politely until they get something sorted if they haven't already. And if you have them time, you could always volunteer to make that link a reality. Foodbanks always need people willing to go and collect whatever supermarkets have to give.

And after all that, surely it goes without saying, support your local zero waste shop. Buying packaging free reduces your waste, not just in wrap and plastic, but also by allowing you to purchase just what you need for each meal, thereby reducing risk of not using something up before it goes off. It's a win-win that we need much, much more of.

As with many of the subjects we've touched on, food waste is an area where change is starting to happen, but it is far too slow. Supermarkets are beginning to take some responsibility for finding an outlet for the still edible food they consider to be waste, but they are not yet willing to address the fundamental flaws in the system they have created which embeds waste into their operating models. This would represent a fundamental challenge to the way they do business.

Such change is hard to bring about without concerted pressure and alternative models showing they are financially viable. In the meantime, there are plenty of individual actions we can take to minimise waste at the household level that will also save us money in the process. There is really no argument against learning to treat food as a far more precious and useable a resource than we currently do. The false abundance of supermarkets has led us to a way of thinking that is highly linear when what we need to do is embrace the circular thinking espoused by Ellen MacArthur and others. Waste is a mindset we are trapped in. We need to turn it into an opportunity.

Oh, and get yourself some ducks. Just don't forget to stock up on the frozen peas.

13

Sustainable water consumption

Mainly Going Nuts

In June 2021 Bloomberg news ran a story on their website about water shortages in California and their devastating impact on almond growers in the region.[145] They began their report by focusing on the direct experience of one farm who are having to take huge risks to survive:

"'Farming's very risky,' said Christine Gemperle, who will undertake the arduous process of pulling out all her trees on the orchard this fall, replacing them with younger ones that don't need as much moisture. It's a tough decision. Almond trees are typically a 25-year investment, and if it weren't for the drought, these trees could've made it through at least another growing season, if not two. Now, they'll be ground up into mulch."

It is a tough story. A farmer struggling against the elements and facing into the harsh realities of fighting a losing battle against a record breaking drought. In such circumstances it's hard not to feel some sympathy for Christine and her farm. The problem is that commercial almond growing in California is destructive to the local water table even at the best of times. This industry, feeling the crushing effects of a lack of water falling from the sky, has been sucking unsustainable amounts of water from grounds sources for years. It is a brutal cycle of despair.

If you eat almonds, it's likely they come from the United States. America is responsible for more than 80% of almonds grown globally, all of them are the product of California.[146] The industry contributes more than $11 billion dollars a year to the local economy and is vital to the area. According to the Food Revolution blog: "A single almond takes about 1.1 gallons of water to produce. Or close to 10 gallons for a handful. California dedicates about 8% of its total agricultural water supply to growing almonds. Almond trees need water year-round, even when they are not producing almonds. And more almond trees are being planted in California, with the number of almond orchards doubling in the last 20 years."[147]

The water consumption associated with growing almonds has made the headlines quite a bit over the past few years. The Almond Hullers & Processors Association (AHPA), a regional trade body representing the industry released an 8 point factsheet in defence of its members stressing that more water efficient practices were being introduced by a majority of farmers and the amount of water taken to produce the end product had reduced by 33% over the last few years.[148] All this is true and other industries do use more water in total. Dairy accounts for a bigger amount of the agricultural water used in the state but that is slightly misleading. The problem with almonds is their impact on the water table driven by the year round moisture needs of the trees. However, it is also possible to conclude that a glass of milk from a cow in California may have a higher water use associated with it than a similar amount of almond milk.

If you search online to try and learn more about this subject, a bewildering range of options appear hosting argument and counter thrust. The industry has become proactive in defending itself whilst the spotlight being shone upon them has only grown over the last decade. It is not that easy to pick the truth from the carefully placed statistic used in isolation to give a misleading impression. Once again, the well intentioned consumer is at a disadvantage when trying to make the best decisions.

Maybe, instead of being sucked into a black hole of bad information, we can step back for a moment and try to learn about where we can get good quality water use statistics. For that we can turn to the Water Footprint Network, which is the world most comprehensive water use database using only peer reviewed data.[149]

Our first nugget of knowledge is that a water footprint is made up of three parts, Grey, Green and Blue. They are defined in the following way:

"Blue Water Footprint: The amount of surface water and groundwater required (evaporated or used directly) to produce an item – for food this mainly refers to crop irrigation.

Green Water Footprint: The amount of rainwater required (evaporated or used directly) to make an item – for food this refers to dry farming where crops receive only rainwater.

Grey Water Footprint: The amount of freshwater required to dilute the wastewater generated in manufacturing, in order to maintain water quality, as determined by state and local standards – for food this refers to things like field and farm runoff."[150]

If we then take a practical example of this method being used, it becomes clearer to see why such delineation is necessary.

According to a 2012 report, 80% of cattle in the United States is reared in what we consider a 'traditional', intensive manner.[151] This involves spending six months on pasture and the other half of the year on smaller plots being fed high calories feeds designed to fatten them up quickly. These are usually soy based. In contrast, the remaining 20% of herd are pasture grazed all year round, leading to slower growth but a lower environmental footprint associated with the meat. As a result of these different methods of rearing the animals, different water outcomes are produced. The intensively reared cows have a high blue water footprint because of the water used to grow the crops that become their feed. They may also have a notable grey water cost if indiscriminate nitrogen based fertilizer use has taken place somewhere along the food chain. In contrast, the pasture grazed cattle have a higher green water footprint as most of their water use is based on growing the grass they munch on. This isn't much of problem except in times of drought.

If we apply this information to the almonds of increasingly drought stricken California, then our new understanding casts a harsh light. The nut trees need as much green water as they can get, but it is in increasingly short supply as climate change makes the necessary rainfall less and less common. Because of that they use ever more blue water in the form of irrigation which depletes ground water sources across the area. On top of that, grey water runoff is a further issue, tainting shallow and slow moving water courses so that pollutants do not run off quickly. It is a bad combination. Oh, and as an aside, their intensive farming is horrifically punishing to the bees required as pollinators, with many travelling huge distances and dying as part of the process.[152]

Nuts are important part of a balanced, nutritious diet. No one is suggesting we don't eat them but, as consumers, we need once more to think about all the costs associated with them. We have already seen how the hidden costs of what we eat warp our sense of value and price when we looked at the health impacts of our diets earlier in the book. We need to consider the hidden cost of water use in the same way. Luckily, we don't have to give up nuts, we just have to be pickier about them.

As we saw earlier, nuts are something the UK could easily grow more of given its climate. We could reduce our dependence on imported nuts by re-establishing our traditional cobnut industry or by increasing the quantity of walnuts grown here. Both options are eminently feasible. We've been planting walnuts at home, and we know others are experimenting with them as laid out in the sections on agroforestry and silvopasture. We can also choose oat and hemp milk instead of almond milk to reduce our footprints even further. These are readily available in pretty much every supermarket now.

Even if we feel we have answers to the specific issue of almonds, there are bigger problems for consumers here and that is the reason that water use remains our 'aspirational eighth' when we discuss our 'Sustainable Seven' in store. You, the diligent shopper, are going to have to do all the legwork on this because no one is making this information obvious to you at the shelf edge. There is no labelling, no agreed standard, no obvious measurement. As we head into the next couple of decades where research suggests growing areas that we rely on for a lot of our imported produce will come under increasing climate strain and associated water supply disruption, we have no straightforward way of knowing if we're contributing to the problem or not. It's enough to drive anyone… nuts.

Water, water everywhere

The Water Footprint Network has produced a range of highly detailed papers on national water use both for the production and consumption of food. I can't pretend that they make light reading, but they are fascinating in a policy wonk, don't-get-out-much sort of way.

In terms of food production, the headline summary is as follows:

"China, India, and the US are the countries with the largest total water footprints within their territory, with total water footprints of 1207, 1182 and 1053 Mm3/yr, respectively. About 38% of the water footprint of global production lies within these three countries. The next country in the ranking is Brazil, with a total water footprint within its territory of 482 Mm3/yr. India is the country with the largest blue water footprint within its territory: 243 Mm3/yr, which is 24% of the global blue water footprint. Irrigation of wheat is the process that takes the largest share (33%) in India's blue water footprint, followed by irrigation of rice (24%) and irrigation of sugarcane (16%). China is the country with the largest grey water footprint within its borders: 360 Mm3/yr, which is 26% of the global grey water footprint."[153]

Water Footprint by Product

(Per 500g of food purchased)

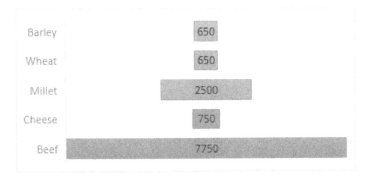

Source: Water Footprint Network[154]

Those figures make a lot of intuitive sense. China, India, the US, and Brazil are all large food producers with giant agricultural sectors. It also highlights some of the hardest to fix issues. India relies massively on irrigation to produce its staples of wheat and rice. Most of that water comes from rivers fed by run off generated from snow and glacier melt high in the Himalayas. The effects of climate changes are disrupting those traditional water flows, with as much as 75% of Himalayan glaciers in retreat according to a study by Anjal Prakash of the Indian School of Business, Hyderabad.[155] This has a corresponding impact on the water available for agriculture.

But food is a global commodity. If we considering the challenge of understanding water use from a consumer's perspective, then we need to think about who is exporting a lot of high water footprint foods, and who benefits from these flows of trade. Once again, the Water Footprint Network have crunched the numbers:

"The US, Pakistan, India, Australia, Uzbekistan, China, and Turkey are the largest blue virtual water exporters, accounting for 49% of the global blue virtual water export. All these countries are partially under water stress… This raises the question whether the implicit or explicit choice to consume the limited national blue water resources for export products is sustainable and most efficient. Closely related to this is the question to what extent the scarcity is reflected in the price of water in these countries. Given the fact that all the externalities and a scarcity rent are seldom included in the price of water, most particular in agriculture, one cannot expect that production and trade patterns automatically account for regional water scarcity patterns."[156]

The flip side of this is that some countries are effectively saving their own water resources by importing copious quantities of high water footprint foodstuffs instead of growing it themselves. The UK falls into this category, with the Water Footprint Network estimating that we save ourselves "53 Gm3/yr (75% green, 15% blue, 9% grey)"[157] of our own water consumption each year in this manner. It is another strong argument in favour of us growing more of our own food and taking responsibility for all the costs associated with it. Our continued choice to not increase our own fruit and veg production is just that, a choice. There are plenty of other countries around the world who have large water footprints associated with the food imports, but they are reliant on rainwater that falls elsewhere in the world. No one is suggesting that Kuwait, Jordan, or Israel, to name but three, should be using more of their own rainfall to feed themselves. Unlike us, sat here in moist, temperate Great Britain, they don't have that option.

The upshot of all these detailed figures is that, in layman's terms, water isn't priced appropriately where food is grown so the hidden cost isn't present in the price we pay at the shelf edge. A lack of visibility also prevents us from moderating our shopping habits as we would in a world of perfect information. Of course, this is true for our high profile almonds, as well as much more. Understanding water use is a global challenge because our food arrives on our plates from around the world. It seems an obvious statement to make but the reality of the detail assembled by researchers makes it clearer than ever.

Turning the taps off at home

All those figures show, in general terms how the UK imports food that has a high water footprint, increasing the water shortage problems faced by other nations. We understand how this is the classic example of a hidden cost associated with our food. Now, we need to have a closer look at our own behaviour.

Avocados are one of my pet peeves. I have never had avocado on toast, and I don't intend to. Why the UK has developed such a fascination with the things baffles me.

That might seem a touch irrational, but they are a great example of what we are not doing right when it comes to food. And it's not just avocadoes, we are importing food with high water costs without any real awareness of the problem. In 'Feeding Britain' Tim Lang cites researchers at Cranfield University who "calculated that the water consumption associated with the UK's intake from just five countries was 25 million cubic metres – equivalent to 10,000 Olympic swimming pools."[158]

It's not just fruits that are a problem. There are other high profile examples. Over the last fifty years the UK has embraced the curry with a fervour that leads to some calling it our national dish. That's great but we grow pretty much no rice ourselves. (There is one poor soul in Scotland attempting this heroic feat of agricultural optimism, good luck to him.) As a result, our rice comes from nations such India, Pakistan, and Spain, all which are facing a worsening water crisis over the next decade. To put the impact into perspective, according to figures calculated by the UNESCO-IHE institute for Water Education and quoted by Tim Lang again, the average UK person has a daily water footprint of around 2757 litres. To produce 1kg of imported rice takes 2672 litres by itself![159] In addition Mike Berners-Lee found that the carbon footprint of producing a kilo of rice is higher than burning a litre of diesel.[160] None of this is to suggest we give up rice but there are less impactful staples to use, and it seems fair to say that the vast majority of curry eaters are oblivious to this silent impact caused by their regular enjoyment.

And how about the most obvious consumption of water of all? The stuff we drink. Over the last twenty years the UK has developed an astonishing taste for bottled water, plenty of it imported. According to 'Feeding Britain': "In 2017-18 UK bottled water sales were £243.5 million for still water (which) duplicates tap water."[161]. This is astonishingly wasteful from water resource, packaging, and transportation perspectives. Mike Berners-Lee crunched the numbers again and found that bottled water was one thousand times more impactful compared when to tap water. At the most basic level of quenching our thirst, we are doing water badly at a huge cost that isn't reflected in the price we pay at the till.

On top of all this, our own water supply is threatened by climate change and population growth. In 2019 the head of the Environment agency was quoted in an interview with the BBC's Countryfile as saying "Within 25 years, England will reach the "jaws of death – the point at which, unless we take action to change things, we will not have enough water to supply our needs".[162] With the faster growing population and largest existing teeming mass of people, this stress will fall soonest on the south-east of England. It is a sobering thought that even within the bounds of the United Kingdom we could well be discussing the political and social impacts of water transfers from one region to the other before too long. We were not that far away from such conversations by the end of the long, dry summer of 2022.

For too long the impact of the food we eat on the water supplies of nations around the world and our own backyard have been hidden from view. A dirty blue secret no one wants to mention aloud. The climate emergency will force the subject into the open over the next decade, leaving us no choice but to face up to another of the hidden costs associated with what goes on our plate. In such a world it seems likely that being seen to eat certain foodstuffs will become socially unacceptable for many, whilst those on lowest incomes may be left with no choice if action is not taken now to ramp up the production of less thirsty alternatives. For less essential items (yes, we're looking at you avocadoes with your massive footprint), the idea that such impactful foods were once 'fashionable' will hopefully come to seem laughable to us and the generations to come. A luxury once afforded by western consumers who hadn't learned to take what they eat seriously.

The more visible the impact of our outsourced water use becomes the more pressure should build for high quality information to be available to consumers at the point of purchase. A traffic light scheme, similar to that used for nutritional guidance needs to become the norm so that customers with good intentions aren't left to guess or spend their own time doing endless research. Once again, taxation needs to target the sources of highest impact.

We live on a blue planet, water defines how we view our world when we picture that image of a fragile ecosystem suspended in space. If that is not to seem a bitter irony in decades to come as water shortages compound existing inequalities and drive conflicts, we need to educate ourselves and change how we eat.

Retail Revolution

Part 3

The Foodifesto
Retail Revolution

- ➤ Establishment of a network of 1 metre household liquid refilling stations across the UK.
- ➤ Creation of a government backed (Green Investment Bank etc) Sustainable Food Franchise to provide a viable choice for consumers across the UK.
- ➤ New Green Business funding for green start-ups in all industries including food retail and production.
- ➤ Increased use of 'rent free first year' schemes for retail start-ups, including food retail.
- ➤ Full review of business rates.
- ➤ Strategic backing where appropriate for the creation of regional supermarket chains with emphasis on Celtic Nations.
- ➤ Strategic industries block on any purchase by non-UK company of a UK based food retailer with under 100 stores in order to protect local identity as it is put back into the system via other parts of this plan.
- ➤ Individuals to place an high emphasis on shopping locally, supporting small businesses and zero waste stores.   .

Retail Revolution
A New Ecosystem

Reformed Large Multiples

Food Hubs

Regional Winners

Government Backed Franchises

Independent Zero Waste Retailers

1 Metre Miracles

14

Starting from the bottom

At the shelf edge

The previous chapters have (hopefully) armed us with an understanding of both the concept of sustainability and an insight into how our food retail industry has come to be the planet squishing behemoth that it is. We have also considered the nature of the structural changes we need and the sort of food we'd like to be selling and eating if we want to create a sustainable food ecosystem in the future. The final question is where would we sell all this great, sustainable food if all our ideas came to fruition?

We could simply attempt to sell it in our existing supermarkets. If the food is that good, then surely it will find a market? Sadly, history shows us that isn't what happens in the existing model. As we discussed way back in the first section of this book, supermarkets will always gravitate towards selling well established products with long sales histories. The more data they have on a product the easier it is for the computerised ordering systems to keep the shelves full. It's not romantic but it is brutally effective at keeping us well stocked with indiscriminate calories. On top of that, such centralised ordering systems mitigate against truly regional differentiation by creating high barriers to entry in the form of large quantity demands a small supplier may not be able to meet or increased retail price (and hence profit for the supermarket) to compensate for the perceived extra complication and cost of stocking such lines, thus rendering them uncompetitive against more established alternatives.

Because of this in-built inertia, our food retail revolution will need to start somewhere else, taking root and growing in size until it puts pressure on the big retailers to change their ways. That is not just wishful thinking. The majority of the big retailers have done trials with packaging free dry goods over the last few years because they are keenly aware of all trends in the sector, and they have noted the rise of the zero waste retailers. As always, they are determined to preserve their existing market share by co-opting any organic change that appears. To force them to really take such change seriously and drive it out across their huge estates of stores we, the consumer, need to make that market pressure too big to ignore and worth the culture shift needed to allow it to be successful in such settings.

To do that it will be necessary to create a network of diverse types of food shops, more attuned to local demand and suppliers. These outlets would be better able to respond nimbly and be more focused on offering knowledgeable service given by staff with a real understanding of what they are doing and why it matters. If we return to where it all started, in the introduction of this book, this is how to make selling different beans, in a different way, a widespread reality.

In small shops up and down the country we can see a glimpse of these ideas already being put into practice and the existing small shops are making a difference. We know that. Ours does, and so do hundreds of others on a daily basis. If we extrapolate out from our little empire, it's clear that zero waste shops and other ethical retailers are responsible for hundreds of thousands of pieces of packaging being saved. These are genuine achievements made in the face of overwhelming odds. But if we consider the challenge of the world reaching Net Zero by 2050 can a network of independents really get us where we need to be fast enough?

The short answer to that rhetorical question is no. Independent retailers full of great, well informed staff and owners are absolutely part of the answer but what we need is bigger than that. The clock is ticking on cutting those emissions by 50% in time for the end of the decade. What we need is to reimagine the whole sector from the bottom up and that includes using the pressure of our actions to force movement in the big multiples who are going nowhere in the next decade or more. We must hit them in the pocket to co-opt them into our journey and that is only done by driving change from below. And we need to start that sort of revolution than right from the smallest retailing scale of all: 1 metre.

1 metre miracles

Think about a metre. It is really not a lot. If metric blows your mind, I'll let you visualise 3 feet instead. Either way, one metre could be the start of changing the world. Most modern metal shelving that you see in shops works on a 1m shelf length. It is the basic unit of measurement for a lot of retailing and it's a great place to begin. It is where we began our zero waste journey too.

One of the simplest changes a household can make is to refill its household liquids; washing up liquid, fabric conditioner and the like. Whilst not strictly food, they are almost always purchased from a supermarket alongside the weekly shop and it is an easy starting point that gives an obvious, measurable win. In a world where much of we have discussed it complicated or involves trade-offs, this is simple. We know how to eliminate that plastic bottle waste. Refill points for those products have been around for years now and the good news is that a simple set up only needs one metre of space. To get an idea of the potential scope of this simple swap, our little shop fills over 2500 bottles a year. That's 2500 items not being produced with the associated GHG footprint saved. 2500 receptacles not accidentally ending up in landfill because they haven't been recycled properly. Now multiply that up to a national scale and the numbers get mind boggling. In 2015 the UK spent more than £400 million on washing up liquid alone[163], that is a lot of bottles and doesn't even include all the other types of household liquids it's possible to refill. Imagine what would happen if we scaled up what our one little shop (and others like it) are doing.

Well, we can do that. Picture where you live. It might be a village, town, or city. What if every village of five hundred people and more found a metre for a refill and information hub? It could be in a shop, but it doesn't have to be. It could be in a community centre, pub, church, doctors' surgery, or school. You can put that metre anywhere you like. I happily bet a punnet of our freshly grown autumn raspberries that if you live in a village of that size or larger then right now you can come up with a least one place that a refill station could go.

So why isn't it there?

The simple answer is twofold and familiar; a lack of imagination and a lack of drive to make it happen. It's the good old story of inertia again. It is a great example of much of what we've discussed through the book. There are multiple wholesalers of bulk cleaning and household liquids which cover the whole of the UK. Many of those brands make their products here as well so there can be a lower transportation footprint with these lines compared to products produced by multinationals. On top of that, the majority of them take back their large plastic containers (typically either 20 litres or 5 litre) and reuse them, creating a closed loop system. They are a textbook example of the circular economy in the real world. The availability of the product isn't a barrier. Instead, it is a failure to realise how accessible change can be and the complete absence of any level of government producing the impetus and seed funding to make it a reality. If a country decided to it could eliminate huge swathes of plastic bottle waste within a year for less than £500 per location start-up cost and with no need to invest in extra space. All it would take would be a national network of suppliers, retailers, and volunteers in the smallest locations to make it a reality. All of which can be drawn together most easily by the convening power of local authorities and/or central government.

We know it is this simple because it's what happened to us. We were selling 'standard groceries' with a slight twist when a customer mentioned the idea of liquid refills one afternoon. A quick internet search later we had come across a large multinational offering the service with free setup and we were away on our journey. It took less than an hour.

But this first step of our plan has an impact beyond the easy elimination of plastic waste (as great and worthy a goal as that is in its own right). Our 1 metre miracles would also create an inescapable cultural movement. Such a network would mean refilling becomes normalised and information on making sustainable choices becomes available everywhere. From there wide swathes of the population have their minds opened to others sorts of change. Making refilling an everyday act, even if it is a food adjacent set of products to start with, is the foundation stone of nation-wide action. Our one metre miracles can open minds to the possibilities of doing things a little differently whilst delivering a clear sustainability win on everyone's doorstep.

15

Zero Waste Independent Retailers

Doing it Everyday

As we move on to the next step on our figurative ladder of change, we come home again to what we do in our haphazard way on a daily basis. It is time to look at all those independent zero waste and sustainable food retailers who are already out there trying every day to make a difference and see what we can do to create even more of them.

The UK has somewhere in the region of three hundred 'zero waste' or similar type shops at the time of writing. That figure is a best estimate based on our participation in and knowledge of the sector. It spans the length and breadth of the UK and is stunning triumph of hope and credit card debt over reality. At some points it feels like there is a shop like us opening somewhere in the UK most weeks, if new entrants to the industry Facebook group we are part of is anything to go by. Equally, however, lots don't make it beyond their first year or so. Whilst that's normal for all new small independent business to some extent, it's also a signifier that this is not an easy movement to be part of. The burn out following the Covid pandemic has also taken a real toll on those who managed to keep plugging away through the worst of the restrictions.

Definitions of zero waste shops vary and each individual retailer will have their own boundaries on what they are comfortable stocking and what they feel is best left alone. Many sell items other than food such as household products, deodorants, soap bars and so on. The tag 'zero waste' can be a little confusing to some, but it is the best moniker we have for this entire sector of the food retail industry that has sprouted organically, driven almost exclusively by passionate, informed individuals and their desire for change. It doesn't matter how they define themselves precisely, it is enough right now that they are out there trying to create a different sort of future for us. These shops all sell a range of packaging free grocery staples such as rice and pasta, lentils and beans, seeds, and nuts. On top of that they will probably add the sort of liquid refill option we saw in our 1 metre miracles. From there the offering you'll find varies as different shop owners deliver their own take on what sustainability means to them and how they marry that with keeping a roof over their heads.

As we saw in the chapter on what sustainability is, we cast our net a little wider than some. By using our Sustainable

Seven bullet points we give ourselves licence to sell a range of organic tinned goods, locally produced condiments, bread flours to encourage people to bake themselves, loose coffee roasted a few miles away, local ales brewed within twenty miles of the shop, and so on. We sell our fresh veg from our great nearby growers and we are on the lookout for a bakery to supply us as well. In our mind we're always looking at how we can replicate as many aisles of a supermarket as we can in a more sustainable fashion. The idea is that the larger percentage of a family's weekly basket we can cater too, the more chance we have of them thinking it is worth the effort to shop with us. At the moment we're doing ok on this mission although a sustainable biscuit option continues to elude us. If you're a manufacturer of biscuits made in the UK that aren't wrapped in plastic, feel free to get in touch with us. There is a definite market waiting to be exploited.

In nearly all cases these shops have received no funding unless they have been lucky in tapping into a source for things like co-operatives or not for profit organisations. Post austerity Britain has nothing as lovely as Green Business funding or any sort of rate relief for businesses trying to do the right thing by the planet. If you want to set up your own ethical food retailer you either need moderately deep pockets, a nice bank loan or a passion that runs so deeps it doesn't balk at scary amounts of credit card debt. The fact that more than a handful of these shops currently exists is a miracle considering the brutally competitive nature of the food retail industry and the structural barriers that exist. For these reasons and more, it is fair to estimate that probably 75% of the UK's zero waste stores are either losing money or only break even because the owner effectively works for free.

It is not a place to be if you want to get rich fast.

Despite all these challenges, we need more of them, not less. Think of it like this, there are roughly three thousand Co-op's in the UK. Add on the Spars, Nisa, McColls and all the other small food retail franchise brands that are out there and you have a huge sector that is currently selling £1 bars of unethical chocolate and industrial quantities of internationally brewed beer with the taste and texture of stuff found in a pub urinal at 11pm on a Friday night. This is a ripe target for our brave and passionate independent retailers, this might be the sector they could disrupt the most.

To put it in simple numerical terms, an average sized Co-op (I'm not picking on them, I believe passionately in the theory of them, they are just the best proxy for an industry standard of local retailing) will cover between 1500 and 3000sq foot of space and will stock somewhere in the region of 3-5000 products. Taking that on is a huge challenge. Most independents in the zero waste/ethical sector cover a space under 500sq foot and stock two to five hundred items. That is a huge disparity and challenge to tackle. If we're expecting these small independents to replace a full supermarket shop, that's more like replicating the experience of 10,000 products. Even with a healthy dose of simplification that is really hard and involves fridges, freezers, alcohol licences and so on. The barriers are high and expensive.

But what if we don't expect independent zero waste retailers to take on that huge, supermarket sized challenge, despite it feeling very much like that right now for everyone in the sector. What if we saw them as part of revamped food retail industry with a series of different sized and funded options all working together to create a more sustainable food future? Then, we could let these independent retailers focus on what they are best at. Being hyper local, extremely nimble, champions of great food being produced within a short range of their location, combined with a really strong offer on packaging free basics. If every town had somewhere they could buy genuinely local alcohol and a sustainably sourced chocolate option, plus a loaf of bread baked with twenty miles, you are going a long way towards challenging convenience retailers straight away. Throw in a washing up liquid refill and a packaging free bit of pasta for tonight's tea and you're really getting somewhere. We need that offer everywhere. In our new food universe let's aim for three thousand of them instead of the current 300 and place them within a wider context that they can actually succeed in.

With that goal in mind, we need to think about how we start to grow this sector. To create a wide network of independent zero waste stores that offer a meaningful alternative will take funding. This fledgling beacon of food change is struggling right now and as we have already mentioned, many aren't making ends meet. Small business grants for ethical start-ups could power this industry for amounts in the £10000-30000 region. Tax breaks for green business and rate relief would also help massively. Schemes run by local councils to pay the rent of new businesses for a year in empty shop units are also good. Making that first year affordable is often the key to any small retailer making it, ethical or not. Banks could offer free business banking to sustainable businesses from any sector, not just retail. VAT rates could be adjusted to support sustainable businesses. A nebulous idea at risk of manipulation I know but we can't chuck out ideas just because fears of bad faith implementation exist. The list of possible ideas is huge, urgently needed and could easily be extended to support genuinely sustainable suppliers as well. Without such help, the reality of the brutally price competitive nature of food retailing multiplied by the financial challenges for households in a post pandemic, post Brexit world will see the sector buckle under the strain of making change a reality. There is also a need for industry adjacent not for profit organisations and charities to help with co-ordination, lobbying and the sharing of best practice in order to help all those trying hard to be part of a better future to succeed.

If we cast our minds forward in positive fashion it feels possible to dream of a time where, amongst all those people motivated to make refilling a normal part of their daily lives with our network of 1 metre miracles, we can find some who are inspired or mad enough to take on the challenge of becoming part of the solution by having their own zero waste shop. But for that to happen we'll need to make it a far more attractive proposition than it is now. Well targeted financial support for green and ethical start-ups would go a long way towards that alongside a range of complimentary measures. As we have said before, we also need the wider context of the food retail industry to be right.

There is no viable, sustainable, food future without the option of refilling and packaging free shopping being accessible to most of the population. Change is only possible if it's realistic. Currently it isn't and we need to alter that. However, even that huge shift won't be enough. Independent zero waste stores are part of the answer, not all of it. With that in mind it is on to the next, larger rung of our new look food shopping world. It's time to mimic an existing success story that rarely gets mentioned in this context; it's time to consider franchising.

16

Franchising the Dream

A Rules Based Empire

Franchising is all around us. Most of the local stores you such as Spar, Costcutter and so on are franchises. Quite a few McDonalds are and so are Subways. Put simply a franchise is an agreement to use an existing brand and their products by an independent retailer.

When we first opened our own shop, we had a choice, did we want to be truly independent with all the risk and freedom that brings, or did we want to sign up with a franchise to take advantage of their nationally recognised branding and supply networks? We chose independence and that led us down the path to zero waste retailing but that is not to say that franchising wouldn't have had its commercial advantages and may well have made us more money in the short term.

According to Franchise UK, an industry group, there were 48,000 franchises in operation in the UK at the start of 2020[164], so it's a well-established model used by a wide variety of sectors not just the food industry. In the last few years the Co-op and Morrisons have looked at using franchises as a way of expanding its store base with some success, even if the numbers are still small.

All of which fact setting leads us to our next idea. A sustainable retail franchise owned by the state through either a Green Development Bank as proposed by Labour, the new UK Infrastructure Bank laid out by Rishi Sunak in 2021[165], or some variation upon those two options. We have established that to change our food ecosystem we need both more local retailers and more ways of exerting market pressure upon large supermarkets. Franchising offers a way to gain scale whilst using the power of government to lay down standards. This idea is a dramatic state intervention, diametrically at odds with prevailing orthodoxy over the last 40 years that the state shouldn't be meddling in individual businesses or picking winners and losers. Such an analysis holds that the role of the state is to set the rules of the game (preferably as few as possible) and get out the way as wonders of free market economics generate trickle down wealth for all.

Well, that hasn't worked. The start of this book reeled off the litany off issues with our food industry from supply to retail and all areas in between. A policy of minimal intervention actually means leaving outcomes in the hands of the most dominant players in any given industry. In the case of food, that means an awful lot of power rests with supermarkets, and their incentives as private companies are tied to maximising profit. Beyond public pressure or interest, they have little reason to tackle issues in our food system, such as the depletion of our planetary resources at an unsustainable rate, or the health inequalities that makes many overweight, unhealthy, and ignorant about what they're consuming. And on top of that, it does not even make sure everyone is fed, hence the rise in foodbank use. Under such conditions it does not seem unfair or radical to suggest doing something different. In fact, it is more surprising if we don't challenge such a rotten status quo.

But, even if we accept the need for change, why is a government owned franchise scheme the answer? Isn't it all a bit communist to expect our leaders to provide our daily bread? Earlier we outlined the need for systemic change. In the terms of our analogy about free market orthodoxy, we need the rules of the game overhauled and that must be done by government. If we accept that premise it surely isn't a big leap to say that a government owned financial institution could set the terms of a retail franchise. We are basically asking a government backed financial organisation to act like the McDonalds head office, offering a shop kit available for retailers to buy and benefit from providing they follow the (in this case sustainability) rules that are part of the contract. If you want an example to prove that a government can interact with franchises in such a fashion, think of the post office.

One of the major advantages that large brands have is uniformity. We've discussed this mostly as a negative that prevents genuine regional variations and support for small suppliers but there is a flip side. There has to be otherwise big successful companies wouldn't do it. Think about when you go on holiday or out for the day and you want something for lunch. You have two broad choices. You can either find a small, local, independent restaurant, scan the menu to make sure there will probably be something everyone likes, attempt to make a value judgement based on how the place looks and then dive in hoping for a great, one off, experience. This, in retail terms, is the current zero waste sector. Alternatively, you get your lunch from Subway or Greggs. You know what they sell, the menu is the same in every town in the land. The price will be the same, the ingredients standardised and the experience dependable. Sometimes, when it has been raining all morning and the kids have been playing up, there is nothing more you want in the world than the simple, reliable, comfort of that familiar experience and there's nothing theoretically wrong with that. Everything has its place.

Creating a sustainable food retail franchise scheme captures these benefits for our nascent sector. Familiarity would encourage the feeling of safety and security that time-pressed shoppers often crave and tightly drawn franchise contracts would minimize the downside of excessive homogenisation. To achieve this mythical balancing act it would be desirable for a panel of food retail, environmental and health experts to be assembled by the UK government to draw up the terms of the franchise agreement. After doing so the Investment or Green bank would be in charge of running the franchise process and signing contracts with any potential franchisees. On top of that they could offer cheap loans to get such businesses off the ground. Franchisees (the people actually running the shops on a day to day basis) would need to put up some of their own capital but would benefit from an established brand, collective marketing and purchasing power. All the standard benefits of franchising, backed by government finance and security.

On top of those positives, a franchise scheme offers a way of scaling up which is a key part of taking on the supermarkets. Individual shop owners could run up to ten or fifteen franchises in a geographical area for example. It seems sensible to set some sort of upper limit on this as we would want to keep the advantages of local retailer and the nimbleness and small supplier progression that offers. It may vary from region to region.

Such shops would scale up the existing zero waste concept, looking to create a functioning format for a shop anywhere between 2500 and 20,000 square feet. That is a co-op to small supermarket in general terms. By working at scale, they could not only offer chances to small retailers to bridge one of the gaps in existing food retail landscape, but they could also spark innovation with existing suppliers by offering a test bed for innovative ideas. Depending on the recommendations of our expert panel setting the terms of reference for our franchises, such an idea may also embrace the possibility of operating along a co-operative model.

Nor would this idea need to squeeze out genuine independent retailers who want to stay that way. Any aspiring franchisee would need to demonstrate they are aiming to satisfy unmet demand, not cannibalising the trade of an existing zero waste retailer. In fact, the opposite could be true, such shops could provide a way of independents scaling up and a home for butchers or bakers to trade on a commission basis within their store.

Even with such safeguards it is possible to see how franchising sustainable shopping options would be contentious, who gets to set the rules and definitions would doubtless be the subject of fierce discussion. However, it offers a realistic, proven way of scaling up an industry. This isn't an anti free market or anti privately owned retailer idea. It is designed to address an existing failing of the market. The food retail sector in the UK has had decades to prove it can marry the positives of capitalism with genuine social responsibility. It has failed. Our franchise scheme aims to reverse that failure by creating a genuinely new option that can grow, rather than slapping heavy and potentially counter-productive new restrictions on existing operators within the market.

With our one metre miracles of refilling, our blossoming small scale independent zero waste retailers and our government back franchisees spreading sustainability throughout the land, we're starting to build the picture of a vastly different type of future for the UK food retail industry. However, there is still more to be done. We need a vision of what a group of our franchises or a collective of independent retailers might look like. We need to find a way to harness the best of our geographic differences within the country. We need a regional success story.

17

Regional Winners

Setting an Example

So, what does a regional winner look like? Aren't all our wonderful independents up and down the land doing their local thing, winners? Well, yes they are, but that isn't what we mean in this section of our change manifesto. What we are referring to here are the next stage up the ladder. Locally rooted retailers with 5-25 outlets of a size roughly equivalent to a Waitrose, all under one brand and owner, acting as a complement to those independents we've talked about already. Here, at this stage of our plan for change, we find an option that can take on the existing supermarkets with the help of our franchising idea if they want it.

Let's conduct another thought experiment. Can you think of a chain of small supermarkets with less than 50 shops in the UK? Unless you live in one specific area, the answer is probably not. But why aren't there smaller scale supermarket brands with the ability to really focus on stocking local products and what would be the benefits of having them?

The answer to the first part of the questions lies once again in the competitive nature of the UK food retail industry and the lack of safeguarding of regional identity by the monopoly and mergers authorities over the years. The biggest players in the sector have been able to swallow up smaller competitors on their way to growth over the past 50 years. Think of brands like Somerfield, Safeway, Kwik Save amongst others who have disappeared from our high streets and there were plenty more that were gobbled up as well. From a purely profit point of view such actions might well make complete sense but they create a landscape of national homogeneity, when what our new food ecosystem needs is to reintroduce regional differences in order to allow more consumers to shop easily for locally produced food made by independent suppliers.

The big national food retailers are really, really bad at doing local food. It goes against everything they are set up to achieve and it shows. In many ways this is understandable. If you have 800 stores you want to know what they are all doing at any one time. The easiest way to do that is to have them all doing the same thing. It keeps costs under control and minimizes risk of store managers doing crazy things when no one is looking. It's a natural human instinct on the part of the head office bureaucracy that runs every large business, and it reassures customers, giving them a base set of expectations whether they're visiting the branch in Inverness or Truro. The outcome of this instinct are national retailers who, to use an example from here in Wales, results in a beer brewed four hours' drive away in Cardiff being sold as 'local' just because it is made in Wales. This is not the sort of behaviour that will drive down food miles and result in thriving local food networks.

Smaller sized supermarket chains would be able to indulge in more flexibility simply because of their size. It is possible to keep a close eye on the impacts and legal requirements of 10 experiments. It's not feasible to do the same for five hundred. On top of that, locally rooted retailers of the sort we are envisaging would be able to build close links with their suppliers offering a pathway to growth. If you're a small food producer looking to expand, how do you do so? You might get yourself stocked in a local store but if they only have one shop then it's either a case of painstakingly building up a local network of independent stockists for yourself or trying to get listed by one the big retailers. The problem is almost no small producer can go from stocking one or two small stores to a couple of hundred supermarkets in one big leap. Rungs on the ladder are missing which stop growth.

All of this might sound a little utopian. Smaller scale supermarket operators holding their own against the might of the major chains whilst offering their customers a diverse range of local, ethical products. What happened to keeping this grounded in the reality of the world we live in now? Well, the reality is such an alternative does exist in one part of England. Remember when we first asked the question at the start of the chapter; could we conceive of such a thing? Well, the people of Lancashire and Cumbria can. It's called Booths.

Follies and Emotions

The small town of Keswick in the Lake District nestles between Cumbrian fells and the beautiful Derwent Water. All year round it is busy with visitors keen to explore a slice of nature that has been part of the English national identity since Wordsworth went a' wandering. The high street and numerous assorted alleys are packed with outdoor retailers full of brightly coloured Gore-Tex designed to keep out the worst of the rain that often seems to sweep through these parts. Luckily, the town also does a fine line in tea rooms and cafes to help you shelter or dry off depending on your luck that day. In short, it's a very nice place to be if you're that sort of person. But if you walk away from main pedestrianised area, past the eternal discounts offered by the big chain outdoor retailers, ignore the lure of the particularly good independent book shop on the opposite side of the road and round the corner by the pet shop, you'll find the only supermarket in town. It is a slightly squat, slate grey tiled building that sits comfily in its surroundings without totally dominating them. This is the first Booths we ever went to.

Now, I should pause here and point out a couple of things. Firstly, this book is not sponsored by Booths (although we are very open to bribery by cake if anyone from the

292

company is reading), and we have never worked for them or received any endorsement from them (although I did once have an unsuccessful job interview with them a decade ago). Our slightly odd love affair with them is all our own and we can blame no one else for it. They are not perfect and could do plenty more than they do but they are the best example of what the sort of retailer we are arguing for in this section of the book looks like.

All of this goes to explain why my wife and I are back in Keswick on a wet Monday afternoon, indulging our own personal folly. We're here because we are not normal. We are ridiculously set in our ways and hopelessly prone to romanticising something like a food shop. It's ok, we know we're not quite sane, it is just a couple of decades of selling beans can do this to you if you're not careful.

What we find inside the store is part throw back, part throw forward. There are still meat and fish counters staffed by people who have a vague idea what they're talking about, a sight that has disappeared from our largest food retailers almost entirely over the last five years. There is more loose unpacked veg than you will find anywhere other than a very large Morrisons. (And even that's not guaranteed. Morrisons have been a bit freaked out at times by the amount of waste their experiments with unpacked fruit and veg have caused, hence the very short lived dry ice counters in the produce sections that now sit turned off and just used as normal shelving. But I digress…) Booths have genuinely local suppliers stocked in both the fresh and grocery parts of the store. There are products often only found in independent stores such as Two Farmers crisps which come in compostable packaging and Ecover refill points for your household liquid refills down the aisle with all the other household products. A totally normal part of a medium sized supermarket environment. This is some of what is possible if you put your mind to it, even if Ecover is far from the most ethical option available.

And these are places people do their weekly shop. They aren't a novelty. You wouldn't walk in and think you were in an unfamiliar setting. That is exactly what we're hoping for at this stage of our masterplan. It is possible to take what we think of as a normal shop and subvert it sufficiently that it can change habits almost unnoticed. There are more examples too. Over the years Booths have dabbled with loose bulk coffee that you can fill a bag with, juicing machines so you can make your own fresh orange juice there and so on. Their range of regional ales is mind blowing and seasonality is a key feature of their fresh food counters. Truth be told, it is a bit disappointing they aren't doing refillable loose grocery staples yet, but it probably isn't long before they do. This is a supermarket sized operation, anchored in its location, attempting to do food the right way. Like I said in our disclaimer, it's not perfect, but it is the best template that could evolve into what we need that we've found so far.

Our trips to various Booths have taken on the air of a slightly comical pilgrimage. We know it's a bit nuts to have such an emotional attachment to a place selling food, but we can't help it. In fact, thinking about it, sat outside one of their shops, munching on a cake, one of the main premises of this book is that the world would be better if more people had a bond with how and where they buy what they eat. Maybe the problem isn't us and our indefensible milage to visit these places, maybe the problem is that 'normal' food shopping is so soulless and empty of passion. How can we love what we eat if we don't have any bond with where we buy it? Perhaps that explains why we now do our Christmas food shop at one of these little retailing gems every year.

Based on that justification we head back to the car after a few hours enjoying Keswick and set off in the direction of home. On the way back we will stop off in one of the Lancashire stores as well because they'll have a slightly different mix of products, with a handful of different local suppliers. Even though Booths have just twenty-seven stores spread predominantly across two counties, they aren't content with calling everything within that area 'local' for every store. They are demonstrating that a multiple retailer can actually do local really well which is an eye opener if you're used to the industry norm.

As we drive home, dusk turning to dark and the lights of Elsmere Port twinkling as we pass, I lose myself in a pleasant daydream. Imagine if this was happening across the UK. Why aren't there a couple of well known, well defined Scottish food retailers replicating this? Why isn't there a Welsh supermarket brand of twenty-five stores shouting about the great food made locally and providing a path for growth for local suppliers? Why isn't it happening in the West Country? Yorkshire? Norfolk and Suffolk? How about a London based supermarket brand specializing in promoting all the amazing fusion and world inspired food happening in every borough of capital? Why shouldn't we work to make this a reality? If we had these chains operating across the UK, selling the best of what is locally produced alongside ethical products that can make a real impact on waste and food miles it would a game changer. Such alternatives would be all the more powerful and accessible for being change within a format, the supermarket, that all shoppers are used to and familiar with. These could be the biggest of our new government backed franchises or they could outgrow them and establish their own brands. Either way, the dream is a tantalising one.

The reality of course, is that such an outcome will need to be specifically planned for and worked towards as part of a long term strategy. The big national retailers won't want such a vision to succeed but that is no reason not to do it. Indeed, it is only because of the incumbent's current resistance to change that such plans are now necessary. Love is a crazy mad thing, but it also the most powerful force in the universe. Why can't we all have love stories about where we go food shopping? Let's bring orange juicing machines and five hundred types of genuinely local ale to the masses.

18

Food Hubs

Knitting the Web

We've got 1 metre tops ups, independent shops, regional retailers, and a host of wonderful things going on. What next for our new food system?

Now we need to think about joining the dots. Taking a series of individual successes and joining them together. Taking our single wins and turning them into a self-supporting, nurturing, force multiplying web of magnificent. It is time for food hubs.

Food hubs are a nice way of saying that we want people to talk to each other a bit. They can take many different forms and be shaped to whatever a location needs but they all have the same aim in mind. To link local producers, sellers, and consumers of food with each other in order to provide more opportunities for everyone involved. A good food hub can create new markets for a small scale grower, open up new suppliers for an independent retailer and find more ways for local

297

customers to enjoy great food that has been produced on their doorstep. The best way to think of them is as the spider's web linking the efforts of others together. A hub might know a shop willing to take a farmer's surplus, they might run a farmers' market in a part of their target area that lacks a permanent outlet for local fruit and veg, or they could support advertising drives or open days to showcase what is available locally.

Throughout this book we have talked about a better food ecosystem for the future and hubs are a crucial part of that. If we think of an ecosystem covering the whole country, then food hubs are the next level under that. Hubs link areas together, ecosystems tie the hubs into a national whole. As we have progressed through our ideas for a better way of doing food, we can start to see how bottom up action can be turned into something bigger. We may have spent time discussing one metre miracles, single farms and educated consumers. Now we're talking about how that knits together and creates real change through scale and multiplier effects.

A lot of food hubs take the form of not for profit organisations that are set up purely to facilitate the links that bind people together. These bodies often collaborate closely with local councils, charities and health boards. The best food hubs look to go beyond just what we sell and where, they seek to tackle some of the deeper problems which we looked at the beginning of this book and which are particularly well set out in the Dimbleby report on food. By linking with charities and health boards, food hubs seek to tackle the issues that cause obesity and ill health as well as providing opportunities for food education. It is all very well telling people they need to eat less processed food but if someone has never been given the tools to cook a meal from scratch for themselves then you're just setting them up for frustration and failure. Food hubs can be a key part of how we tackle these ingrained, often multi-generational issues, going forward. As we saw when we talked about our local community growing space that lacked the ability to eat what they had managed to grow, these barriers are real and more prevalent than it is widely assumed. Food hubs are a tool to drive action across multiple areas so that food is not only grown, but also eaten locally.

There are various organisations working at setting up food hubs across the UK. The Open Food network has been seeding hubs for a number of years and has had success supporting and nurturing groups which have had real impacts on their communities. They continue to find ways to finance the growth of this key part of our future food reality helped set up five more hubs across Wales in the first half of 2022. Sustainable Food Places also does a lot of excellent work helping nascent local food partnerships and hubs get off the ground. They have a complete range of resources and support to hand which can guide groups through the process of bringing a hub to life. In Wales, they've helped a really good food hub come to life in Cardiff which was symbiotically linked to the local health board from the very beginning.[166] This is a great example of how acknowledging the wider impact of the food we eat can shape an organisation from the start.

Another, already flourishing food hub can be found in Cambridge. Alongside all the sorts of activities we have already mentioned, it has set up a veg boxed scheme specifically targeted to people who received healthy start vouchers[167]. This is an excellent demonstration of a hub trying to directly tackle the problem of accessibility and cost. It shows that with a little creativity there are ways of making sure good food is available for all parts of the community. It is an idea that needs replicating nationally.

The driving force behind the Cambridge Hub is Duncan Catchpole and he has authored a book on the subject of food ecosystems.[168] In it, he talks in detail about how the theory and the practice of creating food hubs and joined up systems can work, as well as sketching out how such schemes could be financed. Early on he touches on issues of resilience. He notes that, in the context of the global pandemic we have been living through, such concepts matter more than ever. To him, and plenty of others, such global challenges are even more of a reason to embrace hubs and local food networks: "As we look to rebuild in the aftermath of coronavirus, projects such as the food hub seem more relevant that ever; the Local Food Ecosystem creates opportunities for people to start their own small food businesses... It improves the resilience of the food system, ameliorating our chances of coping with the next pandemic... But most importantly, it shows a way in which we can 'build back better' which is kinder to the planet. Without doubt, the *right time* for the Local Food Ecosystem is *right now*."[169] It is an inspiring call to arms for all of us involved in this fledgling, fragile part of the food system. We need these changes more than ever, for ourselves, for our communities and for the planet.

By tapping into the knowledge of existing leaders like Duncan Catchpole and the work already done by various charities and third sector organisations, the convening power of government at regional and local level could be used to drive the roll out of more hubs. By prioritising action at that level, we can aspire to create solutions that genuinely match the needs of each location. The aim being to maximise the impact of existing facilities and infrastructure, whilst working to fill the gaps in provision and strengthen links in our spider webs of co-operation.

Once we get beyond the theory of what a food hub is, we can see that they are an intensely practical idea. They take all the promising ideas we've come up with so far and magnifies their reach and impact. They can drive local engagement by getting people involved with the food they eat and target support at the area's most in need of them. Whilst they can seem a slightly ephemeral concept, neither making nor selling the food themselves, they are a key part of creating a better food ecosystem in the future. As part of our work investigating how to create a food hub in our area, some of our first discussions involved such 'nuts and bolts' issues as how many minibuses are they locally? Do we have any community kitchens? Is there anyone with the resources to provide a growing guide to the burgeoning number of community gardens about? These are not lofty, abstract ideals. Hubs are the glue that is needed between our sustainable cogs, and they provide much needed resilience, strength and support because our new vision isn't operating in a vacuum, it will have to fight for survival in the world as it is, not the one we'd like. We need people doing those little things that turn into something much bigger. Hubs are how we do that.

19

The Big Retailers

Pressure Pays

Supermarkets are not going away. No matter how much we might wish for a world where their price distorting, market squashing dominance didn't exist, it is not going to happen. Or certainly not on a time scale that will be relevant to the challenge to reach net zero by 2050. As this book has sought to acknowledge from the start, they are part of the landscape we must seek to reshape in order to change our food industry.

Alongside their negative impacts, supermarkets are both a modern miracle and thoroughly underappreciated when placed within the historical context of how we shopped previously. 363 days a year we can go into one and be almost certain of getting what we want, a choice of thousands of products. In terms of human history, that is deeply abnormal. We, as shoppers, are blessed with an abundance unmatched at any point in time.

And how has that cornucopia come to pass? By the magic trick that is modern, just in time, logistics. Food arrives at large, regional distribution centres every hour of the day. It might have flown halfway around the world, been transferred onto a lorry and driven to the warehouse. It might have been shipped from Europe in a refrigerated truck, temperature controlled to ensure freshness for as long as possible. It may have been bought direct by a UK based producer in their own lorry to the site. However it arrives, it is delivered to giant, aircraft hangar sized buildings which sit perched innocuously somewhere near a big motorway junction at various strategic points across the country.

And then what? Well, it doesn't stay there for long. No large supermarket sits on big supplies of anything. Most stock comes in one door and goes back out the other within twenty four hours, a head spinning procession of food and drink matched by computer ordering systems with the individual store that needs it. Staff (or for a firm like Ocado, robots) 'pick' the stock from where it is temporarily stored in the warehouse, building up a delivery specific to each shop based on sales history over the preceding six to eight weeks and a forecast that may well include local weather, events, and season. This order is then loaded onto a supermarket branded lorry and dispatched on a route devised by a computer program to be as efficient as possible, each truck visiting multiple stores in a day.

When a lorry arrives at a store there needs to be staff waiting at the right time to unload it and work it onto the shelves. If the lorry runs behind or gets cancelled it may turn up at time when the staff aren't available causing a backlog. Moving food around is a complex dance that only works if every step runs to schedule, every time. The moment one part of the jigsaw fails, a late delivery to a distribution centre, a large number of lorry drivers calling in sick, a road closure that causes big delays, unexpected sales causing unforeseen demand or staff shortages in store, then customers face empty shelves. Now think how often you see empty shelves in your local supermarket. The miracle is that you don't see them every day.

I am deeply sceptical of the ability of the large retailers to offer refillable grocery products and ethical, healthy options successfully. Having worked in large supermarkets, personal and often painful experience shows that they are the toughest types of retail jobs out there. The hours can be long, especially in any sort of position of responsibility and the workload huge. Physically it can be crushing. I always remember chatting to the wife of my line manager years ago and saying that I didn't know how he kept up his pace as I was flat out on the sofa every evening. She made it very clear that he was exactly the same, he had just grown better at hiding it than me. This is the reality of those low prices. The week before Christmas the shop floor work that goes into the fresh sections of supermarkets is the most intense that I have experienced. Decent sized stores will be receiving pallets of just coleslaw *every day!* Add onto that the pallets of cream, party food, cooked meats. Then factor in a couple of lorries per day of veg. On Christmas Eve I used to have one member of staff for eight hours just filling the milk section alone. It is a ridiculous environment kept afloat only by hours of unpaid overtime done by all those middle level supervisory roles that have been so brutally cut over the last decade or so. It is always worth remembering that without thousands of people working up to ten hours or more a week for free on top of their full-time contracts, the existing supermarket model would fall over. Back in my days as a fresh food manager for one of the big retailers, I always felt a week where I did less than 50 hours was an achievement. Opting out of the working time directive, meant to limit European workers to no more than an average of 48 hours a week, was standard practice. Is that really the sort of human price we are willing to pay for our food?

It should be obvious that these places are not set up to provide the level of staff and training need to make such a zero waste shopping experience a happy one for the average, time pressed shopper. However, that doesn't mean that the positive side of the supermarket experience; the low prices, the familiarity, the convenience, will not remain a major draw for a lot of families. With such a strong, existing customer base it can be hard to imagine meaningful change but as we laid out at the start of this section, it is possible. We, the average Joe or Joanna pushing a trolley around endless aisles, are not powerless. Far from it. We wield the biggest power of all, yet we barely realise it. It is the power of our money. Every pound we spend is a choice. Every decision a chance to make a difference, but only if we can make the alternatives enough of a realistic option for everyone. By building the other parts of our hypothetically reshaped food retail industry we can open up a world whereby our purchasing decisions can force change on the large players. And they will change. Their reason to exist is to create shareholder value. Anything that threatens that on a large enough scale will provoke a response. But until we reach that point, they will vigorously defend the profitable status quo.

As we have touched on when discussing reductions in plastic waste, the biggest UK food retailers are starting to change and that is a result of public pressure and awareness. The new sustainability rating system by Which, launched in February 2022, will help drive this process even further.[170] In year one, a couple of well-known names lost out because they didn't have the relevant information available in the right format to allow comparison. You can be sure that by year two they will have fixed that issue and made sure they demonstrate improvement. Peer pressure and heightened reporting of performance can be useful tools in our battle for change within the existing food retail environment. Combine this with the power of the pounds in our pocket and there is a glimmer of hope.

It is not just our money that can loosen the grip of the biggest operators on what we eat. Creating a wider base of locally focused food producers and growers will weaken the purchasing power of supermarkets by shifting the emphasis away from huge purchases of best-selling, multinational lines. A wider choice of ethical retail outlets will take some market share away, forcing the loss of a small number of stores. Laws enforcing the inclusion of the environmental footprint of a product in its final cost will nullify the biggest players advantage in price wars. There isn't one blow that takes down the existing supermarket industry, and nor is that dream practical. What we can do is cut them down to size by growing the alternatives. It is our only meaningful option.

In such a scenario, we would see supermarkets forced by competitive pressures and meaningful legislation to adopt better, more sustainable practices for staff, customers, and suppliers. One useful measure that could be driven by legislation would be to make ethical and sustainable company reporting meet standardised criteria in order to allow customers to really understand what the big brands they buy from are really up to. This would obviously have wider impacts than just the food sector but would be another tool in our work to demonstrate the true value of what we buy, not just the price. At present nearly all the big supermarket retailers produce some sort of annual ethical report. They look lovely, trumpet myriad achievements that are impossible to compare, and mean absolutely nothing to average shopper.

I have a food retail background and am clearly a little obsessed, and even I found attempting to make sense of these documents a tortuous experience so I shall spare you any snippets. Suffice to say that such reports are filled with items which seem the very definition of that old term, 'comparing apples and oranges'. Standardising such reporting will help shine a light on who really is pursuing best practice and making a meaningful difference. Without such clarity we will struggle to know how to use supermarkets in the best way possible as part of our improved food retail industry.

Bezos's behemoth

Amazingly, we've got this far barely mentioning one of the biggest forces likely to impact on how we buy our food over the coming years. That is not by accident. To face up to the elephant can be to feel a level of powerlessness. It is so big, has such deep pockets and is driven by such a relentless need to control all of commerce everywhere that resisting it can seem hopeless. I am, of course, talking about Amazon. It is fair to say that we've not really touched upon online retailing at all despite it being a growing player for a decade or more, particularly in the UK grocery market.

Despite that increasing ubiquity, food retailers really don't like online sales. For a start, like every other type of retailer, they struggle to make it profitable. How do you sell food for the same price and yet pay for a van, a driver and website whilst maintaining the same profit margin on a product that you would if someone just steps off the street and picks it from the shelf? Answer: you probably can't. It also adds a layer of complication to the operation and supermarkets work on simplification. Now you've got all those home delivery pickers clogging up the aisles when you are trying to put stock on shelves in the most efficient manner. It's not ideal even if they have all got much better at it over the last few years, including with the creation of 'dark stores' designed only for staff to fulfil internet orders despite looking like a standard supermarket in many respects.

Our mantra of acknowledging the world as it is means we have to recognise that home delivery is now an established part of the food retail landscape and will remain so forever more. The genie will never go back in the bottle. Research by Statista showed how online sales as a percentage of total food purchases in the UK jumped from around 4% in January 2020 to more than 12% at the peak of lockdowns. It has since fallen back a bit but remains at double the level it was pre-covid[171]. Because of this hyper charged trend, the UK grocery sector has attracted even more attention from the biggest online retailer of them all.

Amazon sells food. You know that, right? It doesn't necessarily sell a lot, but the amount is growing, and it has tie ups with a number of UK retailers including Morrisons. This seems a classic case of it being better to sleep with the bear than find him wandering into your cave unannounced at 3am. It might be more comfortable, but you still run the risk of being eaten in the end. For Morrisons, the risk is worth it given their failure to develop a meaningful online offering as quickly some of their rivals. Not content with just flogging beans and toilet roll online, Mr Bezos behemoth also owns food shops. In America

Amazon owns the Whole Foods chain of shops as well as a number of Amazon Fresh outlets. It has conducted trials in the UK. In response to the shift in buying habits driven by pandemic lockdowns. Some of these stores, particularly in convenience locations are free of shop floor staff as far as the customer experience is concerned. They don't even have checkouts. A serious of cameras and sensors track your movements around the store, recording what you place in your basket and then you Amazon account is charged once you leave the building. Efficient, cost effective and soulless. If we cast our minds back to the pandemic and how the customers in our little shop benefited from human interaction at a tough time, these seems too high a price to pay for saving a minute or two at a checkout. The hidden cost here is the very real mental wellbeing we derive from social interactions as human beings.

Industry analysts have long suspected that Amazon has eyes on a large physical food retailing presence in the UK, although it has not always been obvious to see how that would come about. The direction of travel is clear though, Amazon wants a bigger slice of the pie in multiple countries, ours included. As such they represent a clear risk to the food future we're laying out. To negate this danger, we will probably find ourselves dependent on government intervention and the actions of the monopolies and mergers authorities. It should be a clear strategic red line, enforced by legislation well in advance, that the protection of our independent retailers from takeover by non-UK based companies is in the national interest. There is no point creating great regional, sustainable options, just to see them swallowed up by global companies that pay little or no tax and have no interest in the fostering of food diversity across the UK.

Meals on Wheels

The other massive change within our food landscape over the last five years is the unstoppable rise of home delivery services such as Deliveroo and Just Eat. These firms now have links with major retailers and networks of delivery riders and drivers across large parts of the UK. In fact, if you cannot tap your phone and get food delivered to your doorstep in under an hour, you're now in the minority. As part of this trend Amazon also has expanded its food delivery service, offering better terms to its Prime subscribers[172]. The march of the delivery moped seems unstoppable.

There are positives to this. People with mobility issues and other disabilities can access food more easily than they previously could but that is a small bonus compared with the normalisation of instantly available junk food. We are far too early into this brave new future to have reliable statistics, but the long term prognosis can't be good. Anecdotal evidence shows that people are not using the ability to order healthy food from the convenience stores that have tie ups with these firms. Most people aren't sat on their sofa on a Sunday evening, after the supermarkets have closed, saying to themselves 'I think I'll order some bananas for pudding via my app of choice'. They're ordering beer, cigarettes, and cheap chocolate. We have already seen in this book how our ever expanding obesity crisis can't be solved by willpower alone. We need restrictions on the availability of foods high in sugar, salt, and fat, accompanied by curbs on advertising in order to help people make better choices. Instead of doing that, we are chauffer delivering the stuff to people's doorsteps 24/7. From a public health point of view this is utter madness. We are once again allowing private companies, driven only by the profit motive, to accentuate one of the largest hidden costs of the food we eat because we fear regulating our free market economy.

It is another glaring example of government being unwilling to take responsibility for helping us create a better food ecosystem.

Having said that, technological innovation and change is inevitable, and this is not a call for a luddite-esque return to the days when the only way to buy food was from someone wielding a pencil and piece of paper. Technology, used correctly, as part of a long term plan, can be a key part of increasingly access to better choices for people who have health and wellbeing issues.

However, that isn't what we are seeing. The proliferation of online shopping and the rise of numerous, quick, home delivery options via apps, is enabling more the damaging behaviour and decisions that have caused so many problems over recent decades. There is no way we can fix the health implications and costs of our current bad food choices without regulating the ability for people to have junk food dropped at their front doors every hour of the day. Once again, we need to make positive choices that lead to a better tomorrow, rather than blindly following the path of instant convenience. But to do that we need to view our food choices as part of an all-encompassing ecosystem rather than just an industry ripe for profit.

A note on Butchers, Bakers and the like.

The rise of the supermarkets had many effects but one of the biggest was to banish a lot of independent butchers, fishmongers, greengrocers, and bakers from our high streets. Is there a way of making them part of our new look food ecosystem? Are they part of this future?

The theoretical answer is obviously yes. Locally reared, fished and grown food sold by knowledgeable people is exactly what we are aiming for. The reality is, there aren't many viable ways of sparking into life a vibrant world full of amazing local butchers and bakers in every town and city in the land overnight. If there was, someone would have done it long before this book was written. The convenience and pricing of supermarkets is too compelling for the vast majority of cost conscious, time short shoppers to ignore. As we have said before, it's important we don't blame them for making that choice. Life is really hard for a lot of people on a day to day basis for a whole host of reasons. If we're going to make a difference, then it has to find solutions that acknowledge that reality.

Fixing that conundrum, as always, is a multi-faceted jigsaw puzzle featuring more emphasis on the skills required to make these jobs a visible career for school leavers, more funding for start-ups, more co-operation on a local level to make shared spaces available to multiple small specialists and of course the structural changes needed to put a price on products that major retailers sell that reflects their carbon footprint and planetary cost. In short, if we fix all the other problems in the food sector, we will also create the space for our butchers, bakers, fishmongers and greengrocers to once again exist. However, it will take a long time to replace all the specialist knowledge lost over the last few decades if that is ever realistically possible.

It would also take decades to remove supermarkets. Time we don't have to save the planet, but we can change the environment around them and the largest online operators, forcing a spotlight on what they do and using our purchasing power to drive change. Creating a widespread system of alternatives seems the only realistic option open to us if we want to create a better food future for ourselves and the planet we depend upon. As part of that process we need to harness our own choices and the power of our hard earned cash to send clear signals to the profit orientated private companies that provide the bulk of our food. By making ethical choices where we can and using whatever nascent parts of our improved food ecosystem exist in own areas, it will be possible to start to show these big beasts how future profitability rests on making a different set of decisions, not on continuing on a path that even the boss of Iceland, Richard Walker, admits is unsustainable. It is a hard road, starting one metre and one spending choice at a time, but the end results would be a reshaping of a retail ecosystem that currently disguises massive harm and perverse incentives under a siren call of seemingly endless cheap calories.

20

Retail Revolution Knowledge, Skills & Pride

Cultural revolution

We have already touched on life working in a supermarket. There are positive sides to it, you can have really fun days if you embrace the pace and challenge and are working with a small group of people willing to muck in and get the job done. In that sense, it is like almost any job, the quality of it is dependent on the people you're working directly with. But in other ways, it's a world sucked of a lot of the things we would ideally look for in meaningful work. There is often a lack of training, recognition and pride. Crucially, there sometimes isn't a great deal of respect either.

The Coronavirus pandemic has shone a light on many parts of society and at various points it has seemed that we may be edging closer to an appreciation of the things that really matter in life. It has been heart-warming to see the love shown towards those working in the NHS in such tough times and all of that warmth, and more, is well deserved. However, we haven't always seen such gratitude towards other sectors of society that may also fit the term of key worker even if they seem less glamorous than saving lives. One example might be our attitudes as a country towards care workers and they horrific way they, and those in their care, were left unprotected in the early stage of the pandemic. Another might be those who sell us our food.

Food retail is not, by any stretch of the imagination, a heroic calling. There is no comparison in life or death impact between those in the NHS and those staffing our supermarkets but that does not mean the latter are not vital to our wellbeing and the functioning of society. Just look at the first meaningful reaction to the news of the virus' spread. Panic buying of pasta and other staples. Food is essential to our survival and those selling it should be recognised as key to our daily lives. We should treat those who serve us according. However, this is not a call for all of us to stand on our doorsteps and cheer supermarket home delivery drivers as they come up the street. Instead, it is a plea for basic respect and value to be placed on jobs that most of us take for granted and some actively make unpleasant. Working in food retail during the global pandemic has not been fun. Staff have been abused, physically and verbally, and worn down by the challenge of keeping going when so much else of daily life seemed to stop. There have been no widespread furloughs for checkout staff, no calls for shop floor workers to be protected from unvaccinated customers coming within less than two metres of them, in contrast to some other industries. These people have kept going, day in, day out, and our food retail system has kept functioning throughout. If you stop and think about it, it is a miracle that large supermarkets haven't been forced to close because of widespread outbreaks of covid amongst store teams. That is not the same as saying those outbreaks haven't happened, they've just been covered for by more staff on low hours, highly flexible contracts, going above and beyond to keep the show on the road. Maybe that is a little heroic after all.

And then they get abused if they ask a customer why they are not wearing a mask.

We need to rethink our attitude to those who make sure we have something to eat. We shouldn't live in a world where retailers are investing in body cameras for staff in order to counteract anti-social and threatening behaviour. Food retail work is never going to be a sexy job, but it can be one where we restore those values of pride and respect, both for those working in the industry and for customers.

First of all, we can make sure people are being paid for what they work. Legislation is needed to prevent the abuse of those on salaried contracts from working consistently over their contracted hours. Companies should be forced to declare the number of hours their salaried staff are working and face fines if they are shown to be heavily reliant on what is effectively unpaid overtime. At the same time, such legislation should enshrine the right to one nominated protected day a week for all workers. At present supermarket workers (along with those in other sectors) are being asked for, and pressured into, offering up 24/7 availability in order to get a job. What this means is that a person on a 16 hour a week contract can find themselves working a totally different sixteen hours each week. Or if they have ticked a box to say they are available for overtime it could be 20 hours one week, 32 in the second and 16 in the third. All spread over different shift patterns on different days. This is justified as responding to 'the needs of the business'. What about the needs of the employee? Legislation should give all staff the right to one protected day a week that they can nominate when they begin working for a company (and can change whenever they wish) which is free from work. Surely, six days a week of availability is enough for any employer? Such a law would lessen the pressure felt to be as flexible as possible to get a foot in the door which many currently experience. I have written the schedules for teams working in big and small supermarket environments, such a law wouldn't cripple any operation in my experience.

There is also a need for wider use of existing training opportunities and standardisation of practices across the industry. Such moves would make it easier to bring pride and recognition to these workplaces. As we mentioned earlier in the book, relevant NVQ's do exist and more people should be encouraged to sign up to them, but there is room for more industry norms and processes to be recognised with publicly visible reward and recognition. A world where people can see the staff they are interacting with are well trained and knowledgeable is a world where they are more likely to be given the respect they deserve rather than the current reality.

There is also another angle to pride within the workplace. The pride staff feel in the employer they work for. If we create the changed retail ecosystem that has been laid out in the last few chapters, then we give more opportunities for people to work for companies they can feel proud of. We give more chances for staff to feel they are part of something that makes a difference. If I think back to my days in supermarket management this was always a challenge I couldn't find an answer to. I would sit at home reading inspiring tales of leadership in various sports teams (nope, I didn't get out much back then either) looking for little titbits on how to manage people but it never seemed relatable. Top end athletes had pride in their work and the high performance environments that they functioned in. How is that relatable to a weekend stock boy in a supermarket? Where is the point of pride or emotional attachment? It just doesn't exist. If we had better food retailers, doing better things, not only would customers derive an emotional connection (like us and our Booths pilgrimages) but so would the staff employed there. Engaged staff are proven to give better service as well. It is a virtuous circle for all. Better quality interactions driving increased sales and knowledge. Those precious intangibles, pride, and respect, coupled with meaningful training, can lift our food retail industry to better heights and improved public recognition.

The food retail industry – Putting it all together

The food retail industry needs huge structural change and the best way to achieve that is to start from the bottom up by building a network of various sized outlets dedicated to showing what a different future looks like. By creating new ways for people to use their purchasing power, change can be driven upwards, forcing adaptation upon the biggest retailers in the sector.

For such a scheme to work we would need to marry an array of bottom up action with a deliberate, government led, strategy aimed at creating a range of retailers and spaces dedicated to bringing genuinely sustainable food to our neighbourhoods. By grounding these offerings in their locality, mandating them to focus on local suppliers and producers, a web of positive social change could be kickstarted. This of course, would require investment, legislation, and political will, all of which can seem in short supply. It is long past time that we started treating the food industry as strategically important and food retail falls within that recalibrated mindset. Investment in strategic industries is not new or unheard of. The only real change is recognising that what we eat deserves such a designation.

In our revamped food future lost skills could be recaptured and spread across the country. New connections with our food, stimulating original and captivating ways of interacting with what we buy may open up. We can find ourselves changed by what we shop for and the environments we do it in. That is a genuinely exciting set of outcomes based around the simple idea of forming an emotional connection with how we buy our dinner.

But this isn't a set of proposals founded in make believe or the recreation of a non-existent past. By utilising existing space and already successfully operating business models on a wider scale it is realistic to envisage change on a scale big enough to make the difference needed, but it will take co-ordinated effort to make it happen. We will have to harness the power of government, the knowledge of experts across myriad fields and, perhaps most importantly, the imagination of wide swathes of the public as a tool to batter down the power of the inertia that leaves our food retail industry currently stuck in such an unimaginative and harmful place. Within such a future, jobs of worth are created, communities are rekindled, and value can take the place of cost.

We have the templates we need to bring such change to life. Refill points for liquids exist up and down the land. Zero waste shops open weekly somewhere in the country, regional retailing does happen as our petrol bill can testify.

As with so much of our response to the climate crisis, the challenge lays not in discovering novel solutions, but in using those we already have in different, more widespread ways. We have the answers. Examples of success already exist. What we need is the will to spread change across the nation in a coherent manner, harnessing the power of all, bringing to life a food revolution.

Tomorrow

Part 4
A Final idea
Food Future

The Foodifesto

Engagement & Education

➤ Information drive to make 'Green' options available on all ballots.

➤ Report into the creation of scheme to link summer agriculture work to further education admissions schemes or gap year options.

➤ Creation of Food, Ecology & Sustainability syllabus as part of standard curriculums for years 7-11 to replace 'Food Tech'.

➤ Creation of Ecology and Sustainability syllabus at 'A' level.

➤ Funding for the wider provision of Food Policy degree level courses

➤ Tax and other incentives increased to increase take-up of employers signing employees up for NVQ level courses.

➤ Embedding of Regenerative Agriculture principles in standard farming/ecology education.

➤ National accreditation created for retail management skills to drive best practice nationally.

21

A Final Idea

To achieve all we have discussed, the hard tangibles of new shops across the land and the intangible benefits to the places we live and work, we need to draw all these ideas together in a way that captures the scale of the problem and the attention of those needed to fix it. We need to take what we've learned and imagined into being across these pages and show concisely what all this fine talk of a new food ecosystem would look like. And then we need a way to spark all that change into life...

Over the years the UK, not unlike other nations, has had plenty of grand festivals or exhibitions to mark various jubilees and celebrations. Their planning has included the building of marvels such as the original Crystal Palace back in 1851 and the slightly less loved Millenium Dome nearly 150 years later. We've got form on these things. So why not a year long Great Festival of Food to function as the ignitor for our cascade of disruptive, enriching program of change? Such a festival would draw together the various strands of our food landscape into one compelling whole. By shining a light on the wide impact food has on us and the landscapes we live in, it would be the perfect opportunity to engage people and kickstart individual action such as personal education, lifestyle choices, refilling, growing your own, supporting local producers and so much more.

Such a festival should be a moveable feast. We don't need a great monument to the British farmer or a diamond encrusted supermarket of magnificence. We need a travelling circus filled to bursting with the life affirming tales of what is already happening up and down the land, skilfully woven into one compelling national narrative. That doesn't mean this is a festival of jingoistic Britain First nonsense. Far from it. Such a story needs to place the food we eat in its global context to help us all understand why our dinner choices affect so many people around the world. There is no place here for narrow nationalism.

As this exhibition visits as many places as possible over the course of a year it should carry growers, makers, sellers and educators and health workers in its wake. A great retinue of people unleashed in the service of a great national good. There could be exhibits on regenerative agriculture, small scale growing, understanding the hidden costs of our food, the health impacts of our choices, the education opportunities that are out there, and so much more. Online information can give people access to their local choices once they have visited so that they're able to connect with agents of change whilst they're still in the first flush of motivation. We could even have people dressed as Fairtrade bananas. Just not me.

This idea could also be a turning point in our relationship with our own landscapes. The festival could educate and engage people so that they learn to seek out wild and healthy parts of our islands instead of seeing a heavily managed and commercially farmed monoculture dominated by large fields as an aesthetically pleasing norm.

Our festival would harness the skills of one great British industry, the creative arts, in service of another. We produce great food already, we just need to do more of it and learn to harness that goodness in pursuit of the wider goal of a just society where people don't have to rely on charity for food or suffer health problems because they lack the skills and options to access better outcomes. A festival of food can be a great public good that starts the transformation of our country into a place where fantastic food, ethically produced gives people the basis of healthy fulfilling lives.

This travelling show of food fabulousness would spend a year igniting a conversation and acting as the starting point of a new story by shining a light on what has gone before and what is possible tomorrow. The festival would be an inflection point in our national tale of food and would offer up glimpses of what could be if we come together and act at all levels of society. It could be a huge, highly visible, transformative moment to take abstract ideas of change and individual efforts at better outcomes into a meaningful whole. Ideas on a page are great but to engage people we need to bring them to life. The Foodifesto listed ideas for change, some of which are based on individuals deciding to take responsibility for their own decisions and do things differently. Standing alone that may look unrealistic. Why are people going to magically decide to support their local zero waste shop or plant some veg in their garden. The truth is they aren't unless they are given a reason and a motivation to do so. That is the ultimate purpose of our Great Food Festival. It is our spark that might make much of what we've talked about in these pages plausible instead of possible.

22

Food Future

Writing a book is not a particularly quick process. During the course of turning my thoughts on the future of the food we eat in this country into something that might hang coherently together, a whole host of things happened. Wildfires ripped through the west coast of America and the eastern seaboard of Australia. Polar temperatures reached new highs, ice shelves and glaciers melted. Flooding disrupted large communities in south east Asia, particularly India and Pakistan. Droughts hit multiple continents at various points, all of them inflicting damage to crops and forcing rises in prices for consumers globally. In short, it was a normal year or so in the life of planet as it is today.

Faced with such news, and the climate models available to scientists, it is clear that our food future is increasingly uncertain as our planet creaks and strains under the pressures created by Anthropocene warming. Areas of the world that currently grow vast numbers of crops are forecast to see changes which cast severe doubt on their ability to continue to feed big chunks of humanity. The modern miracle of just-in-time supply chains is under threat like never before.

Such an onslaught of negative events and projections is enough to leave anyone feeling drained and hopeless. The challenge is too big, the spread of events to wide to get an easy grasp on. As laid out at the start of this book, humans are, in evolutionary terms, still tribal animals. Asking us to conceptualize as series of individual events and tipping points spanning the whole Earth is a stretch for a species use to thinking about its close relatives and neighbourhood. It's all just too much.

Yet, it doesn't have to be that way. The future is not set in stone. We can decide to challenge what scares us and find a way to write a different story. To do that we need to take on board the information that is out there regarding the scale of change happening to the natural world, and in response use the best of human nature to produce a positive path to a better future. This is true for any number of challenges we face, but it is especially so when we talk about food. There is a far more positive, sustainable food ecosystem waiting for us if we rise to the moment. It is still viable to envision a future where we are fed nutritious, rewarding calories that don't harm us or the wider world. Our food can be a source of local pride and jobs as well as acting as a source of resilience in tough times. What we eat can become something we take great care over and a deep well of knowledge could be passed on to future generations. But time is running out.

The changes required to make this a reality are not easy. As the old saying goes, nothing of any value ever is. And yet what alternative do we have? Do we want to live in a world increasingly rocked by shortages and uncertain supply of the foods that we've previously taken for granted? Do we want to find ourselves losing diversity of crops and species as pollinators and plants fall out of sync in reaction to changing weather patterns? The answer surely is no.

To meet this moment we will need different choices at all levels. This will require political engagement both nationally and locally, as well as changes at the level of individual households. We will need to find a new balance in how we grow our food. The next couple of years offers a chance to steer a new course which balances landscape management with sustainable food production. Right now, we're threatening to learn the lesson of protecting biodiversity and soil health without finding a place to produce our own food within the mix. This is one of the key battles in front of us. A generation of opportunities may be lost if we get it wrong. Famers are our indispensable allies in this fight, but they need the right tools just like we all do as consumers.

We need to arm ourselves with an understanding of real value, learning to look beyond shelf edge price to all the hidden costs associated with calories that seem too cheap to be true. As part of that we will need to shop in different ways, in different places, building again connections with those who supply us with food.

There is so much change within our own hands that it feels impossible to submit to the negativity totally. We can do this, one small choice at a time. And then we can harass, challenge, and eject our political leaders until they follow our example and enact the laws that will accelerate the pace of change to something that meets the need for net zero emissions by 2050. Hopefully the Foodifesto helps give an outline of what all that work can look like.

As I write these words, fired up anew by the positive possibilities of an informed, engaged electorate bringing a better future to life, I am sat where this book started. Up on our hillside there is sunshine in the air, cabbages are growing in the polytunnel, new life has arrived in the form a family dog, projects big and small continue their unequal path towards eventual completion. All of us, big, small, furry, and feathered have come through another winter in one piece. The long nights have slowly given way to the watery light of a tentative change in seasons. Whilst, looking out of the window, much appears calm, but in reality the natural world is moments away from bursting into a spate of action. Spring is coiled, about to be sprung. The summer stretches out before us full of endless possibilities. It might be a bumper year for fruit or a great season for veg. The damson trees may yield a crop that fills every jar we have with jam, or they may give us nothing. Maybe we'll coax another couple of new born chicks out of our old hens before their time is up. It certainly seems likely this will be our first year of regular duck eggs.

And there are other simple pleasures to come. One of my favourite joys of the summer is to sit at our back door as dusk drapes itself across the hills and the sun dips towards the sea on the horizon. At this magical time swallows, who nest in our barn, come out to feed on the wing. They alternate between serene calmness and a diving, ducking frenzy, not unlike hyped up teenagers on an invisible rollercoaster. They return to us every year now, a reminder of our place in a much bigger scheme of things. A pinprick on a life that spans huge distances. A manifestation of the maxim that our future lies in the global and the local.

But before all of that comes to pass, back here in spring, there is an obvious analogy to draw. The earth sits at its own tipping point. The future stretches out before us. Will it be filled with abundance and balance or a continuation of the path that has caused environmental damage, poverty, health inequalities and a widespread detachment from the food we eat? Are we capable of being the generation of storytellers who find a way to conquer the negative with an exciting vision of what could be? At its simplest, what sort of people do we want to be? Spring is the season of hope and renewal. It is also a season of action as every gardener and grower knows. Now is the time to put in the effort that gives us the best possible chance of positive outcome. It's time to put away the keyboard and get to work. The best stories are those bought to life.

Acknowledgements

Although only one name appears on the cover, writing a book is a collaborative experience in many ways. The Foodifesto wouldn't exist without the input of many other people, knowingly or unwittingly.

First of all, a big thank you to all my customers. You come into the Sustainable Weigh/Siop y Glorian to buy groceries and make a difference. As a by-product of that, a whole host of interesting and stimulating conversations have taken place across the last 3 years which have shaped this book. Even if I can't remember all your names individually, rest assured, I will recognise your distinctive Tupperware options anywhere.

An even bigger debt of gratitude goes to the select few who were helpful enough to take a very rough draft of the Foodifesto home and give feedback on it. Your words and ideas were invaluable. Two brave souls, Laura and Lucinda, sacrificed their time to do a full edit of the book, including all its repetitions, spelling mistakes and grammatical follies. Because of both of you I will never look at a semi colon or apostrophe the same way, although I do now cast covetous eyes at Oxford commas. Any remaining errors are mine alone, they did the best anyone could.

The final thank you goes to the person who is more responsible for the ideas in these pages than anyone else, and yet would claim utter surprise at such a thought. My wife, Cherise, planted the seeds long ago for a life where we owned land and animals, and many years on that is the dream we're living. None of that, or this book, would be possible without her love, support, knowledge, and priceless ability not to take any nonsense from her husband. Thank you for everything. Even the ducks.

Selected Bibliography

Braiding Sweetgrass *Robin Wall Kimmerer*

Call of the Reed Warbler *Charles Massy*

Dirt to Soil *Gabe Brown*

Farm to Fork *Joe Stanley*

Feeding Britain *Tim Lang*

Green and Prosperous Land *Dieter Helm*

How Bad are Bananas *Tim Berners-Lee*

How to Avoid a Climate Disaster *Bill Gates*

How to Save our Planet *Mark Maslin*

Manifesto *Dale Vince*

Native *Patrick Laurie*

Rewild Yourself *Simon Barnes*

Silent Spring *Rachel Carson*

The Green Grocer *Richard Walker*

The Day the World Stops Shopping *J.B. MacKinnon*

The Future we Choose *Christiana Figueres*

The Malay Archipelago *Alfred Russel Wallace*

The Missing Lynx *Ross Barnett*

Wilding *Isabella Tree*

Index

Footnotes

[1] The Economist, 2021. *Food Crisis Briefing, page 20*. 21st May 2022.

[2] Dimbleby, H (2021). *National Food Strategy*. Available at: https://www.nationalfoodstrategy.org/ (Accessed 4th October 2022).

[3] Dimbleby, H. National Food Strategy. Available at: https://www.gov.uk/government/publications/government-food-strategy/government-food-strategy (Accessed 4th October 2022).

[4] Wells, Jonathan C. K, Stock, Jay T. (2020). "Life History Transitions at the Origins of Agriculture: A Model for Understanding How Niche Construction Impacts Human Growth, Demography and Health".

[5] Steel, C (2008). *Hungry City* page 13

[6] Britannica, The Editors of Encyclopaedia. "agricultural revolution". *Encyclopaedia Britannica*, 4 Dec. 2015, https://www.britannica.com/topic/agricultural-revolution. Accessed 4 October 2022.

[7] Wilson Quarterly (1997). The Birth of the Supermarket. *Wilson Quarterly*, Summer 1997

[8] Smart, A (2018). Remembering when the first supermarket in Britain opened in West Bridgford. *Nottingham Post*, 20th January 2018.

[9] Evans, Bryce (2017) The British 'National Kitchen' of the First World War. *Journal of War & Culture Studies*.

[10] Lang, T (2020). *Feeding Britain* pages 38-39

[11] Lang, T (2020). *Feeding Britain* page 36

[12] Lewis (2016). *Woodlands.co.uk*. 26th October 2016. https://www.woodlands.co.uk/blog/flora-and-fauna/hedgerow-loss/#:~:text=They%20suggested%20that%20hedgerows%20were%20lost%20perhaps%20at,one%20million%20kilometres%20of%20hedgerow%20%28in%20the%20U.K%29. Accessed 4th October 2022

[13] Yurday, E (2022). Average UK Household Cost of Food, *Nimblefins.co.uk*, 20th July 2022. Available at: https://www.nimblefins.co.uk/average-uk-household-cost-food. Accessed 4th October 2022

[14] Bedford, E (2022). Consumer spending on food in the United Kingdom from 2005 to 2021, *Statista.com*. 22nd September 2022. Available at: https://www.statista.com/statistics/289911/expenditure-on-food-in-the-united-kingdom-uk/ Accessed 4th October 2022.

[15] https://www.thegrocer.co.uk/top-products/fresh-fruit-and-veg-top-products-2019/600230.article

[16] The Grocer (2022). Britain's Biggest Brands 2022: the top 100. *The Grocer*, 25 March 2022. Available at: https://www.thegrocer.co.uk/britains-biggest-

brands/britains-biggest-brands-2022-the-top-100/665829.article. Accessed 4th October 2022.

[17] UNFCC (2022). The Paris Agreement. Available at: https://unfccc.int/process-and-meetings/the-paris-agreement/the-paris-agreement. Accessed 4th October 2022

[18] Mulgan, G (2022). *Four ways societies can use our collective imagination to improve how society works*, 18th April 2022. Available at: https://www.jrf.org.uk/blog/four-ways-we-can-use-our-collective-imagination-improve-how-society-works. Accessed 3rd October 2022.

[1919] Wrap (2015). Food Waste Data, *wrap.org.* 2nd March 2015. Available at: https://wrap.org.uk/resources/guide/waste-prevention-activities/food-love-waste-data. Accessed 4th October 2022.

[20] Alston, P (2018). *Statement on Visit to the United Kingdom, by Professor Philip Alston, United Nations Special Rapporteur on extreme poverty and human rights.* 16th November 2018.

[21] The Food Foundation (2022). *Broken Plate report 2022*, page 8. 19th July 2022.

[22] DEFRA (2022). *Origins of food consumed in the UK 2019.* Available at: https://www.gov.uk/government/collections/family-food-statistics. Accessed 4th October 2022.

[23] Sustainable Food Trust (2022). *Feeding Britain from the Ground Up.* Available at: https://sustainablefoodtrust.org/our-work/feeding-britain/ Accessed 4th October 2022.

[24] Defra (2020). *Agriculture in the UK 2020.* Available at: https://www.gov.uk/government/statistics/agriculture-in-the-united-kingdom-2020. Accessed 4th October 2022.

[25] Montaigne, F (2019). *Yale Environment 360*, 4th September 2019. Available at: https://e360.yale.edu/features/will-deforestation-and-warming-push-the-amazon-to-a-tipping-point. Accessed 4th October 2022.

[26] Stockholm Resilience Centre (2022). *Planetary Boundaries: An Update.* Available at: https://www.stockholmresilience.org/research/research-news/2015-01-15-planetary-boundaries---an-update.html. Accessed 3rd October 2022

[27] Millenium Ecosystem Assessment (2005). *Millenium Ecosystem Report.* Chapter 1 pages 27-30. Available at: https://www.millenniumassessment.org/en/Reports.html. Accessed 2nd October 2022.

[28] Mackinnon, JB (2021*). The Day the World Stops Shopping*, page 83.

[29] Victor, P (2008). *Managing without Growth: Slower by design, not disaster.*

[30] Global Footprint Network (2022). www.overshootday.org/ Accessed 4th October 2022.

[31] Mackinnon, JB (2021*). The Day the Word Stops Shopping,* page 32-33

[32] Collins English Dictionary (2022). *Definition of Sustainability.* Available at: https://www.collinsdictionary.com/dictionary/english/sustainability. Accessed 4th October 2022.

[33] LexisNexis (2022). *Sustainable development (Brundtland definition) definition.* Available at: https://www.lexisnexis.co.uk/legal/glossary/sustainable-

development-brundtland-definition. Accessed 4th October 2022.

[34] Kimmerer, R W. (2020) *Braiding Sweetgrass*, Page 190.

[35] House of Commons Library (2022). *Food Banks in the UK*, 14th July 2022. Available at: https://commonslibrary.parliament.uk/research-briefings/cbp-8585/ Accessed 4th October 2022.

[36] House of Commons Library (2022). *Food Banks in the UK,* 14th July 2022. Available at: https://commonslibrary.parliament.uk/research-briefings/cbp-8585/ Accessed 4th October 2022.

[37] Office for National Statistics (2022). *Consumer Price Inflation: 2022*. Available at: https://www.gov.uk/government/statistics/consumer-price-inflation-uk-september-2022. Accessed 4th October 2022.

[38] Monroe, J (2022). We're pricing the poor out of food in the UK – that's why I'm launching my own price index, *The Guardian*, 22nd January 2022.

[39] ITV (2021). *Good Morning Britain*, Jan 21st, 2021

[40] Department for Work and Pensions (2022). *Benefit expenditure and caseload tables 2022,* 24th May 2022. Available at: https://www.gov.uk/government/publications/benefit-expenditure-and-caseload-tables-2022. Accessed 4th October 2022.

[41] Public Health England (2022). *The Eatwell Guide*, 25th September 2018. Available at: https://www.gov.uk/government/publications/the-eatwell-guide. Accessed 1st October 2022.

[42] Public Health England (2022). *The Eatwell Guide*, 25th September 2018. Available at: https://www.gov.uk/government/publications/the-eatwell-guide. Accessed 1st October 2022.

[43] BBC Food (2022). *Calculator: Are you getting all the nutrients you need?* Available at: https://www.bbc.co.uk/food/articles/nutrition_calculator. Accessed 2nd October 2022.

[44] Global Nutrition Report (2021). *Country Nutrition Profiles, United Kingdom of Great Britain and Ireland.* Available from: https://globalnutritionreport.org/resources/nutrition-profiles/europe/northern-europe/united-kingdom-great-britain-and-northern-ireland/ Accessed 4th October 2022.

[45] Global Nutrition Report (2021). *Country Nutrition Profiles, United Kingdom of Great Britain and Ireland.* Available from: https://globalnutritionreport.org/resources/nutrition-profiles/europe/northern-europe/united-kingdom-great-britain-and-northern-ireland/ Accessed 4th October 2022.

[46] Scrinis, G (2018). *Ultra-processed foods and the corporate capture of nutrition*. Available at: https://www.bmj.com/content/371/bmj.m4601. Accessed 4th October 2022.

[47] Steenson, S and Buttriss, J (2021). *Healthier and more sustainable diets: What changes are needed in high-income countries?* 15th August 2021.

[48] NHS Digital (2020). *Statistics on Obesity, Physical Activity and Diet, England, 2020*. 5th May 2020. Available at: https://digital.nhs.uk/data-and-information/publications/statistical/statistics-on-obesity-physical-activity-and-diet/england-2020. Accessed 4th October 2022.

[49] Diabetes UK (2021). *Diabetes diagnoses double in the last 15 years,* 5th April 2021.

[50] Dimbleby, H (2021) *National Food Strategy*, Page 48, Figure 4.4.

[51] Rauber F, da Costa Louzada ML, Steele EM, Millett C, Monteiro CA, Levy RB (2018). *Ultra-Processed Food Consumption and Chronic Non-Communicable Diseases-Related Dietary Nutrient Profile in the UK (2008⁻2014). Nutrients.* 2018 May 9

[52] The Lancet (2020). Available at: https://www.thelancet.com/journals/langas/article/PIIS2468-1253(22)00169-8/fulltext. Accessed 5th October 2022

[53] The Sustainable Food Trust (2019). *The Hidden Cost of UK Food*. Available at: https://sustainablefoodtrust.org/our-work/true-cost-accounting/ Accessed 5th October 2022

[54] Garthwaite, K (2016) *Stigma, shame and 'people like us': an ethnographic study of foodbank use in the UK, Journal of Poverty and Social Justice*, vol 24, no 3, 277–89

[55] DEFRA (2021). *70th annual report to Parliament on smallholdings in England*, 23rd February 2021. Available at: https://www.gov.uk/government/publications/70th-annual-report-to-parliament-on-smallholdings-in-england. Accessed 5th October 2022.

[56] Ipsos (2021). *Ipsos MORI issues index* August 2021.

[57] BBC (2019). *Election 2019*. Available at: https://www.bbc.co.uk/news/election/2019/results. Accessed 5th October 2022

[58] van Haute, E (2016): *Green Parties in Europe*, London: Routledge 2016, p. 118

[59] The Guardian (2021). *German election 2021: full results and analysis*, 27th September 2021.

[60] DEFRA (2022). *About us*. Available at: https://www.gov.uk/government/organisations/department-for-environment-food-rural-affairs/about. Accessed 5th October 2022

[61] DEFRA (2021). *Department for Environment, Food and Rural Affairs Outcome Delivery Plan: 2021 to 2022,* 15 July 2021

[62] Page 32, Figure 2.2. Henry Dimbleby Food report for UK Government 2021

[63] Dimbleby, H (2021) *National Food Strategy*, Page 32, Figure 2.2.

[64] Future Generations Commissioner for Wales (2022). *Well-being of Future Generations (Wales) Act 2015.* Available at: www.futuregenerations.wales/about-us/future-generations-act/. Accessed 5th October 2022

[65] Farming UK (2021). *Half of farmers face ruin from subsidy cuts, warn experts*, 25 October 2021.

[66] Office for National Statistics (2018). *Labour in the agriculture industry, UK: February 2018,* 6 February 2018.

[67] Ritchie H, Roser, M and Rosado, P (2017) *Crop Yields*. Available at: https://ourworldindata.org/crop-yields. Accessed on 5th October 2022.

[68] RSPB (2020). *Biodiversity loss report,* BII index. 2020.

[69] DEFRA (2022). *Emissions of air pollutants in the UK – Ammonia (NH3).* 18 February 2022.

[70] Forgrave, A (2019). *Farming anger forces Rewilding Britain to pull out of Summit To Sea project in Mid Wales*, North Wales Live. 21st October 2019

[71] Rewilding Britain (2022). *Four in five Britons support rewilding, poll finds.* 19th January 2022. Available at: https://www.rewildingbritain.org.uk/news-and-views/press-releases-and-media-statements/four-in-five-britons-support-rewilding-poll-finds. Accessed 5th October 2022

[72] Knepp Estate (2022). *Knepp Wildland*. Available at: https://www.kneppestate.co.uk/knepp-wildland. Accessed 5th October 2022.

[73] Knepp Estate (2022). *Regenerative Agriculture*. Available at: https://www.kneppestate.co.uk/regenerative-agriculture. Accessed 5th October 2022.

[74] Regenerative Food and Farming (2022). *Learn More*. Available at: https://regenerativefoodandfarming.co.uk/carbon-ghgs/ Accessed 5th October 2022.

[75] Permaculture Association (2022). *The Basics*. Available at: https://www.permaculture.org.uk/knowledge-base/basics# Accessed 5th October 2022.

[76] Soil Association (2022). *Agroforestry*. Available at: https://www.soilassociation.org/causes-campaigns/agroforestry/ Accessed 5th October 2022

[77] Ellen MacArthur Foundation (2022). *Making Nature Positive Food the Norm.* Available at: https://ellenmacarthurfoundation.org/resources/food-redesign/overview. Accessed 5th October 2022

[78] Ellen MacArthur Foundation (2022). *The Big Food Redesign*, page 34.

[79] Ellen MacArthur Foundation (2022). *The Big Food Redesign* page 35.

[80] Sustainable Food Trust (2022). *Feeding Britain*. Available at: https://sustainablefoodtrust.org/our-work/feeding-britain/ Accessed 5th October 2022.

[81] Dimbleby, H (2021) *National Food Strategy*, Page 42.

[82] Berners-Lee, T ((2010). *How Bad are Bananas*, Profile Books, London, pages 27&83

[83] Shahbandeh, M (2022). *Percent of UK consumers planning to shop local 2019-2020,* 17th March 2022. Available at: https://www.statista.com/statistics/1285643/percent-of-uk-consumers-planning-to-shop-local/ Accessed 5th October 2022.

[84] Simpson, E (2021). *Almost 50 shops a day disappear from the hight street,* 5th September 2021. Available at: https://www.bbc.co.uk/news/business-58433461. Accessed on 5th October 2022.

[85] Smith, L (2022). *Plastic Waste, House of Commons research briefing*, page 6. 11th January 2022.

[86] Smith, L (2022) *Plastic Waste, House of Commons research briefing*, pages 10-11 11th January 2022.

[87] Greenpeace (2021*). What really happens to your plastic recycling,* 21st April 2021. Available at: https://www.greenpeace.org.uk/news/plastic-recycling-export-incineration/ Accessed 5th October 2022

[88] Ross, A (2018). *Unearthed*, Greenpeace, 21stOctober 2018. Available at:

https://unearthed.greenpeace.org/2018/10/21/uk-household-plastics-found-in-illegal-dumps-in-malaysia/ Accessed 5th October 2022.

[89] U.S. National Ocean Service (2021). *What is the great pacific garbage patch?* 26th February 2021. Available at:
https://oceanservice.noaa.gov/facts/garbagepatch.html. Accessed 5th October 2022

[90] Ellen MacArthur Foundation (2016). *The New Plastics Economy: Rethinking the future of plastics and*
catalysing action, page 23

[91] DEFRA (2021). *Carrier bags; Why there's a charge*, 21st May 2021. Available at:
https://www.gov.uk/government/publications/single-use-plastic-carrier-bags-why-were-introducing-the-charge/carrier-bags-why-theres-a-5p-charge.
Accessed 5th October 2022.

[92] Simmonds, E and Lawrence, K. (2022). *What are supermarkets doing about the environment,* 3rd February 2022. Available at:
https://www.which.co.uk/reviews/shopping-sustainably/article/what-are-supermarkets-doing-about-plastic-ahzAC2s22tXv#how-they-compare-on-plastics. Accessed 5th October 2022.

[93] WRAP (2022). *The UK plastics pact.* Available at: https://wrap.org.uk/taking-action/plastic-packaging/the-uk-plastics-pact. Accessed 5th October 2022.

[94] WRAP (2022). *The UK plastics pact.* Available at:
https://wrap.org.uk/resources/report/uk-plastics-pact-annual-report-2020-21.
Accessed 5th October 2022.

[95] Zero Waste Scotland (2022). *Deposit Return Scheme*. Available at:
https://depositreturnscheme.zerowastescotland.org.uk/ Accessed 5th October 2022.

[96] Siegle, L (2018). *Turning the tide on Plastic*, Orion Publishing Group, Page 213

[97] Dimbleby, H (2021). National Food Strategy, page 76.

[98] Lancet Planetary Health (2020). *Trends in UK meat consumption: analysis of data from years 1–11 (2008–09 to 2018–19) of the National Diet and Nutrition Survey rolling programme*

[99] Irish Times (2022). *Seaweed has the potential to sharply reduce agriculture emissions*, 18th August 2022. Available at:
https://www.irishtimes.com/business/innovation/2022/08/18/seaweed-has-potential-to-sharply-reduce-agricultural-emissions/ Accessed 3rd October 2022.

[100] Lemetayer, M (2021). *Gas giants: Can we stop cows from emitting so much methane?* 27th October 2021. Available at: www.ibtimes.co.uk/gas-giants-can-we-stop-cows-emitting-so-much-methane-1695765. Accessed 3rd October 2022.

[101] ABC news (2021). *Sydney brewery algae reducing methane from cattle experiment*, 25th Oct 2021. Available from: www.abc.net.au/news/2021-10-26/sydney-brewery-algae-reducing-methane-from-cattle-experiment/100567164. Accessed 5th October 2022.

[102] Shahbandeh, M (2022). *Soybean production worldwide 2012/13-2021/22, by country*, 11 February 2022. Available at:
https://www.statista.com/statistics/263926/soybean-production-in-selected-countries-since-1980/ Accessed 5th October 2022.

[103]Greenpeace (2022). *Soya.* Available at: www.greenpeace.org.uk/challenges/soya. Accessed 5th October 2022.

[104] Ritchie, H and Roser, M (2021) *Forests and Deforestation.* Published online at OurWorldInData.org. Available at: 'https://ourworldindata.org/forests-and-deforestation' [Online Resource]. Accessed 5th October 2022.

[105] Financial Times (2020) *Climate graphic: Brazil denudes rainforest further in 2020*, March 2020

[106] Lang. T (2020). *Feeding Britain,* page

[107] Rebanks, J (2021). *English Pastoral*, Penguin, pages 238-239

[108] Dimbleby, H (2021). *National Food Strategy*, page 42

[109] Fink, L (2022). *Letter to investors 2022*

[110] Ritchie, H (2022). *Dairy vs. plant-based milk: what are the environmental impacts?* 19th January 2022. Available at: https://ourworldindata.org/environmental-impact-milks. Accessed 5th October 2022.

[111] Berners-Lee, M (2010). *How Bad are Bananas*, Profile Books, page 72

[112] The Economist (2021). *Technology Quarterly*, 2[Nd] October 2021, page 6.

[113] The Economist (2021). *Technology Quarterly.* 2nd October 2021, page 4.

[114] Mordor Intelligence (2022). *Meat substitutes market - growth, trends, COVID-19 impact, and forecast (2022 - 2027).* Available at: https://www.mordorintelligence.com/industry-reports/meat-substitutes-market. Accessed 5th October 2022.

[115] KBV Research (2022). *Global Plant-based Meat Market By Source (Soy, Wheat, Pea, and Others), By Type (Chicken, Fish, Beef, Pork, and Others), By Product (Burgers, Sausages, Patties, Grounds, Nuggets, Tenders & Cutlets, and Others), By Regional Outlook, Industry Analysis Report and Forecast, 2021 – 2027*, January 2022. Available at: https://www.kbvresearch.com/plant-based-meat-market/ Accessed 5th October 2022.

[116] The Economist (2021).*Technology Quarterly*, 2nd October 2021, page 6.

[117] Fairtrade Foundation (2022). *Facts and figures about Fairtrade*. Available at: https://www.fairtrade.org.uk/what-is-fairtrade/facts-and-figures-about-fairtrade/ Accessed 5th October 2022.

[118] Fairtrade Foundation (2022). *Facts and figures about Fairtrade*. Available at: https://www.fairtrade.org.uk/what-is-fairtrade/facts-and-figures-about-fairtrade/ Accessed 5th October 2022.

[119] Fairtrade Foundation (2022*). Get involved in your communities*. Available at: https://www.fairtrade.org.uk/get-involved/in-your-community/communities/ Accessed 5th October 2022.

[120] Gilbert, H (2017). *Green and Blacks launch prompts 'ethical scheme' confusion fears*, 3rd August 2017. Available at: https://www.foodmanufacture.co.uk/Article/2017/08/04/Fairtrade-lookalike-schemes-could-confuse-shoppers. Accessed 5th October 2022.

[121] Channel 4 (2022). *Cadbury Exposed: Dispatches*. First broadcast 4th April 2022. Available at: https://www.channel4.com/programmes/cadbury-exposed-dispatches. Accessed 5th October 2022.

[122] Lang, T (2020). Feeding Britain, Penguin, page 172

[123] FAO, IFAD, UNICEF, WFP and WHO. (2021). *The State of Food Security and Nutrition in the World 2021. Transforming food systems for food security, improved nutrition, and affordable healthy diets for all.*

[124] Wallace, A R (1876) *The Geographical Distribution of Animals.*

[125] Wallace A R (1869*). The Malay Archipelago,* Penguin Classics, 2014, page 47.

[126] Wallace, A R (1869). *The Malay Archipelago.* Penguin Classics, 2014, page 50.

[127] Wallace A R (1869). *The Malay Archipelago.* Penguin Classics, 2014, page 50.

[128] Wallace, A R (1869). *The Malay Archipelago.* Penguin Classics, 2014, page 53.

[129] Wallace, A R (1869). *The Malay Archipelago.* Penguin Classics, 2014, page 54.

[130] Wallace, A R (1869). *The Malay Archipelago.* Penguin Classics, 2014, page 54.

[131] WWF (2022). *The Heart of Borneo under siege.* Available at: https://wwf.panda.org/discover/knowledge_hub/where_we_work/borneo_forests/borneo_deforestation/ Accessed 7th October 2022.

[132] Wallace, A R (1869*) The Malay Archipelago.* Penguin Classics, 2014, page 74.

[133] Current Biology (2018). *Global Demand for Natural Resources Eliminated More Than 100,000 Bornean Orangutans,* 5th March 2018. Available at: https://www.cell.com/current-biology/fulltext/S0960-9822(18)30086-1. Accessed 7th October 2022.

[134] University of Michigan Museum of Zoology (2022). *Nasalis larvatus, proboscis monkey.* Available at: https://animaldiversity.org/accounts/Nasalis_larvatus/#2fade67e293477cb4089b077c77c37f4. Accessed 7th October 2022

[135] Borneo Nature Foundation (2012). *The Orangutan tropical peatland project Position Paper,* July 2012

[136] Food and Agriculture Organisation of the UN (2022). *Food loss and waste database.* Available at: https://www.fao.org/platform-food-loss-waste/flw-data/en/ Accessed 7th October 2022.

[137] Wrap (2022). *Food surplus and waste in the UK – key facts.* Available at: https://wrap.org.uk/resources/report/food-surplus-and-waste-uk-key-facts. Accessed 5th October 2022.

[138] Cohen, D (2021). *Revealed: UK's largest supermarkets throw away enough food for 190 million meals each year,* Independent, 27th February 2021.

[139] WRAP (2022). *Food surplus and waste UK, key facts.* Available at: https://wrap.org.uk/resources/report/food-surplus-and-waste-uk-key-facts. Accessed 5th October 2022.

[140] Lang, T (2020). *Feeding Britain*, Penguin, page 315

[141] Dimbleby, H (2021). *National Food Strategy*, page 42, fig 3.3.

[142] Lang, T (2020). *Feeding Britain,* Penguin, page 323

[143] Ellen MacArthur Foundation (2022). *Circular economy introduction.* Available at: https://ellenmacarthurfoundation.org/topics/circular-economy-introduction/overview. Accessed 8th October.

[144] Ellen MacArthur Foundation (2022). *How to run a profitable circular farm: one-acre farm.* Available at: https://ellenmacarthurfoundation.org/circular-examples/one-acre-farm. Accessed 7th October 2022.

[145] Elkin, E (2021). *California's Drought Is So Bad That Almond Farmers Are Ripping Out Trees*, Bloomberg, 13th June 2021

[146] U.S Sustainability Alliance (2022). *Fact Sheets U.S. Almonds - A Global Leader in Sustainability*. Available at: https://thesustainabilityalliance.us/u-s-almonds-fact-sheet/. Accessed 6th October 2022

[147] Robbins, O (2019) *Are Almonds Sustainable?* Food revolution network, 7th June 2019. Available at: https://foodrevolution.org/blog/almonds-sustainability/ Accessed 6th October 2022.

[148] Farm Progress (2015). *8 facts about almonds, agriculture, and the drought*, 8th April 2015. Available at: https://www.farmprogress.com/tree-nuts/8-facts-about-almonds-agriculture-and-drought. Accessed 6th October 2022.

[149] Water Footprint Network (2022). *WaterStat - water footprint statistics* Available at: https://waterfootprint.org/en/resources/waterstat/

[150] https://www.watercalculator.org/footprint/foods-big-water-footprint/ Accessed 6th October 2022

[151] Matthews, K and Johnson, R (2013) *Alternative Beef Production Systems: Issues and Implications*, United States Department of Agriculture, April 2013.

[152] McGivney, A (2020). *'Like sending bees to war': the deadly truth behind your almond milk obsession,* Guardian, 8th January 2020. Available at: https://www.theguardian.com/environment/2020/jan/07/honeybees-deaths-almonds-hives-aoe. Accessed 7th October 2020

[153] Water Footprint Network (2022). *National Water Footprints,* Vol 1, Section 3.1.

[154] Water Footprint Network (2022). *School Resources*. Available at: https://waterfootprint.org/en/resources/school-resources/ Accessed 7th October 2022

[155] Prakash, A (2020). *Retreating Glaciers and Water Flows in the Himalayas: Implications for Governance,* Observer Research Foundation, 15th September 2020.

[156] Water Footprint Network (2022). *National Water Footprints*, Vol. 1, page 21.

[157] Water Footprint Network (2022). *National Water Footprints* Vol 1, page 22.

[158] Lang, T (2020). *Feeding Britain*, Penguin, page 226.

[159] Lang, T (2020). *Feeding Britain*, Penguin, page 228-229

[160] Berners-Lee, M (2010*). How Bad are Bananas*, Profile Books, page 89.

[161] Lang, T (2020). *Feeding Britain*, Penguin, page 232

[162] Rowe, M (2019). *Water shortage in the UK: what's the problem and how to save water,* 3rd October 2019. Available at: https://www.countryfile.com/news/water-shortage-in-the-uk-whats-the-problem-and-how-to-save-water/ Accessed 7th October 2022.

[163] Statista (2015). *Sales value of dishwashing products in the United Kingdom (UK) from 2011 to 2015*, 3rd November 2015. Available at: https://www.statista.com/statistics/438945/sales-value-dishwash-united-kingdom-uk/ Accessed 7th October 2022.

[164] Franchise UK, 2020. *UK franchises – four key statistics to consider,* 9th January 2020. Available at: www.franchise-uk.co.uk/buying-a-franchise-uk/uk-franchises-four-key-statistics-to-consider/ Accessed 7th October 2022.

[165] BBC.co.uk (2021). *Budget 2021: UK Infrastructure Bank to be based in Leeds*,

03 March 2021. Available at: www.bbc.co.uk/news/uk-england-leeds-56269234. Accessed 7th October 2022.

[166] Sustainable Food Places (2022). *Resources kit, partnership structures*, Page 6. Available at: https://www.sustainablefoodplaces.org/resources/ Accessed 6th October 2022.

[167] Cambridge Food Hub (2020). *Healthy Start veg box scheme*, 8th September 2020. Available at: https://cambridgefoodhub.org/2020/09/08/healthy-start-veg-box-scheme. Accessed 6th October 2020.

[168] Catchpole, D (2021) *Local Food Ecosystems*.

[169] Catchpole, D (2021). Local Food Ecosystems, page 2.

[170] Simmonds, E and Lawrence, K (2022). *What are supermarkets doing about the environment?* 11th July 2022. Available at: https://www.which.co.uk/reviews/shopping-sustainably/article/what-are-supermarkets-doing-about-plastic-ahzAC2s22tXv#how-they-compare-on-plastics. Accessed 7th October 2022.

[171] Statista (2022). *Online grocery shopping in the United Kingdom (UK) - statistics and facts*, 29th July 2022. Available at: https://www.statista.com/topics/3144/online-grocery-shopping-in-the-united-kingdom/#dossierKeyfigures. Accessed 6th October 2022.

[172] Smithers, R (2020). *Amazon plans big expansion of UK online grocery service*, Guardian, 28th July 2020.